PRAISE FOR *THE TROJAN WAR*

"To pull off such a radical new take on the Trojan War requires three things: scholarly expertise that allows intimate knowledge of the Greek text of Homer, along with familiarity with thousands of scholarly books and articles that frame the age-old Homeric question of authenticity; a writer's flair for imagery and engaging prose; and a most non-academic willingness to experiment. . . . We are fortunate that Barry Strauss possesses all three gifts, and the result is that his Trojan War really is a 'new history' that is as different as it is welcome."

    —Victor Davis Hanson, *The New Criterion*

"The second best book about the Trojan War I have ever read."

    —Steven Pressfield, author of *Gates of Fire: An Epic Novel of the Battle*
      of Thermopylae and *The Afghan Campaign*

"Barry Strauss boldly treats the Trojan War not as mythology or poetry but as history. To the epics of Homer and other Greek sources he adds a broad knowledge of the Bronze Age, of its physical remains and of written evidence from the Hittite and Egyptian archives. The result is an exciting tale written in a lively style that brings Homer's heroes and the world in which they lived to vibrant and colorful life."

    —Donald Kagan, Sterling Professor of Classics and History, Yale University

"Barry Strauss reminds us that little is new in warfare—names and dates change, but the soul of combat remains the same across millennia. By capturing the sublime tranquillity and thunderous violence of the ancient world, he makes Homer feel fresh and more relevant than ever. *The Trojan War* is a lyrical, entrancing book, ringing with arms, and also with truth."

    —Nathaniel Fick, author of *One Bullet Away: The Making of a Marine Officer*

"This is as good an account as we are likely to get of one of the most famous wars in history. A must-read for anyone interested in war, history, or ancient times."

    —Max Boot, senior fellow in national security studies, The Council on
      Foreign Relations, and author of *War Made New: Technology, Warfare,*
      and the Course of History, 1500 to Today

ALSO BY BARRY STRAUSS

The Battle of Salamis: The Naval Encounter That Saved
Greece—and Western Civilization

What If?: The World's Foremost Military Historians Imagine
What Might Have Been
(contributor)

Western Civilization: The Continuing Experiment
(with Thomas F. X. Noble and others)

War and Democracy: A Comparative Study of the Korean War
and the Peloponnesian War
(with David McCann, co-editor)

Rowing Against the Current: On Learning to Scull at Forty

Fathers and Sons in Athens: Ideology and Society
in the Era of the Peloponnesian War

Hegemonic Rivalry: From Thucydides to the Nuclear Age
(with Richard Ned Lebow, co-editor)

The Anatomy of Error: Ancient Military Disasters
and Their Lessons for Modern Strategists
(with Josiah Ober)

Athens After the Peloponnesian War: Class, Faction and Policy, 403–386 B.C.

THE TRO

JAN WAR

A New History

BARRY STRAUSS

SIMON & SCHUSTER PAPERBACKS
NEW YORK · LONDON · TORONTO · SYDNEY

Simon & Schuster Paperbacks
1230 Avenue of the Americas
New York, NY 10020

First Simon & Schuster trade paperback edition August 2007

Simon & Schuster Paperbacks and colophon are registered trademarks of Simon & Schuster, Inc.

For information about special discounts for bulk purchases, please contact Simon & Schuster Special Sales: 1-800-456-6798 or business@simonandschuster.com

Designed by Dana Sloan

Manufactured in the United States of America

3   5   7   9   10   8   6   4

The Library of Congress has cataloged the hardcover edition as follows:
Strauss, Barry S.
The Trojan War : a new history / Barry Strauss.
p. cm.
Includes biographical references and index.
Contents: War for Helen—The black ships sail—Operation beachhead—Assault on the walls—The dirty war—An army in trouble—The killing fields—Night moves—Hector's charge—Achilles' heel—The night of the horse
1. Trojan War. I. Title.
BL793.T7S78 2006
939'.21—dc22
2006044389
ISBN-13: 978-0-7432-6441-9
ISBN-10:   0-7432-6441-X
ISBN-13: 978-0-7432-6442-6 (pbk)
ISBN-10:   0-7432-6442-8 (pbk)

Map of Troy on page xxvi from *Celebrating Homer's Landscapes: Troy and Ithaca Revisited* by J. V. Luce, Yale University Press, page 94, © 1998, used by permission.

For Scott and Karen, Judy and Jonathan,
Larry and Maureen, and Ronna and Richard

CONTENTS

AUTHOR'S NOTE

Most of the quotations from the *Iliad* and the *Odyssey* are from Alexander Pope's translation. A few have been translated by the author for greater accuracy.

Homer never uses the word "Greeks," referring instead to Achaeans, Danaans, Argives, and, occasionally, Hellenes. Modern scholars refer to the Greeks of the Late Bronze Age as Mycenaeans. This book generally refers to them as Greeks.

All dates in this book from the Bronze Age (ca. 3000–1000 B.C.) are approximate unless otherwise stated.

TIMETABLE OF EVENTS RELATING TO THE TROJAN WAR

Bronze Age	3000–1000 B.C.*
Height of Mycenaean civilization	1450–1180
Linear B writing	1450–1180
Submycenaean Period	1180–1050
Troy VI a–h	1740/1730–1300
Troy VIi (formerly known as Troy VIIa)	1300–1210/1180
Troy VIj (formerly known as Troy VIIb1)	1210/1180–1130
Troy VIIb2	1130–1050
Trojan War	1210–1180
Hittite Empire	1380–1180
Egyptian New Kingdom	1550–1070
Battle of Megiddo	1479
Amarna Letters	1382–1334
Battle of Qadesh	1274
Height of Assyria's Bronze Age power	1300–1200
Ugarit destroyed	1187
Greek palaces destroyed	1180
Sea Peoples	1200–1100
Greek Dark Ages	1150–750
Greek Renaissance	800–700
Greek alphabet invented	750
Homer	700s
Iliad and *Odyssey* written down in Athens	560–527

*All dates are approximate.

A NOTE ON ANCIENT HISTORY
AND ARCHAEOLOGY

Ancient Greek history traditionally begins in the year 776 B.C., when the first Olympic Games are supposed to have been held. By coincidence, the earliest example of the Greek alphabet dates to about 750 B.C. So both tradition and scholarship would agree in labeling everything that happened before the early eighth century B.C. in Greece as "prehistory." But thanks largely to archaeology, we know a great deal about the history of the "prehistoric" Greeks. And some of our knowledge even comes from written sources, because centuries before the Greek alphabet, scribes used a primitive writing system for record-keeping in Greek. Called Linear B, it was in use from about 1450 to about 1180 B.C., after which it disappeared. Much more sophisticated writings also survive from other so-called prehistoric cultures, and they offer important historical information about prehistoric Greece.

But more on that later. First, let us quickly scan the historic period of ancient Greece. The Greek city-states reached their heyday in the centuries between about 750 and 323 B.C. The period between 750 and 480 is known as the Archaic Age, while the years from 480 to 323 are called the Classical Period. At the end of the Classical Period, King Alexander III of Macedon, known today as Alexander the Great, conquered all of Greece as well as the Persian Empire to the east. Alexander's conquests began a new era of Greco-Macedonian kingdoms known as the Hellenistic Age, 323–30 B.C. That gave way, in turn, to the Roman Empire, which lasted until A.D. 476, when it split into barbarian kingdoms in the West and the Byzantine Empire in the East.

Almost all ancient written testimonies about the Trojan War date to the 1,200-year period from the start of the Archaic Age to the end of the Roman Empire. But in order to understand what really happened, we must look backward. The four centuries before the start of the Archaic Age are known collectively as the Greek Dark Ages (ca.1150–750 B.C.). "Dark" refers to the absence of writing, but the physical evidence uncovered by archaeologists sheds light on that era.

Another important term is Iron Age, used for the millennium from about 1000 B.C. to A.D. 1. In this epoch, new technology made iron the most durable metal for tools and weapons. The earlier two millennia, from about 3000 to about 1000 B.C., are known as the Bronze Age, after that era's most widespread metal for tools and weapons; iron was known but rare. The Bronze Age is the setting for this book.

In Greece, the Bronze Age is commonly divided into three periods, Early (3000–2100 B.C.), Middle (2100–1600), and Late (1600–1150). Naturally, it is difficult to assign dates to events that took place so long ago. Most dating is relative and approximate rather than absolute: that is, we can say that A is older than B or even that A comes from the period of, say, 1600–1500 B.C., but rarely can we be more specific.

Sometimes we get help from surviving written records, such as lists of Egyptian kings and their reigns (although even in that case we are not completely sure about dating). On occasion we hear of an eclipse, which can be dated by astronomers. In rare instances, it is possible to find samples of once-living material (from bone to shells to minerals) that can be dated by laboratory testing through radiocarbon dating, neutron activation analysis, or dendrochronology (counting tree rings, based on tree physiology as well as on rainfall and other environmental factors). By the last technique, for example, the tremendous volcanic explosion that destroyed most of the island of Thera has been dated to 1627–1600 B.C.

But these cases are few and far between because they depend on the quality of the sample and because testing is very expensive. Dendrochronology requires having both a number of comparative ancient tree samples as well as having nearby living trees with identical ring patterns to the sample in question. And radiocarbon testing can narrow dating to about a century but not a year.

So most dating of material dug out of the earth has to be done by more rough-and-ready methods. Fortunately for historians the remains of past civilizations tend to be deposited in layers. For example, if a house is built in A.D. 1700 and then torn down and replaced in 1800, the remains of the old house will be located below the remains of the new house. Any glass, wood, bricks, artwork, or other material found together with the foundations of the old house can be dated to the period 1700–1800. If we could take a "slice" of history in the soil of an ancient land, like Greece, we would find layers of history stacked up one above the other. The technical name for these layers is strata, and the careful study of them is called stratigraphy. Stratigraphy is one of the most important tools in the archaeologist's kit for assigning dates.

The city of Troy, for example, consists of a dozen separate levels in the Bronze Age. Each corresponds to the city during a particular era. Troy I, for example, is the city as it was ca. 3000–2600 B.C., while Troy VIi (formerly called Troy VIIa) is the city of ca. 1300–1180 B.C. The division between two layers is sometimes sharp and sometimes barely distinct. For example, there is relatively little difference between Troy VIh (ca. 1470–1300 B.C.) and Troy VIi but Troy VIj (ca.1180–1130 B.C. and formerly called Troy VIIb1) was very unlike Troy VIi, which it followed.

The most common item found in the layers of ancient civilization is pottery. By carefully tracing changes in the shapes and styles of pottery, and by vigilantly recording the layer in which a particular potsherd is found, experts can date archaeological strata, sometimes fairly narrowly, to as little as a generation.

Through a combination mainly of pottery analysis and stratigraphy, scholars have devised a system of relative dating for the Greek

Bronze Age. Anchored by a few absolute dates, the periods known as Early, Middle, and Late Helladic are the building blocks for dating Greek prehistory. They are subdivided in turn into such subperiods as Middle Helladic III, Late Helladic IIB1.

Pottery dating is sometimes specific to a particular region, and these periods apply mainly to the Greek mainland and islands. In Anatolia, where Troy is sited, pottery dating is based on locally produced pottery, much of it imitations of the popular and widely traded pottery of Greece. So Trojan pottery dating differs from Greek.

Archaeology is mostly a matter of digging in the soil, but it can also mean going beneath the sea. Underwater archaeology in the Mediterranean has exploded with dramatic discoveries in the last few decades. For the background to the Trojan War, three Bronze Age shipwrecks, two off the coast of Turkey and one off the coast of Greece, stand out in importance. The Ulu Burun wreck (Turkey), a ship of about 1300 B.C., the Cape Gelidonya wreck (Turkey), and the Point Iria wreck (Greece) each date to about 1200 B.C.; all offer intriguing evidence.

With so many factors involved, dating events in the Bronze Age is complicated and often controversial. Consider these as rough guides: From about 2000 to 1490 B.C., civilization flourished on the island of Crete. Organized around several great palaces, this civilization is known today as Minoan. The Minoans were great farmers, sailors, traders, and artists. Although their ethnicity is not clear, we do know that they were not Greek.

The first speakers of Greek arrived in Greece from points east around 2000 B.C. They were a warlike people and took over the Greek peninsula from its earlier inhabitants. In the Late Bronze Age (ca. 1600–1150 B.C.) the newcomers' civilization dominated Greece in a series of warrior kingdoms, of which the most important were Mycenae, Thebes, Tiryns, and Pylos. We call their civilization Mycenaean. Linear B (a writing system representing syllables) shows that their language was Greek, and that they worshipped the same gods as their Archaic and Classical Greek descendants. In short, they were

Greek. Evidence suggests that the Mycenaeans called themselves Achaeans or Danaans, the two terms which, along with Argives, Homer uses for them. New Kingdom Egyptian texts refer to the kingdom of "Danaja" and to such cities in it as Mycenae and Thebes. This is independent confirmation of Homer's political framework.

The Mycenaeans were sailors, soldiers, raiders, and traders. Around 1490 B.C. they conquered Minoan Crete and took over its former colonies in the eastern Aegean islands and on the Anatolian mainland (present-day Turkey) at Miletus. Over the next several centuries, they engaged in war, diplomacy, commerce, cultural exchange, and dynastic intermarriage with the great kingdoms of the eastern Mediterranean. At least one Mycenaean king was addressed as an equal in diplomatic correspondence from the Hittite king. Although Linear B texts do not allow the identification of specific events, they provide an abundance of data about weapons and warfare. If the Trojan War really happened, it was an event in the Mycenaean Age—one of the last great events before the decline and fall of Mycenaean civilization in the 1100s B.C.

The Mycenaeans' main rival was the greatest kingdom in Anatolia, Hatti, also known today as the Hittites. The Great King of the Hittites was important enough to correspond on an equal footing with the rulers of Assyria, Babylon, Mitanni, and Egypt and powerful enough to make war on them. These six kingdoms were the perennial powers of the region in the Late Bronze Age.

From their stronghold high in the central Anatolian plateau, the big city of Hattusha, the Hittites looked down and competed for the rule of what was then the world. Their main interest was in expanding southward to the Mediterranean coast of Anatolia and eastward into Syria. But they found themselves drawn willy-nilly into the ever-shifting politics of western Anatolia. Thanks to the evidence of archaeology and epigraphy, this story is much richer than most people would guess—but largely untold.

The most important source is the Hittite royal archives from Hattusha, from which thousands of clay tablets survive, as do hundreds of similar tablets from other Hittite cities. Most of them are written in the Hittite language, in a writing system called cuneiform, which employs about five hundred wedge-shaped symbols. We also have Hittite inscriptions from various places carved on stone or inscribed on metal. Some of these are written in hieroglyphics, a rebuslike system of picture-writing, but not in the famous Egyptian hieroglyphics: rather, they are written in a language called Luwian. Luwian is closely related to Hittite and was spoken widely in southern and western Anatolia. Luwian survived the Bronze Age, and we have Luwian inscriptions as late as the 200s A.D. Another related Bronze Age Anatolian language is Palaic, spoken in northwestern Anatolia. Little Palaic writing survives.

Other writing systems also existed in the eastern Mediterranean in the Bronze Age. Akkadian, originally a language used in Mesopotamia (modern Iraq), was the international language of diplomacy. Akkadian tablets survive from Cyprus; from Ugarit, a merchant city on the coast of northwest Syria; from Amurru, a border state between the Hittites and Egypt; and from Egypt itself. In addition, texts from the powerful city of Mari (1800–1750 B.C.) abound in information about warfare, although they predate the Trojan War by about five hundred years, so they should be used cautiously. Akkadian inscriptions from the Assyrian Empire of the 1200s B.C. are also a big source of evidence about conflicts and combat, and they are roughly contemporaneous with the Trojan War.

Turning to the Levant, the so-called Amarna Letters (most from 1382–1334 B.C.) are a collection of communications among eastern Mediterranean princes, especially between Pharaoh and his Canaanite vassals. These letters amply document diplomacy and war, especially small wars and low-intensity conflicts. The letters show that the years between about 1450 and 1250 mark the first international system of states in history. For their part, the warrior-pharaohs of New Kingdom Egypt (1550–1070 B.C.) have left a trove of information about military matters.

Finally, various epic poems, myths, and prayers survive from the ancient Near East, from the Sumerian *Gilgamesh* to the Ugaritic *Kirta*, and many are relevant to our story. Although some date to

2000 B.C. or earlier, they reveal continuing behaviors and technologies.

There were various kingdoms in western Anatolia in the Late Bronze Age, but for us, by far the most important was Wilusa. The subject of international conflict and civil war, Wilusa is accepted by many scholars as the place the Greeks called first Wilion and then Ilion—that is, Troy.

Troy was a great city for the two thousand years of the Bronze Age, from about 3000 to 950 B.C. After being abandoned near the beginning of the Iron Age, Troy was resettled by Greek colonists around 750 B.C. and remained a small Greek city throughout antiquity. Wave after wave of different peoples lived in Bronze Age Troy. None of those populations is easily identifiable today, but all left signs of wealth, power, and sometimes tragedy. The city was destroyed from time to time by fire, earthquake, and war, and then rebuilt. The ruins have yielded gold, artistic treasures, and palatial architecture. In the Late Bronze Age, Troy was one of the largest cities around the Aegean Sea and a major regional center—even if not nearly as large as the great cities of central Anatolia, the Levant, or Mesopotamia. Late Bronze Age Troy controlled an important harbor nearby and protected itself with a huge complex of walls, ditches, and wooden palisades. If any period of Troy corresponds to the great city of the Trojan War, this was it.

The most important texts about the Trojan War are two long poems, called epics because they tell of the heroic deeds of men long gone. The *Iliad* is set near the end of the Trojan War, and it covers about two months of the conflict. The *Odyssey* relates the hero Odysseus's long, hard trip home from Troy; it adds only a few additional details about the Trojan War. Both of these texts are attributed to a poet named Homer.

Other poems about early Greece were also written down in Archaic Greece. Known as the "Epic Cycle," six of these poems narrate the parts of the Trojan War missing from the *Iliad* and *Odyssey*. These poems are the *Cypria*, on the outbreak and first nine years of the war; the *Aethiopis*, which focuses on Troy's Ethiopian and Amazon allies; the *Little Iliad*, on the Trojan Horse; the *Iliupersis*, on the sack of Troy; the *Nostoi*, on the return of various Greek heroes, especially Agamemnon; and the *Telegony*, a continuation of the *Odyssey*. Unfortunately, only a few quotations from the Epic Cycle as well as brief summaries survive today. Many, many later writers in ancient times used these and other sources to comment on Homer.

Finally, there is ancient art, both painting and sculpture, which often illustrates details of the Trojan War, sometimes in invaluable ways for historians.

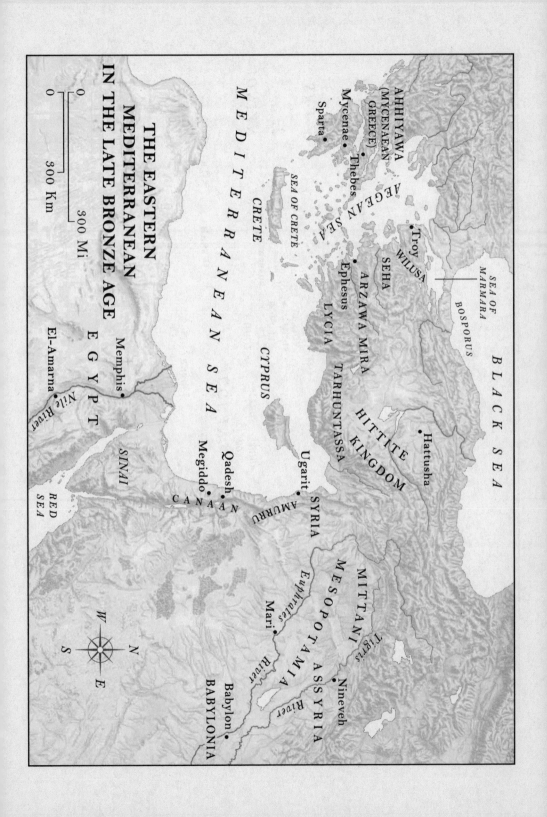

THE EASTERN
MEDITERRANEAN
IN THE LATE BRONZE AGE

0   300 Mi

0   300 Km

MEDITERRANEAN SEA

AEGEAN SEA

SEA OF CRETE

CRETE

AHHIYAWA
(MYCENAEAN
GREECE)

Sparta

Mycenae

Thebes

Troy

WILUSA

SEHA

ARZAWA MIRA

Ephesus

LYCIA

TARHUNTASSA

CYPRUS

HITTITE KINGDOM

Hattusha

SEA OF MARMARA

BOSPORUS

BLACK SEA

EGYPT

Memphis

El-Amarna

Nile River

SINAI

RED SEA

CANAAN

Megiddo

Qadesh

AMURRU

Ugarit

SYRIA

MESOPOTAMIA

MITTANI

ASSYRIA

Nineveh

Mari

Euphrates River

Tigris River

Babylon

BABYLONIA

N
W   E
S

BRONZE AGE GREECE

0 _____ 0

150 Km

0 _____ 0

150 Mi

MACEDONIA

Mt. Olympus ▲

Strymon River

THRACE

Hebrus River

BLACK SEA

BOSPORUS

EPIRUS

THESSALY

IONIAN

SEA

ITHACA

PHTHIA

Mt. Parnassus ▲

GULF OF CORINTH

PELOPONNESUS

Corinth •
Mycenae • • Tiryns
• Thebes
BOEOTIA
• Aulis
ATTICA

ARCADIA **ARGOLIS**

Sparta •
LACONIA

EUBOEA

SEA OF CRETE

Athens •

CYCLADES

AEGEAN

SEA

SCYROS

LEMNOS

IMBROS

SAMOTHRACE

TENEDOS

LESBOS

CHIOS

• Troy

DARDANELLES

Scamander River

SEA OF
MARMARA

Hermus River

ANATOLIA

SAMOS

• Ephesus

Hermus River

• Miletus

Maeander River

• Halicarnassus

DODECANESE

RHODES

CRETE

• Knossos

N
W ✦ E
S

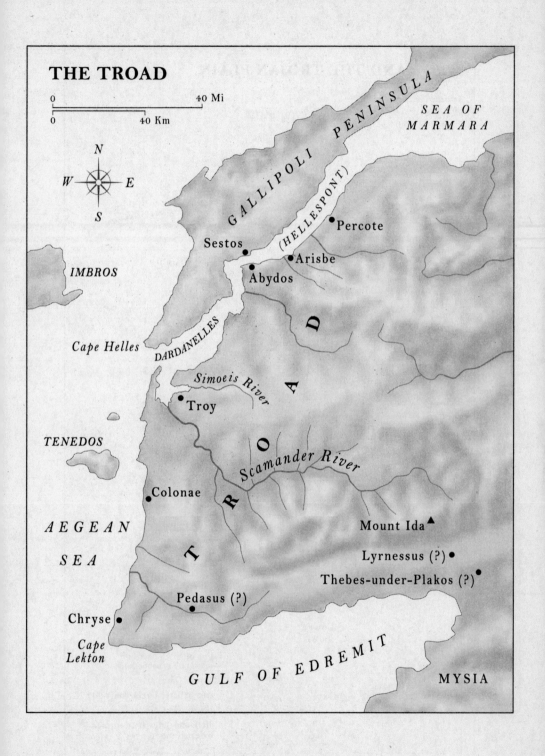

THE TROAD

0 ——————— 40 Mi

0 ——————— 40 Km

N
W *E*
S

GALLIPOLI PENINSULA

SEA OF
MARMARA

(HELLESPONT)

Percote

Sestos

Arisbe

Abydos

IMBROS

DARDANELLES

Cape Helles

TROAD

Simoeis River

Troy

TENEDOS

Scamander River

Colonae

Mount Ida ▲

AEGEAN

SEA

Lyrnessus (?) ●

Thebes-under-Plakos (?) ●

Pedasus (?) ●

Chryse ●

Cape
Lekton

GULF OF EDREMIT

MYSIA

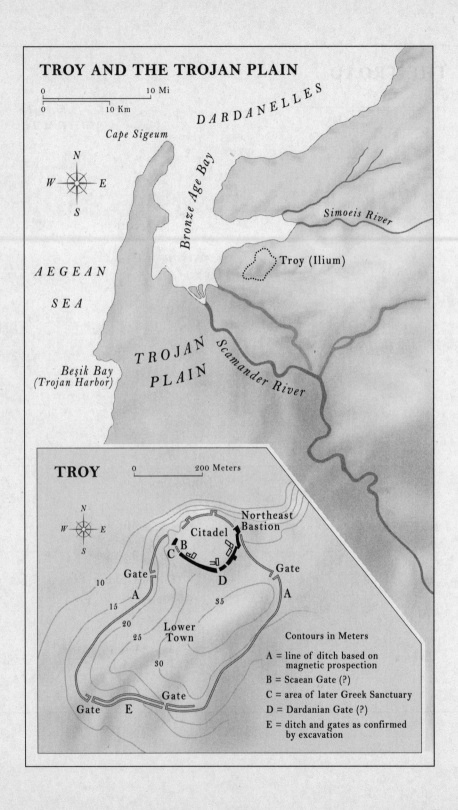

TROY AND THE TROJAN PLAIN

0   10 Mi
0   10 Km

DARDANELLES

Cape Sigeum

Bronze Age Bay

Simoeis River

N W E S

Troy (Ilium)

AEGEAN SEA

Beşik Bay (Trojan Harbor)

TROJAN PLAIN

Scamander River

TROY

0   200 Meters

N W E S

Northeast Bastion

Citadel

B
C
D

Gate
A

Gate
A

10
15
20
25
30
35

Lower Town

Gate
E
Gate

Gate

Contours in Meters

A = line of ditch based on magnetic prospection

B = Scaean Gate (?)

C = area of later Greek Sanctuary

D = Dardanian Gate (?)

E = ditch and gates as confirmed by excavation

THE TROJAN WAR

INTRODUCTION

Troy invites war. Its location, where Europe and Asia meet, made it rich and visible. At Troy, the steel-blue water of the Dardanelles Straits pours into the Aegean and opens the way to the Black Sea. Although the north wind often blocked ancient shipping there, Troy has a protected harbor, and so it beckoned to merchants—and marauders. Walls, warriors, and blood were the city's lot.

People had already fought over Troy for two thousand years by the time Homer's Greeks are said to have attacked it. Over the centuries since then, armies have swept past Troy's ancient walls, from Alexander the Great to the Gallipoli Campaign of 1915.

And then there are the archaeologists. In 1871 Heinrich Schliemann amazed the world with the announcement that a mound near the entrance to the Dardanelles contained the ruins of Troy. Schliemann, who relied on preliminary work by Frank Calvert, was an inspired amateur, if also something of a fraud. But the trained archaeologists who have followed him by the hundreds in the 130 years since have put the excavations on a firm and scientific basis. And they all came to Troy because of the words of a Greek poet.

But are those words true? Granted that ancient Troy really existed, was it anything like the splendid city of Homer's description? Did it face an armada from Greece? Did the Trojan War really happen?

Spectacular new evidence makes it likely that the Trojan War indeed took place. New excavations since 1988 constitute little less than an archaeological revolution, proving that Homer was right

1

about the city. Twenty years ago, it looked as though Troy was just a small citadel of only about half an acre. Now we know that Troy was, in fact, about seventy-five acres in size, a city of gold amid amber fields of wheat. Formerly, it seemed that by 1200 B.C. Troy was a shabby place, well past its prime, but we know now that in 1200 the city was in its heyday.

Meanwhile, independent confirmation proves that Troy was a byword in the ancient Near East. This outside evidence comes not from Homer or any Greek source but from Hittite texts. In these documents, the city that Homer calls Troy or Ilion is referred to as Taruisa or Wilusa—and in the early form of the Greek language, "Ilion" was rendered as "Wilion."

A generation ago scholars thought that the Trojans were Greeks, like the men who attacked them. But new evidence suggests otherwise. The recently discovered urban plan of Troy looks less like that of a Greek than of an Anatolian city. Troy's combination of citadel and lower town, its house and wall architecture, and its religious and burial practices are all typically Anatolian, as is the vast majority of its pottery. To be sure, Greek pottery and Greek speakers were also found at Troy, but neither predominated. New documents suggest that most Trojans spoke a language closely related to Hittite and that Troy was a Hittite ally. The enemy of Troy's ally was the Greeks.

The Greeks were the Vikings of the Bronze Age. They built some of history's first warships. Whether on large expeditions or smaller sorties, whether in the king's call-up or on freebooting forays, whether as formal soldiers and sailors or as traders who turned into raiders at a moment's notice, whether as mercenaries, ambassadors, or hereditary guest-friends, the Greeks fanned out across the Aegean and into the eastern and central Mediterranean, with one hand on the rudder and the other on the hilt of a sword. What the sight of a dragon's head on the stem post of a Viking ship was to an Anglo-Saxon, the sight of a bird's beak on the stem post of a Greek galley was to a Mediterranean islander or Anatolian mainlander. In the 1400s B.C., the Greeks conquered Crete, the southwestern

Aegean islands, and the city of Miletus on the Aegean coast of Anatolia, before driving eastward into Lycia and across the sea to Cyprus. In the 1300s they stirred up rebels against the Hittite overlords of western Anatolia. In the 1200s they began muscling their way into the islands of the northeastern Aegean, which presented a big threat to Troy. In the 1100s they joined the wave of marauders, known to us as the Sea Peoples, who descended first on Cyprus, then on the Levant and Egypt, and settled in what became the Philistine country.

The Trojan War, which probably dates to around 1200 B.C., is just a piece in a larger puzzle. But if the resulting picture builds on Homer, it differs quite a bit from the impression most readers get from his poems. And "impression" is the right word, because much of the conventional wisdom about the war, from Achilles' heel to Cassandra's warnings, is not in Homer at all.

Consider what Homer does say: He tells the story in two long poems, the *Iliad* or Story of Ilion (that is, Troy) and the *Odyssey* or Story of Odysseus. According to Homer, the Trojan War lasted ten years. The conflict pitted the wealthy city of Troy and its allies against a coalition of all Greece. It was the greatest war in history, involving at least 100,000 men in each army as well as 1,186 Greek ships. It featured heroic champions on both sides. It was so important that the Olympian gods played an active role. Troy was a magnificent city and impregnable fortress. The cause of the war was the seduction, by Prince Paris of Troy, of the beautiful Helen, queen of Sparta, as well as the loss of the treasure that they ran off with. The Greeks landed at Troy and demanded the return of Helen and the treasure to her husband, Sparta's King Menelaus. But the Trojans refused. In the nine years of warfare that followed, the Greeks ravaged and looted the Trojan countryside and surrounding islands, but they made no progress against the city of Troy. Ironically, the *Iliad* focuses on pitched battle on the Trojan Plain, although most of the war was fought elsewhere and consisted of raids. And the *Iliad* concentrates on only two months in the ninth year of the long conflict.

In that ninth year the Greek army nearly fell apart. A murderous epidemic was followed by a mutiny on the part of Greece's greatest warrior, Achilles. The issue, once again, was a woman: this time, the beautiful Briseis, a prize of war unjustly grabbed from Achilles by the Greek commander in chief, Agamemnon. A furious Achilles withdrew himself and his men from fighting. Agamemnon led the rest of the army out to fight, and much of the *Iliad* is a gory, blow-by-blow account of four days on the battlefield. The Trojans, led by Prince Hector, took advantage of Achilles' absence and nearly drove the Greeks back into the sea. At the eleventh hour, Achilles let his lieutenant and close friend Patroclus lead his men back into battle to save the Greek camp. Patroclus succeeded but overreached himself, and Hector killed him on the Trojan Plain. In revenge, Achilles returned to battle, devastated the enemy, and killed Hector. Achilles was so angry that he abused Hector's corpse. King Priam of Troy begged Achilles to give back his son Hector's body for cremation and burial, and a sadder but wiser Achilles at last agreed. He knew that he too was destined to die soon in battle.

The *Iliad* ends with the funeral of Hector. The *Odyssey* is set after the war and mainly describes the hard road home of the Greek hero Odysseus. In a series of flashbacks, it explains how Odysseus led the Greeks to victory at Troy by thinking up the brilliant trick of smuggling Greek commandos into Troy in the Trojan Horse, an operation which he also led. Achilles did not play a part in the final victory; he was long since dead. The *Odyssey* also shows Helen back in Sparta with Menelaus. But Homer leaves out most of the rest of the war. One has to turn to other and generally lesser Greek and Roman poets for additional detail.

Aeneas is a minor character in the *Iliad*, but the hero of a much later epic poem in Latin, written by Vergil, the *Aeneid*. Vergil makes Aeneas the founder of Rome (or, to be precise, of the Italian town that later founded Rome). But in Homer, Aeneas is destined to become king of Troy after the Greeks depart and the Trojans rebuild.

Now, consider how new evidence revises the picture: Much of what we thought we knew about the Trojan War is wrong. In the old view, the war was decided on the plain of Troy by duels between champions; the besieged city never had a chance against the Greeks; and the Trojan Horse must have been a myth. But now we know that the Trojan War consisted mainly of low-intensity conflict and attacks on civilians; it was more like the war on terror than World War II. There was no siege of Troy. The Greeks were underdogs, and only a trick allowed them to take Troy: that trick may well have been the Trojan Horse.

The *Iliad* is a championship boxing match, fought in plain view at high noon and settled by a knockout punch. The Trojan War was a thousand separate wrestling matches, fought in the dark and won by tripping the opponent. The *Iliad* is the story of a hero, Achilles. The Trojan War is the story of a trickster, Odysseus, and a survivor, Aeneas.

The *Iliad* is to the Trojan War what *The Longest Day* is to World War II. The four days of battle in the *Iliad* no more sum up the Trojan War than the D-day invasion of France sums up the Second World War. The *Iliad* is not the story of the whole Trojan War. Far from being typical, the events of the *Iliad* are extraordinary.

Homer nods, and he exaggerates and distorts too. But overly skeptical scholars have thrown out the baby with the bathwater. There are clear signs of later Greece in the epics; Homer lived perhaps around 700 B.C., about five hundred years after the Trojan War. Yet new discoveries vindicate the poet as a man who knew much more about the Bronze Age than had been thought.

And that is a key insight because Bronze Age warfare is very well documented. In Greece, archaeologists showed long ago that the arms and armor described by Homer really were used in the Bronze Age; recent discoveries help to pinpoint them to the era of the Trojan War. Like Homer, Linear B documents refer to a Greek army as a collection of warrior chiefs rather than as the impersonal institution of later Greek texts.

But the richest evidence of Bronze Age warfare comes from the ancient Near East. And in the 1300s and 1200s B.C., Bronze Age civilization was international. Trade and diplomacy, migration, dynastic marriage, and even war all led to cultural cross-fertilization. So the abundant evidence of Assyria, Canaan, Egypt, the Hittites, and Mesopotamia puts in perspective the events of the *Iliad* and *Odyssey*.

Some things in Homer that may seem implausible are likely to be true because the same or similar customs existed in Bronze Age civilizations of the ancient Near East. For example, surprise attacks at night, wars over livestock, iron arrowheads in the Bronze Age, battles between champions instead of armies, the mutilation of enemy corpses, shouting matches between kings in the assembly, battle cries as measures of prowess, weeping as a mark of manhood—these and many other details are not Homeric inventions but well-attested realities of Bronze Age life.

Besides recording Bronze Age customs, Homer reproduces Bronze Age literary style. Although he was Greek, Homer borrows from the religion, mythology, poetry, and history of the Near East. By composing in the manner of a chronicler of the pharaohs or the Hittites or Babylon's King Hammurabi, Homer lends an air of authenticity to his poem. For instance, Homer portrays champions on both sides carving paths of blood through the enemy as if they were supermen—or as if they were pharaohs, often described by Egyptian texts as superheroes in battle. Ironically, the more Homer exaggerates, the more authentic he is as a representative of the Bronze Age. And even the prominence of the gods in Homer, which drives most historians to distraction, is a Bronze Age touch, because writers of that era always put the gods at the heart of warfare. Belief in divine apparitions on the battlefield, conviction that victories depended on a goddess's patronage, and faith that epidemics were unleashed by offended deities are all well documented.

Could Homer have preserved the truth about a war that preceded him by five centuries? Not in all its details, of course, but he could have known the outline of the conflict. After all, a remarkably accurate list of Late Bronze Age Greek cities survived to Homer's day and appears in the *Iliad* as the so-called Catalog of Ships. And it survived even though writing disappeared from Greece between about 1180 and 750 B.C.

As for Trojan memories, writing did not disappear from the

Near East, and trade routes between Greece and the Near East survived after 1200. Around 1000 B.C., Greeks crossed the Aegean Sea again in force and established colonies on the coast of Anatolia. Tradition puts Homer in one of those colonies or on a nearby Aegean island. If so, the poet could have come into contact with records of the Trojan War—maybe even with a Trojan version of the *Iliad.*

In any case, writing is only part of the story. The *Iliad* and *Odyssey* are oral poetry, composed as they were sung, and based in large part on time-honored phrases and themes. When he composed the epics, Homer stood at the end of a long tradition in which poems were handed down for centuries by word of mouth from generation to generation of professional singers, who worked without benefit of writing. They were bards, men who entertained by singing about the great deeds of the heroic past. Often, what made a bard successful was the ability to rework old material in ways that were new—but not too new, because the audience craved the good old stories.

We can presume that the Trojan War indeed happened: that is, that a Greek coalition attacked and eventually sacked Troy. But if the Trojan War really happened, how was it fought? What caused it? To answer these questions we will start with Homer and then scrutinize all details in light of what we know about the Late Bronze Age.

Take, for instance, the war's length. Homer says that the Trojan War lasted ten years; to be precise, he says that the Greeks at Troy fought and suffered for nine years and finally won in the tenth. But these numbers should not be taken literally. Among many other reasons, consider that in the ancient Near East, there was an expression "nine times and then a tenth," which means "over and over until finally." It was a figure of speech, much as in today's English the phrase "nine times out of ten" means "usually" rather than the literal numbers. In all likelihood, Homer uses a time-honored expression to mean that the Trojan War lasted a long time. We should not understand it literally. Either that, or the meaning of the phrase was garbled by the time it reached Homer.

So how long did the Trojan War really last? We don't know. All we can say is that it lasted a long time but probably considerably less than ten years. Since they had limited resources, Bronze Age kingdoms are unlikely to have mounted a ten-years' campaign. It was a protracted war. But then, Troy was a prize worth fighting for.

Troy's fortune lay in its location. "Windy Troy," as Homer calls it, was not merely gusty, it was a meteorological miracle. The city rose because it was located at the entrance to the Dardanelles, the water link between the Aegean and the Black Sea. In its prime, Troy covered seventy-five acres and held 5,000–7,500 people, which made it a big city in Bronze Age terms and a regional capital.

The Troad, the hinterland of Troy, was a blessed land. There was fresh water in abundance, the fields were rich with grain, the pastures were perfect for cattle, the woods were overrun with deer, and the seas were swarming with tuna and other fish. And there was the special gift of Boreas, the Greek god of the north wind: Boreas usually blows in the Dardanelles for thirty to sixty days during the summer sailing season, sometimes for weeks at a time. In antiquity, when boats lacked the technology to tack, that is, to zigzag against the wind, Boreas stopped shipping in the Dardanelles. For much of the sailing season, ship captains were forced to wait in Troy's harbor until the wind fell. As lords of the waterfront, Trojans got rich, and they owed it to Boreas.

The Trojans were among the world's great middlemen. Middlemen are rarely beloved, especially if they get rich on bad weather. With the possible exception of textiles, the Trojans had only one good to sell, their famous horses. Horse dealers were the used-car salesmen of the ancient world. The fast-talking Trojans probably found ways to cheat other men that outdid anything thought up in Thebes or Mycenae.

Troy may not have been popular, but with its natural advantages and business savvy, Troy was peaceful and prosperous—or it would have been, had it been wrapped in a bubble. Unfortunately, Troy stood exposed on the bloody fault line where two empires met. There was no more dangerous piece of real estate in the ancient world. To the east lay the Hittites, great charioteers who rode out of the central highlands and dominated Anatolia as well as much of the Near East. To the west lay the Greeks, a rising power whose navy exerted pressure across the Aegean Sea. These two warlike peoples were cousins of a sort. Both spoke an Indo-European language, and both had arrived in the Mediterranean from farther east around 2000 B.C. Although these two rivals never invaded each other's heartland, they took out their fury on the people stuck between them.

Western Anatolia was the Poland of the Late Bronze Age: wealthy, cultured, and caught between two empires. In a region of about forty thousand square miles (roughly the size of Kentucky or about four-fifths the size of England), an ever-shifting set of countries struggled for power—with the Hittites and the Greeks always ready to stir the pot. There was a never-ending series of wars among the dozens of kingdoms that came and went over the years, vying for power in a turbulent no-man's-land.

To the Greeks, who laid claim to the Aegean islands and who held a foothold in Anatolia, the Troad was a threat and a temptation, both a dagger pointed at the Greek heart and a bridge to the Hittites' heartland. It was also the richest source of booty on the horizon. A major regional hub, Troy was a way station for goods from Syria and Egypt and occasionally even from the Caucasus and Scandinavia. How could the predatory hearts of the Greeks not have yearned to plunder it? But it was not a fruit to be easily picked.

Troy was a sturdy fortress. The plain of Troy was broad but, otherwise, it was no place for a bloody brawl. It was soggy for much of the year, which was bad for chariots. It may have been malarial— the evidence is unclear. Add to these factors the Trojan army and Troy's wide network of alliances. But though the city was strong, Troy had weak spots. Twenty-eight towns lay in Troy's rich hinterland, not to mention more towns on the nearby islands, and none of them had fortifications to match the walls of the metropolis. These places overflowed with the material goods and the women whom the Greeks coveted.

Practiced and patient raiders, the Greeks were ready for the challenge of protracted conflict. Living in tents and shelters between the devil and the wine dark sea would be miserable, but no one becomes a "Viking" in order to be comfortable. The Trojans enjoyed all the rewards of wealth and sophistication. But the Greeks had three advantages of their own: they were less civilized, more patient, and they had strategic mobility because of their ships. In the end, those trumped Troy's cultural superiority. And so we come to the Trojan War.

The war probably took place sometime between 1230 and 1180 B.C., more likely between 1210 and 1180. At that latter date the city of Troy was destroyed by a raging fire. The presence of weapons (arrowheads, spearheads, and sling stones) as well as unburied human bones points to a sack—that is, a sudden and violent attack. The towns in the Troad, according to a recent survey by archaeologists, may have been abandoned around 1200, consistent with an invasion.

Yet some skeptics deny the veracity of the Trojan War because few weapons have been found in the ruins of Troy compared to other ancient cities that had been sacked. But we must remember that Troy is no undisturbed site. It was the premier tourist attraction of the ancient world; its soil was dug up in search of relics for such VIP tourists as Alexander the Great and the Emperor Augustus. And later "urban renewal" flattened the citadel for terraces for Greek and Roman temples, a process that destroyed layers of Bronze Age remains. The archaeological evidence fits the picture of a city that was sacked, burned, and, in later centuries, picked through by eager tourists.

The date of the Trojan War sticks in some historians' craws. Around 1180 B.C. the great palaces of mainland Greece, from Mycenae to Pylos, and many places in between, were themselves destroyed. With their own ruin looming, could the Greeks have possibly attacked Troy between 1210 and 1180? Yes. History is full of sudden reversals. For example, most Japanese cities were rubble in 1945, yet only four years earlier, in 1941, Japan had attacked the United States. Besides, the Greek myths say that the Trojan War gave way to civil war and chaos within the Greek homeland, and that might just fit the archaeological evidence. Finally, unrest in Greece in the period 1210–1180 might have made the Trojan War *more*, not less, likely, because it might have tempted Greek politicians to export violence abroad.

History is made up not of stones or words but of people. Was there ever a queen named Helen and did her face launch a thousand ships? Was there a warrior named Achilles who in a rage killed thousands? Did Aeneas suffer through a bitter war only to have the last laugh as a king? What about Hector, Odysseus, Priam, Paris, Hecuba, Agamemnon, Menelaus, and Thersites? Did they exist or did a poet invent them? We don't know, but names are some of the easiest things to pass down in an oral tradition, which increases the likelihood that they were real people. Besides, we can almost say that if Homer's heroes had not existed, we would have had to invent them. There may not have been an Achilles, but Greek warriors used his tactics of raiding cities and of fighting battles by attacking chariots on foot. Whether Helen's face launched a thousand ships or none, queens of the Bronze Age wielded great power and kings made war over marriage alliances. Priam may never have ruled Troy, but Kings Alaksandu and Walmu did, and Anatolian rulers lived much as Homer describes Priam, from his dealings with uppity nobles to his practice of polygamy. So this book will refer to Homer's characters as real-life individuals. The reader should keep in mind that their existence is plausible but unproven. Descriptions of them are based on Homer and, whenever possible, on details drawn from archaeology, epigraphy, art, etc.

And with that, let us meet our leading lady. She is a character who sums up the spirit of her age, and new evidence increases the chances that she really did exist. And that she ran away from home to go to the windy city, blown by Boreas, and the fatal waterway by which it sat, where soldiers stole cattle and hunted men.

CHAPTER ONE

WAR FOR HELEN

S he is the spark that ignited the war. Helen is dressed in a flowing, woolen gown, deftly woven by slave women, in black, taupe, and crimson stripes, and soft and shimmering from the oil with which it has been treated. The sleeves cover her upper arms but leave exposed the pearl skin of her lower arms. The winding bands of a gold bracelet cover each of her bare wrists. Two matching gold brooches hang from the garment's neckline. A tight-fitting bodice and a gold belt emphasize her full breasts. Her face is framed by her long hair, oiled to prevent dryness, and held in place by an elaborate, jeweled headband. Her elegant coiffure consists of pin curls and tendrils about her forehead, and long, glossy curls that fall below her waist. Her maids arrange her tawny hair every morning and night with ivory combs. Her cheeks are glowing with health and rouge, and her shining eyes are lined with carefully applied kohl. She wears a delicate perfume scented with oil of iris and carnation. Love runs after her like puppies, to quote a Hittite proverb.

But on this night, it is a man who pursues her. Paris, prince of Troy, has come to Greece, having commissioned new ships especially for the occasion. He knows that he has to put his best foot forward, because Troy and Greece are rivals, and the Greeks would seize on any sign of weakness. By the same token, Paris is supposed to be at his diplomatic best. By accepting the hospitality of the king of Sparta, Menelaus, Paris has an unspoken obligation to behave like a gentleman. But all's fair in love and war.

Imagine the first meeting of Helen and Paris at a state banquet in his honor, no doubt in Menelaus's palace, which was surely set among the pines in the rich hills of Lacedaemon, the countryside around Sparta. The company sits in the throne room, a large, high-roofed hall with four columns surrounding a central hearth, whose smoke is drawn up and out through an opening in the ceiling. Armed sentries stand along walls frescoed with scenes of lions attacking deer and griffins standing guard. After a procession and offerings to the gods, the guests sit down, in silver-studded chairs. Paris sits in a place of honor, between the king and queen.

Paris and Menelaus are probably each wearing a linen tunic and below it a belted kilt of finely woven wool, possibly made into pat-terned panels and with a fringed edge and a tassel. Menelaus probably wears a diadem in the sign of royalty favored by the Greeks, while Paris might have the horned tiara of royalty common in Anatolia. Each is likely to have a gold signet ring. Menelaus probably has shoul-der-length hair and a trimmed beard but no mustache. Paris might be clean-shaven in the Hittite fashion, but with long hair tied in a knot at the nape of his neck. Greek royalty and nobles all wore leather sandals, while Paris might have worn the boots of an Anatolian king.

Barefoot servants hurry to and fro with oil lamps and silver-and-gold pitchers and bowls for the ritual washing of hands. Then comes the meal. There would be honey, figs, and bread, and a selection of the finest meat from the royal stock: lamb, kid, pork, hare, venison, or wild boar. For a special guest from a royal house, there would be fish. In Greece meat was available even to ordinary people, but fish was food for a king. Fishing was labor-intensive, transport overland was expensive, and fish was not as easy to preserve as meat.

The food would be washed down with plenty of alcohol. The preferred beverage was a cocktail, mixed in a large bowl, of wine, beer, and honey mead, possibly with a taste of pine resin; resinated wine was already popular in Bronze Age Greece. The partygoers drank out of two-handled cups with a wide, shallow bowl above a stem, and made of either the finest painted pottery or of silver or gold. A bard playing the lyre would have entertained the banqueters with heroic song. In between the figs and the lamb, Helen and Paris might have exchanged their first words.

They might well have spoken Greek. Troy's language was probably either Luwian, the main tongue of southern and western Anatolia, or Palaic, the main language of the north. Both were Indo-European tongues, closely related to Hittite. But foreign languages were surely widespread in an entrepôt like Troy, especially Greek, which was spoken by traders and potters as well as nobles who had married into the Anatolian nobility. It seems that Troy's elite were bilingual in their own language and Greek; they had dual names, such as Paris—itself perhaps just Homer's rendition in Greek of a Luwian name, *Pari-zitis*, whose Greek name was Alexander. Troy's elite moved easily in and out of the Greek world, including Menelaus's palace.

In fact, Greeks and Trojans are likely to have forged friendships and kept them going across the generations, because these ties were good for business and they were prestigious. Consider the Greek kingdom of Pylos, west of Sparta, where Linear B texts record a military commander named "Trojan" and a leaseholder of a plot of land named "Trojan Woman." These names may have been bestowed to mark an international friendship, just as in later Greek times an Athenian friend of Sparta named his son "Lacedaemonius," that is, the Spartan.

Some ancient sources insist that Menelaus was about to go abroad: urgent business was calling him away to Crete. If he indeed left Helen alone with Paris, then Menelaus was the most foolish husband since Cronus had trusted Rhea, and *she* took advantage of him by helping their son Zeus overthrow the old man. Menelaus should have paid more attention to Helen's feelings: others surely were doing so.

An indiscreet remark by a Greek ambassador, a letter from a spy, a bawdy song in a Trojan tavern: one or all of these hints of Helen's unhappiness might have spurred Paris to action. The queen of Sparta had a wandering eye and Paris wanted to fill its field of vision. He loved the ladies, whom he handled with the same skill as his famous bow. But in Helen, he had met his match.

According to Homer, Helen was passionate, intelligent, and manipulative. He gives her a pair of hands speedy enough to slip a drug into a man's drink without him noticing. She had a way of leaning back in her chair and resting her feet on a stool, as if she were a judge about to pronounce sentence or a cat getting ready to pounce. She might have been the favorite of Aphrodite, goddess of love, but Helen was nobody's plaything. Although she was young—perhaps still in her early twenties—Helen was not without experience. She was a royal princess, daughter of King Tyndareus of Sparta or, in some versions of the myth, of Zeus himself; her mother was Leda or Nemesis.

That is myth, but the power of certain Bronze Age queens is a historical fact. And nowhere was this truer than in Anatolia. Land of the mother goddess, it was the veritable homeland of strong women. Archaeology may yet document a mighty queen in Greece, but in the current state of the evidence, we have to look eastward for that. And perhaps Helen did so too. Perhaps she was ambitious and saw Troy as a place offering her freedom and power.

Homer's Paris is handsome and amorous. He is stylish, lithe, athletic, and a talented bowman. History lends credibility to the picture. Anatolians were famous as archers. Troy was older than any city in Greece, so Trojans may have found it easy to pour on Old World charm when on the far side of the Aegean. But the other side of the scale held Greek stereotypes about effete easterners and, indeed, Homer makes Paris just a little cowardly in battle. No doubt the real Paris was charming and a hustler, the latter surely not an uncommon figure in a country of horse traders.

But charm is not a word that comes to mind in the case of Menelaus. Helen praised his intelligence and good looks, but that was only after she had been dragged home from Troy to Sparta and was eager to get back in Menelaus's good graces, not that he was fooled. No doubt the *Iliad*'s description of Menelaus is closer to the truth. He was a well-built warrior with distinctive red hair. As a speaker he was no-nonsense. We hear nothing of his skill at the lyre or the figure he cut on the dance floor, as we do of his rival Paris. As a soldier Menelaus was second-rate, incapable of going for the enemy's jugular, let alone fighting the Trojan champion Hector—as he would later have pretensions of doing. He was the kind of warrior who is dismissed again and again in Egyptian texts as "feeble" or "despicable." The god Apollo offers a withering put-down: Menelaus is a "soft spearman." He was, in fact, faintly ridiculous.

She blamed uncontrollable passion for her decision to leave home, husband, and daughter, Hermione, for Paris. But that is what gamblers say when they look back afterward. The real Helen, one suspects, knew just what she was doing.

Paris was no fool for love either. His abduction of Helen may have had less to do with lust than with power politics. By capturing Helen, Paris carried out a bloodless raid on enemy territory. He may have been a knave but he was no pawn: he aimed to use Helen to advance his own position in the royal house of Troy and his country's position in the international arena. Ultimately, her aim was to use him too, so the adulterous couple was less like Romeo and Juliet than Juan and Eva Perón.

The modern reader is skeptical of Homer. Surely, something as big as the Trojan War was about more than a case of wife-stealing. In ancient times others felt similarily, and the Greek historian Herodotus (ca. 485–ca. 425 B.C.) quoted the opinion that the Greeks were fools to make a fuss about Paris and Helen and go to war. And so they would have been if the only reason for the Trojan War had been the beautiful wife of Menelaus. In fact, the Greeks had many reasons to make war on Troy, involving both domestic politics and foreign policy.

Yet Homer is not mistaken but merely authentic. The Bronze Age was an era that preferred to put things in personal terms rather than in abstractions. Instead of justice, security, or any of the other issues that would be part of a war debate today, the Bronze Age tended to speak of family and friendship, crime and punishment. Near Eastern kings proclaim in their inscriptions that they fought to take vengeance on their enemies and on rebels; they fought those who boasted or who transgressed their path or who violated the king's boundaries or raised their bows against royal allies; they fought to widen their borders and bring gifts to their loyal friends. A Hittite king says that his enemies attacked him when he came to the throne because they judged him young and weak—their mistake! Allies are royal vassals, obliged to have the same friends and enemies as the king.

Consider an example from Canaan in the 1300s B.C. When the sons of the ruler of Shechem asked the mayor of Megiddo to join their military campaign against the city of Jenin, they personified the matter: the cause of the war, they said, was the murder of their father by citizens of Jenin. Failure to help would also be personal, as it would turn the sons into Megiddo's enemy.

We would, therefore, expect the Bronze Age to put the causes of the Trojan War in personal terms—murder, rebellion, or even wife-stealing—rather than the aggression, competition, resentment, covetousness, and insecurity that underlay the conflict. But these latter factors were there. They can be traced in Greek and Trojan archaeological finds and in Hittite and other Near Eastern documents. Let's begin with the texts.

Both sides saw conflict looming between Troy and Greece. Hittite texts trace a rising tide of troubles in the 1200s B.C. Around 1280 B.C., Troy gave up its traditional policy of splendid isolation to make an alliance with the Hittites. The king of Troy, Alaksandu, had great wealth but not enough military power to protect his lands, cities, vineyards, threshing floors, fields, cattle, and sheep, not to mention his wife, concubines, and sons—to use the terms of Hittite treaties. The Hittites, in turn, were always looking for allies in turbulent western Anatolia, a region that distracted them from their main interests to the south and east.

So Troy became what the Hittites called a "soldier servant," that is, a Hittite vassal state with military responsibilities, with a promise of Hittite military protection in return. But as the century progressed, Hittite power declined, probably because of a civil war among the various branches of the ruling dynasty. And the Greeks put pressure on Troy, as shown by a letter ca. 1250 B.C. from the king of Ahhiyawa—that is, Greece—to the king of the Hittites. The addressee was probably Hattushilish III (1267–1237 B.C.). The name of the Greek king who sent the letter is unknown. It is possible that he ruled in Thebes. One scholar finds in the text a reference to a famous name of Greek mythology: Cadmus, legendary first king of Thebes. Most scholars, however, reject this reading.

The subject of the letter is the control of the islands off the Anatolian coast, possibly the northeastern Aegean islands of Lemnos, Imbros, and Samothrace. Long ago, the letter says, Cadmus had married off his daughter to an Anatolian king who owned these islands. So according to the Greek king, the islands belonged to him and not to the Hittites. Note that, in typical Bronze Age fashion, the matter is expressed in terms that are personal and familial. The issue is not international law but inheritance.

Note too that any conflict between Greece and Hatti over these islands would pass straight through Troy. And there was other trouble brewing to the south. The brother of the Greek king, a man named Tawagalawa—Eteocles, in Greek?—was pushing out in force from Miletus, aiding a Hittite rebel and trying to make Hattushilish III give Tawagalawa/Eteocles a fief in western Anatolia. Not long afterward, another king of Troy, Walmu, had been forced to flee the city, apparently after a coup. Because Walmu was his vassal, Hittite King Tudhaliya IV (1237–1228 B.C.) wanted to restore him to his throne. But Walmu was stuck in the hands of another king near Troy. We don't know how things turned out and we can only wonder what was at issue in the coup d'état at Troy. Was it simply a power struggle or was some principle at stake? And might that principle have concerned Trojan relations with the Greeks?

Paris's Greek name—Alexander—might mean that he was descended from King Alaksandu, who forged Troy's alliance with the Hittites. Certainly, Paris's mission faced a similar problem: how could Troy achieve maximum security at minimum cost and without undue risk? His answer was to treat the enemy like a rival gang leader, whose power depended on his honor and whose honor meant controlling his woman, at a minimum. Dazed and caught off-guard, the squabbling Greeks would either have to unite—in itself no small thing—and wage a very tough war or they would have to accept one very big but cheap triumph for Troy. Paris had played the game well.

But Menelaus knew the rules too. He went to war not because his bed was cold but because his future was shaky. Paris had not only cuckolded the king but abused his hospitality. The Trojan was like a high roller who openly cheats in front of the casino owner. Unless he punished Paris, Menelaus would be branded as an easy mark. Since he ruled Sparta by marriage and not birth, unless he forced the return of his wife, he would eventually face someone wanting to knock him off his throne. But Menelaus had an immediate problem: his treasury was lighter thanks to Helen's decision to take a queen's ransom with her to Troy.

Just what Helen took is unknown; it was certainly not cash, since coinage had not yet been invented. At a minimum, the hoard included her dowry, which must have been substantial because she was a royal princess. Who knows what other loot she and Paris helped themselves to as they left. The treasures surely gleamed. Greek goldsmiths were famous for their craft, and their masterworks were matched by the pick of the world's imports. Greek kings and queens enjoyed gold and silver vases and cups, bronze daggers inlaid with gold decoration, solid gold earrings, solid gold rings with inlaid amber or lapis lazuli, silver pins with decorated gold heads, ivory plaques and combs, gold diadems and bracelets, gold necklaces with precious-stone pendants. Their shapes were a forest of swirls and rosettes, and decorated with a gallery of ivy leaves, crocuses, figure-eight shields, bulls, lions, hunters, gods, and priests. It was a collection built up over generations, and it was a thief's dream.

Paris not only made off with Sparta's queen, therefore, but with its Fort Knox. Later, Paris describes the Trojan War as a fight

For beauteous Helen and the wealth she brought.

Agamemnon echoes these words. Homer was much too pragmatic to reduce war to romance.

Regional politics also played a role. Agamemnon's Mycenae was the strongest kingdom in Greece, but the other Greek states could and did go their own ways, and in the age's warrior culture, that meant blood. Around 1250 B.C., the great city of Thebes had been sacked by an army that, although largely from other Greek kingdoms, had its roots in a Theban dynastic dispute. Agamemnon would surely rather have the Greeks unite against Troy than turn on one another.

In short, if the question about the Trojan War is, "What's love got to do with it?" the answer is probably, "Nothing."

In later ages Helen was worshipped as a goddess in Sparta, but opinions were mixed elsewhere. The Athenian classical tragedian Aeschylus no doubt spoke for many when he wrote off the woman who had caused the Trojan War with the puns of Helen the "Helandros" and "Helenaus"—Helen the Man-Killer and Ship-Destroyer. Yet the royal princess of Sparta had been an extraordinarily eligible bride. Her dowry was the kingdom.

Like Helen, Menelaus was born royalty, brother of King Agamemnon of Mycenae, but Menelaus did not inherit the kingship. In Hittite society it was possible for a man to marry into the royal family and so win a throne, and the same may have been true for Greece. This usually happened only when a king had no sons, but Helen had two brothers, Castor and Polydeukes. Perhaps they, like Telemachus in the *Odyssey*, were too young to inherit, or more likely, Tyndareus decided it was worth passing them over in order to ally his family with the powerful dynasty nearby. Menelaus became king of Sparta.

Sparta was wealthy and comfortable. Laconia (as the valley in which Sparta lies is known) has yielded many Bronze Age treasures, such as the elegant pair of solid gold cups found in a tomb at a village called Vapheio. These fifteenth-century B.C. masterpieces show scenes of bull-chasing. At Amyclae, near Sparta, stood a Bronze Age mansion; here, centuries later, there rose a structure called the

Menelaion, a shrine to Menelaus and Helen. Many scholars think the palace of Menelaus and Helen once stood there too. Meanwhile, recent excavations in northern Laconia, outside the village of Pellana, have uncovered a Bronze Age cemetery, complete with big and imposing beehive *(tholos)* tombs—the largest such tombs found anywhere. Nearby is a hill on which the excavator believes that he may have found the palace of Menelaus and Helen. This theory is still unproven, but the big tombs of Pellana add to the impression of Bronze Age Laconia's prosperity.

But Laconia was not Troy. Menelaus was a provincial warrior, while Paris was a cosmopolitan prince. Troy was the city of light and life at the meeting place of the world. And it was a good place to be a woman. Women in Bronze Age Anatolia had more freedom and power than their sisters in Mycenaean Greece. The evidence of archaeology, epigraphy, and Homer all agree on this point. Consider a recent and remarkable discovery by the excavators of Troy: a bronze disk, which is convex on both sides, not quite an inch in diameter and just a half inch thick. It weighs only four ounces. Yet it offers an important insight into the society of Troy. Each side of the disk is incised with writing, which shows that it was a seal. The Trojan seal was last used ca.1150–1100 B.C., but it was probably an heirloom. Its style went out of fashion after 1200 and its worn surface suggests long use. So the seal may well tell us about the world of Priam.

The practice of sealing was common in the ancient Near East, including Anatolia. Seals were used to stamp land deeds, court decisions, treaties, royal pronouncements, and even clay "envelopes" in which contracts were stored. Seals were also an important part of commerce, used to mark containers and other merchandise. If the seal was broken, the container had been opened. A respected merchant's seal on a product, then as now, was a guarantee of quality.

The Trojan seal catches the eye for two reasons. First, it is the only writing ever found in Bronze Age Troy. Second the seal is inscribed on both sides. One side bears the name of a man, who was a scribe, while the other side bears the name of a woman, presumably his wife. The writing system is Luwian hieroglyphic, as was standard for Late Bronze Age Anatolia. The bronze is too worn for us to read either name but the signs for "man" and "woman" are each clear. In short, the seal testifies to a degree of freedom and equality for women.

That is not unusual for Bronze Age Anatolia. In the Hittite kingdom, for instance, there was nothing remarkable about married couples, whether royalty or commoners, using seal stones with the husband's name on one side and the woman's on the other. A Hittite woman might even have a seal of her own.

The Greek world had nothing similar to Troy's husband-wife seal. While seals were tools of commerce in Anatolia, in Greece they were used mainly as ornaments. Although Greek bureaucrats stamped goods in the warehouse with seals, in general the Greeks treated their seals as jewelry, as signs of wealth and display, meant to be worn around the neck. Greek seals were not inscribed with writing. Women were sometimes depicted but men predominated, and that seems to fit Mycenaean culture.

In Homer, Trojan men, such as Hector, worry about the opinion of the women of Troy. When Hector's wife, Andromache, asks him to leave the battlefield for her sake and for the sake of their child, Hector replies:

> How would the sons of Troy, in arms renown'd,
> And Troy's proud dames, whose garments sweep the ground
> Attaint the lustre of my former name,
> Should Hector basely quit the field of fame?

Homer's Greeks display no corresponding concern for what their women thought.

Hittite history is punctuated by the careers of powerful royal women. Yes, the Hittite Great King, like other Anatolian monarchs, practiced polygamy. But the power of the chief wife was potentially enormous, especially if she was in charge of raising and marrying off all the royal children. The greatest Hittite queen had those powers and many others: she was Queen Puduhepa, wife of King Hattushilish III. Puduhepa came from a noble family of high priests in southern Anatolia and went on to play a pivotal role in Hittite religion. She also took a hand in law and diplomacy. She had both a joint seal with her husband and her own independent seal. When, for example, Egypt and the Hittites negotiated a peace treaty, which was recorded on a silver tablet, the seal of King Hattushilish appeared on one side of the tablet and the seal of Queen Puduhepa appeared on the other. She corresponded as an equal with Pharaoh Rameses II.

Bronze Age Greece offers the occasional image of a powerful queen like the *Odyssey*'s Queen Arete of the probably fictional kingdom of Phaeacia, but otherwise it had no room for Puduhepas or for gender equality. It was a world whose captains and kings called their bedmates "prizes" and traded them like bric-a-brac. Helen's response was neither to accept nor to protest; Helen's response, one might posit, was to opt out.

From Sparta the lovers fled to Paris's ships, loaded with treasure. They were in a hurry, but found time to stop at Cranae, an island off the coast, where they consummated their passion, or so tradition says. Then came the Aegean crossing. As they neared the Anatolian coast, Helen could hardly have helped noticing the light gleaming on Troy's towers. After disembarking at Troy's harbor, she might have seen, as she rode to town, the wheat fields on the low hills in the distance. Unlike their ancestors, who lived on barley and lentils, the prosperous Trojans of Paris's day grew an abundance of wheat.

As she reached the city, Helen surely found it as foreign as she did exciting. At the gates of the city stood steles, standing stones honoring the gods, a common Anatolian custom but not Greek. Another typical Anatolian feature was the layout awaiting her inside the wooden walls: a lower town around a fortified citadel. Inside Troy's imposing gates, Helen would have found a bustling city of narrow alleys around paved streets with inset drains, a city of shrines, markets, courtyards, ovens, and houses built of stone, mud brick, and wood.

At dawn and sunset the town would have echoed with the din of cattle and sheep and the herders who brought them out to graze and back. The day was filled with the cries of merchants, the talk of slaves and housewives heading out to the springs to do laundry, and the laughter of children. The night rang with the clatter of pottery at the evening meal, the footsteps of the night watch, and the twang of the lute mixed with the whistle of pipes. And on a hot summer afternoon, when anyone sensible was taking a siesta, the city heard nothing at all.

The lower city was so thickly settled that its buildings reached right up to the wall of the citadel, or Pergamos, as Homer calls it. Pergamos rose about one hundred feet above the plain, a half-acre stronghold protected by an 1,150-foot circuit of walls standing 30 feet high. The serpentine path that led up from the lower city would have brought Helen to the royal palace atop the hill.

Helen is likely to have formally divorced Menelaus. Hittite law allowed a woman to initiate divorce proceedings, and society would not have looked kindly on ongoing adultery. The Amarna Letters, for example, consider a woman without a husband as a symbol of desolation, neglect, and futility—like a field without a cultivator. Paris saved Helen from such a fate. The two of them lived in style: Their beautiful house on Pergamos was built by the best craftsmen in the Troad. There they slept in a high-vaulted, perfumed bedroom. She was attended by a group of Trojan handmaids, whom she directed in such household chores as weaving. She enjoyed all the freedom of an Anatolian princess as well as the cosmopolitan pleasures of life in a big city on the crossroads of international trade. Some of Troy's nobles grumbled about her presence, but King Priam was her champion and she called him father. There was only one problem: the long arm of her rightful husband.

Arranged dynastic marriage was a staple of Bronze Age diplomacy. A marriage was, in effect, a treaty. Take, for example, Madduwatta, a wily Hittite vassal king in western Anatolia around 1400 B.C. Madduwatta married off his daughter to King Kupanta-Kurunta of the nearby land of Arzawa. This was the beginning of an alliance between two former enemies, as the Hittite Great King recognized, with no little annoyance. How could he trust Madduwatta to uphold Hittite interests against Kupanta-Kurunta now that the latter was Madduwatta's son-in-law?

If a royal marriage was an alliance, a royal seduction was an act of war. Hittite law uses this striking image for a man who runs off with a woman without her family's consent: "You have become a wolf." It meant, in effect, that he was banished. Adultery was considered an even worse crime, and Hittite law pardoned a husband for killing his wife and her lover if he caught them in the act. But while a man who raped another man's wife got the death penalty, a man who seduced another man's wife got off; in that case, only the wife was executed. If Greek or Trojan law were similar, Helen would have known that she had put her life on the line by running off with Paris. Either she didn't care or she expected to get away with it.

This was not just wishful thinking. It may seem incredible that Helen or Paris thought they could attack the institution of royal marriage without war. But there was precedent. Pharaoh Ay of Egypt had lived down the murder of Hittite prince Zannanza, en route to Zannanza's arranged marriage with Ankhesenamun, the widowed queen of the young Pharaoh Tutankhamun. The murdered prince's father, King Shuppiluliuma I (1344–1322), was one of the strongest of all Hittite kings. Yet his response was a routine attack on Egyptian possessions in southern Syria. Thousands of prisoners were hauled back to Hattusha, but this was no showdown. Shuppiluliuma did not even take part in the campaign, perhaps because he faced other threats on the northern and eastern borders. In short, the Hittite response was little more than a punitive raid, the Bronze Age equivalent of lobbing a few cruise missiles over the border. Pharaoh must have breathed a sigh of relief.

As for the Greeks, it was one thing to threaten to invade Troy and quite another to pull off an invasion. Imagine Priam's reaction to the news of Helen's abduction: whatever his worries, Priam might well have doubted that a Greek army would ever dare appear before Troy's fortifications. If the Greeks did come it would be too late for regrets because backing down would have destroyed Priam's prestige. But Priam surely believed that between Troy's allies and its walls, the city was impregnable. The Greeks would be hard-pressed to carry out more than a few raids, then they would fight over the booty and turn on each other. Surely the expedition would go home after a few months, while Paris kept Helen. Like Pharaoh Ay in the Zannanza affair, Priam might have expected to pay a price for misbehavior but not a very big price.

In any case, Agamemnon would have no easy time persuading the other Greeks into a big and risky war against Troy. A tradition, not mentioned in Homer, records an oath supposedly sworn by all the princes of Greece to uphold Menelaus's claim to Helen, said to be the most beautiful woman in the world, not to mention Greece's premier heiress. The hard-nosed historian Thucydides dismisses this story. He says the other Greeks followed Agamemnon not as an act of grace but because they feared his power.

No doubt Agamemnon was able to twist arms, but Thucydides' analysis is one-sided. The king of Mycenae had the gods on his side. The Bronze Age generally thought of war as a divine drama of law enforcement: war punished criminals who had offended the gods. The Hittites gave this conception a twist and imagined war as a lawsuit before the gods, who would favor one of the plaintiffs with victory. To the Greeks, Paris had twice violated the gods' laws, first by committing adultery and second by abusing his host's generosity. Menelaus's fellow rulers had a clear responsibility to avenge the gods by going to war against Troy unless Helen and the treasures were returned. Anything less would expose themselves to divine punishment.

Even the most pious Greek might have balked at throwing himself against the mighty walls of Troy, but there were compensations. The Greek kings no doubt knew that war would keep their fighting men busy and out of trouble at home. And the potential for plunder outside Troy's walls sweetened the deal. Bronze Age invasions usually included raids, like those carried out under the Hittite King Hattushilish I (1650–1620 B.C.), whose armies plundered the cattle and sheep of an Anatolian enemy's farmers. The Greeks surely relished the chance of doing likewise to the Troad and nearby islands.

They were not likely to have had second thoughts about the pretext for the war, because the Bronze Age was not finicky about the *casus belli.* Conquest was its own reward. It brought glory, honor, and an occasion for king and commoner alike to display what the Hittites referred to as "manly deeds." The victors also got loot, both inanimate and human, including slaves, both male and female. In the reign of Hattushilish III, to cite an example, seven thousand Hittite subjects were transplanted from Lycia (in southwestern Anatolia) to Greece.

In the Bronze Age, women were often regarded as a commodity. The victorious King Zimri-Lin of Mari (in Syria, 1789–1752 B.C.), brought back women captives to serve as weavers and harem mates. In the 1300s, a pharaoh ordered one of his vassals in Canaan to buy him forty "extremely beautiful" female cupbearers; he sent silver weighing sixteen hundred shekels, forty per woman, as well as an escort of archers to bring them back to Egypt. In the Greek kingdom of Pylos, women played a big role in the woolen industry, for instance, as weavers, spinners, and sheep shearers. Linear B tablets from around 1200 B.C. identify about fifteen hundred women and children in these jobs. Some came from places located up and down the coast of Anatolia as well as from the Aegean islands. Others are labeled as "captives," and it is a good guess that they had been seized by Greek raiders. No wonder that, centuries later, the Greek historian Herodotus commented that when Paris ran back to Troy with Helen wife-stealing was an old custom.

Helen was not the cause but merely the occasion of the war. By seducing a Greek princess, Troy had interfered in the politics of the Greek kingdoms and humiliated a powerful man. It was dangerous to hurt an enemy without destroying him; as one of the Amarna Letters says, when an ant is struck it bites back, and on the hand of the man who struck it. And there remained the underlying causes of war: resentment, greed, and power lust. Troy had everything that was dear to the Greeks' rapacious hearts. If Paris had come from

Dogpatch instead of Troy, then the king would have found few tak-
ers for the mission to avenge the gods and uphold Menelaus's honor.
But Agamemnon rallied the Greeks to attack a gold mine.

And so the harbor of Aulis filled up with the black ships in which
the Greeks planned to sail off to war.

CHAPTER TWO

THE BLACK SHIPS SAIL

The king of all Argos and of many an isle stands on the rocky soil and surveys his fleet. Before him in the harbor lie hundreds of wooden ships, their hulls coated with black pitch, their hollow interiors carrying men and supplies, preparing to bring ruin to King Priam and the people of Troy. Or so we might imagine King Agamemnon, son of Atreus, on the eve of the Greeks' departure for war.

The hills echo with the shouts of the harbormaster and the cries of the captains. Horses are whinnying, low, fast, and urgently. Sailors call out curses and every now and then there comes the crack of a stick on the back of some slacking menial. The priests are mumbling something to each other, the oxen bellow, and in the distance, through the noise, there is the sound of the salt sea slapping against the ships.

Agamemnon towers above his servants. He is a big man, healthy and muscular. Homer gives him the broad shoulders of a javelin champion, and as a king he is likely to be well fed and tall—nearly six feet tall, to judge from the skeletons found in the royal graves of Mycenae. That was a great height then, when the average Greek male stood only about five feet five inches. He is a veteran warrior, but if Agamemnon has a broken bone or two from past battles, it doesn't show, because the fractures would have been set by the palace physician and so would have healed perfectly. He has long hair and fiery eyes that offer, in turn, hints of passion, brutality, and resignation. His lips border a beard, his teeth shine gleaming white. He is dressed in a soft, newly made tunic underneath a big, sleeveless cloak. He wears fine leather sandals. A silver-studded sword hangs from an oxhide strap around his shoulders. On sleepless nights, says Homer, when the cares of office weigh, Agamemnon is in the habit of replacing the cloak with a lion skin, a reminder of his power.

He was the greatest king in Greece. Potential rivals ruled in Pylos and Tiryns, but Sparta was in the hands of his younger brother and the power of Thebes had been broken in a civil war the generation before. No wonder Homer reserves for Agamemnon the title *anax*, harkening back to the Bronze Age term for king: *wanax*. Agamemnon was rich and had a big army and navy. His domain was centered in the northeastern Peloponnese but it extended to the islands of the Aegean, perhaps as far east as Rhodes.

Homer's Agamemnon is arrogant, which makes him similar to the many Bronze Age kings whose monuments invited the mighty to look upon their works and despair. Take the king of Mari, Iahdun-Lim (1820–1798 B.C.), who describes himself in an inscription as "opener of canals, builder of walls, erector of steles proclaiming [his] name, provider of abundance and plenty for his people, who makes whatever [is needed] appear in his land, mighty king, magnificent youth." No doubt Agamemnon had an equally high opinion of himself. But he was no autocrat.

Agamemnon's kingdom was typical of its times; it was less a state than an estate, that is, it was essentially a big household. The royal palace had grand staterooms but most of its space was devoted to workshops, storerooms, and armories. It was a manor that produced luxury goods for the *wanax* to trade or give as gifts. Raw materials for the workshops were siphoned off the king's subjects as taxation.

More important, from the military point of view, the palace produced bronze breastplates and arrowheads, manufactured and maintained chariots, and stabled horses. The *wanax* controlled a corps of charioteers and bowmen and possibly one of infantrymen too. In any case, as powerful as he was, the *wanax* probably had no monopoly on the kingdom's military force.

The royal writ was strongest on the king's landholdings, concentrated around the palace. The rest of the territory was run by local big men or *basileis*, each no doubt with his own armed followers. The *wanax* could muster an army and navy out of his own men, but for a really big campaign he would need the support of the *basileis*. In short, the *wanax* was only as strong as his ability to dominate the *basileis*, be it by persuasion or force.

And he had better things to do with his time than learn the rebuslike system for recording Greek that we call Linear B. Homer takes a lot of criticism from scholars who cite the total absence from the epics of the Linear B tablets. But Linear B was used strictly for administrative convenience. Unlike Hittites or Egyptians, Mycenaean Greeks did not put writing on their monuments, boundary markers, wall paintings, or seal stones. So a *wanax* such as Agamemnon was no more likely to know Linear B than Queen Victoria was to know shorthand.

But one text the king might have learned was lines of poetry sung by bards at palace feasts; Mycenaean art shows that bards predated Homer by centuries. Poetry offered the possibility of immortality. Agamemnon already had honor, power, and glory as a "scepter-bearing king"—the term is Homer's, but the royal scepter was already a symbol of power in Sumer, two thousand years before the Trojan War. Agamemnon was a man of many possessions, but now he wanted more.

Greece's pulse quickened as the heralds of the *wanax* made their rounds to call the other kings into action. Agamemnon's peasantry had to look enthusiastic as the king's men rounded them up to serve. The Greek monarchs were no doubt blunter: Troy was an impregnable fortress and only a fool would try to take it. No wonder Homer says that Odysseus kept Agamemnon and Menelaus cooling their heels on rocky Ithaca before he agreed to join the expedition. But in the end, fear, greed, glory, and the gods won out. So they came to Aulis, the best of the Greeks, as perhaps they had never come together before.

There was Nestor, the grand old man of Pylos and most eloquent of the Greeks; Odysseus, the canny lord of Ithaca, Zacynthus, and other islands; Philoctetes, great archer from the rugged country around Mounts Ossa and Pelion; Menelaus, Agamemnon's brother and king of Sparta; Diomedes, the champion "of the great war cry" and the youngest general in the Greek army, who led a contingent from Argos and Tiryns; Ajax son of Telamon of Salamis, the so-called Greater Ajax, known as the Greeks' bulwark if not their brains; Ajax son of Oïleus of Locris, called Lesser Ajax, a hot-blooded bruiser who was spoiling for a fight; and the fearless Protesilaus of Thessaly. A different group of men testifies to the prior Greek penetration of the Aegean: Idomeneus of Crete, the island that Greek arms had grabbed from the Minoans; Tlepolemus son of Heracles, a thug who had murdered his great-uncle on the mainland and moved to Rhodes; and men from the other Dodecanese islands of the southeastern Aegean Sea. Finally, to return to the mainland, there was Greece's greatest warrior, a man known as the best of the Greeks, prince of the central Greek region of Phthia, leader of the fearsome unit of warriors called the Myrmidons: Achilles.

Maybe they are all fiction, but as a group they represent the Bronze Age art of war. Their hands were battle-wise with blood and calloused from stealing cattle. They could trample the enemy like a carpet under their feet or calm the heart of a nervous army under attack. They knew horses like a stable hand and ships like a boatswain, but most of all they knew men and how to lead them. They could be as smooth as the ghee-and-honey paste with which Assyrians cemented rows of mud brick or as rough as the gnarled limbs of an old olive tree. They knew which soldiers to reward with silver rings and which to punish with prison or mutilation. They could inspire the men to follow on foot while they rode in their chariots and to compete for the honor of fighting bravely in their presence.

They could break an enemy's lance or deceive him with words.

They knew how much flour it took to feed an army and how much wood was needed to burn a corpse. They knew how to pitch camp or launch a fleet, how to debrief a spy or send out an informer. They could draw a bow and split a copper ingot like a reed or hurl a spear and pierce the seam in an enemy's armor. They shrugged off mud and snow, towering waves or buckets of rain. They could appraise lapis lazuli with a jeweler's eye or break a merchant's neck with a hangman's hands. They could court a milkmaid or rape a princess. They relished ambushes after dark and noontime charges. They feared the gods and liked the smell of death.

They knew war in all its bloody ways, but they shared a single dream: to set sail home from Troy in ships with timbers creaking from the weight of plunder. Achilles says that he plundered no fewer than twenty-three cities in the Trojan War and Odysseus proudly calls himself "sacker of cities." It was a fitting motto for the Bronze Age way of war, and an inspiration for Agamemnon's commanders. Odysseus and Achilles echoed centuries of predecessors in Late Bronze Age Anatolia. Shortly before 1400 B.C. a Greek called Attarissiya in Hittite—in Greek, perhaps Atreus—landed on the Anatolian coast. He went on a spree of war and plunder through southwest Anatolia with one hundred chariots and a force of infantrymen. Then he crossed the sea to carry out raids on Cyprus. Agamemnon's father was also called Atreus, so perhaps the men were kin. Nearly two hundred years later, ca. 1250, a Luwian general named Piyamaradu continually raided the territory of Hittite vassal kings in western Anatolia. Piyamaradu had the tacit consent and perhaps the help of a Greek royal prince in Miletus called Tawagalawa in Hittite. This Greek might have been Eteocles, a Theban prince of myth, or maybe Teucer, as Greater Ajax's brother was called.

Each of Agamemnon's generals was the leader of a band of warriors; Greek for warrior band is *laos*, a common term in Homer. The warriors were bound by strongly personal ties. We see this, for example, in Homer's emphasis on the loyalty of the Myrmidons to Achilles. Linear B tablets refer to a group of royal officials as "followers" and to the commander of the *laos* as the "man who assembles the warrior band." This latter is, possibly, *lawagetās* in Mycenaean Greek, and some scholars think that the name Laertes, Odysseus's father, is just a contraction of that word. Whereas we, and later Greeks, tend to think of an army as an institution and war as a deployment of men and material, Homer and Bronze Age Greeks tended to think of both in personal terms. For example, the classical Greek word for army, *stratos*, means "encampment," and for war, *polemos* means "engagement of opposing warriors or troops." But both Homer and Linear B avoid these terms, preferring instead "warrior band" and "war spirit" or "war god" (Ares). The army that gathered at Aulis, therefore, was in a real sense, a collection of warrior bands and their chieftains.

It was also a collection of soldiers. Bronze Age documents tend to refer to the army as "the infantry and the chariotry," but that oversimplifies. A well-equipped army around 1200 B.C. had a variety of fighting men, including both heavy and light infantry, charioteers, archers, slingers, specialists in siege warfare (ladder men, sappers, and operators of battering rams and siege towers), scouts, spies, trumpeters, and standard-bearers. As a naval power, the Greeks also had ship's pilots, boatswains, and a variety of seamen as well as marines able to wield long pikes in sea fights.

The support personnel were not small in number. Elite positions were held by priests, diviners, physicians (who also doubled as veterinarians), scribes, and heralds. The masses were made up of carpenters, shipwrights, wainwrights, grooms, stable hands, herdsmen, butchers, cooks, wine stewards, smiths, metalworkers, tinkers, and slaves to handle tasks of every variety, from farming to sewing to maintaining latrines. There might have been a few concubines and prostitutes, but with new sources of women beckoning to the east, it might have seemed unself-confident to bring many bedmates to Aulis.

Aulis sits in the rocky hills at the foot of Mount Messapion, which rises 3,350 feet over the Gulf of Euboea. Watchmen looked down from the mountain, and one day they would light one of the chain of beacon fire messages from Mount Ida to Argos, announcing the fall of Troy. At the shoreline below, at Aulis, a Mycenaean town stood on a rocky ridge separating two harbors. Between them they made Aulis the best port in northern Boeotia, and Boeotia was the logical meeting place for the Greek fleet. The region sits midway between Mycenae, home of Agamemnon, and Phthia, home of Achilles. Boeotia was a wealthy land, rich in warriors for the Trojan expedition. And Aulis faces east, where it looked out on a three-day sail to Troy, when the wind was fair.

But the wind was famously not fair for the Greeks. Aulis was sacred to Artemis, goddess of the hunt. The royal Agamemnon was used to giving commands and thinking later; he had neither the cunning nor the patience of a good hunter. It is not surprising that he fell afoul of the deity.

Homer says nothing about the incident; in fact, he implies that it never happened. But the tale of Iphigenia is preserved in other sources. Like the other Olympians, the goddess Artemis is named in Linear B texts; more intriguing, so is a certain "priestess of the winds," keeper of a cult that might have been important to mariners like the Greeks.

Stories differ as to how Agamemnon offended Artemis, whether by killing one of her sacred animals, by going back on a promise of a special sacrifice, or simply by bragging. The Greeks, like other Bronze Age nations, made substantial offerings to their gods, from oxen, sheep, and pigs to wine, wheat, and wool. In any case, Artemis was angry, so she kept the Greek fleet bottled up in port by making the north wind, Boreas, blow. It is not unusual for Boreas to bluster for a two-week spell in the summer. There is a powerful riptide at Aulis, which would have multiplied the effect of the wind.

In order to appease the goddess and make the wind stop, Agamemnon is said to have coldly consented to the murder of his daughter, Iphigenia. While unverifiable, the tale is plausible. Greece's trading partners in Syria and Canaan practiced child sacrifice, especially in moments of extreme stress. Mycenaeans borrowed many customs from the Near East, as did the Minoans, and the

Greek myths are full of stories of child sacrifice. Archaeology does not prove the myths true but it has found impressive circumstantial evidence.

On Crete, near the palace of Knossos, excavators discovered the bones of four children, all in perfect health. Two can be identified, by their teeth, as having been around ten years old. Their bones had been cut by knives much as animal bones are cut by a butcher's cleaver. Is this a case of cannibalism? And if so, was it part of a religious ritual? Another case comes from four miles away, on the slopes of a mountain south of Knossos, near the village of Arkhanes. Here a temple was discovered and inside were three human skeletons, two men and a woman. Some evidence, such as a bronze dagger and bone discoloration (a sign of death by blood loss), points to human sacrifice. Although not proof positive, the facts suggest human sacrifice on Bronze Age Crete. Admittedly, this evidence is Minoan and not Mycenaean, but the Mycenaeans borrowed heavily from their predecessors. Did Agamemnon?

Agamemnon desperately needed to regain the gods' favor, because he faced a problem that was as much political as meteorological. He knew as well as his men did that a good general has to have good luck. The longer the wind blew, the clearer it was that Agamemnon was unlucky. To galvanize his men and get the attention of the gods, Agamemnon might have wanted to do something bold. Enter Iphigenia.

Legend has her come from Mycenae, riding with her servants on a mule cart—a common Bronze Age conveyance—and thinking that she had been summoned to her wedding. A different kind of altar awaited her. No doubt the girl had expected the feasting, music, and dance that marked a royal wedding. Imagine her, instead, heading for the sacrificial table, white-armed, veiled, dressed in the shimmering gown of a bride, as lithe as Artemis herself, and terrified by the sight of the empty space where there should have been an animal for the slaughter. By killing his own daughter, Agamemnon gave notice of his ruthless dedication to the cause, thereby inspiring and terrifying others. Did he feel remorse as he first washed his hands, then pulled out the knife that hung by his sword scabbard, next lifted the bronze blade to his girl's throat, and finally saw the blood spurt out? Or did Artemis save Iphigenia at the last minute and substitute a deer, as some versions of the story go? All we know is that the wind stopped blowing.

And so the king of Argos and of many an isle inspected his navy. The thought may not have occurred to him, but Agamemnon was looking at one of the glories of ancient Greek civilization. It was technological, it was bloody, and it was new: it was as revolutionary in military affairs as that other Bronze Age invention, the chariot. The 1300s and 1200s were a great age of innovation at sea. The Greeks of that era were the first sea power in history on the continent of Europe. They may have picked up the know-how of ship-building and sailing from Aegean islanders, especially the Minoans on Crete, themselves great seafarers, but the Greeks established a navy in the harbors of the mainland and they invented a new ship: the galley.

The galley is an oared, wooden ship, built for speed, and used mainly for war or piracy. Mycenaean galleys were light and lean. The hull was narrow, as hydrodynamics dictated, and straight and low, to cut down on wind resistance and to ease beaching. A pilot stood in the stern and worked a large-bladed single steering oar. (Incidentally, Homer gets this Bronze Age detail right: in his day galleys used the double-oared rudder.) The hull was decorated with a painted set of eyes in the bows and probably also with an image of the ship's name, such as a lion, griffin, or snake. On the stem post was a figurehead in the shape of a bird's head.

The galley was so successful that its form remained standard in the Mediterranean throughout Roman times. But Bronze Age galleys lacked one refinement that marked their classical Greek and Roman descendants: the ram. The ram wasn't invented until centuries later, possibly by Homer's day. Bronze Age naval battles were decided not by ramming but by crews wielding spears, arrows, and swords and engaging the enemy either from a cautious distance or up close in a hand-to-hand free-for-all.

The galley could be sailed, but the most reliable way to go fast was to row. The most common galley at Aulis was probably the penteconter, a fifty-oared ship about ninety feet long, with twenty-five rowers sitting along each side of the hull. At Aulis there would also have been twenty-oared ships, each with two files of ten rowers on a hull estimated at thirty-five feet long.

Bronze Age Greeks had an advantage in sea battles because of their navies and their know-how. Like today's missiles, airplanes, or tanks, the galley provided strategic mobility. As in modern warfare, the key to much of Bronze Age fighting was to "get there firstest with the mostest." A well-run fleet allowed a king to dominate a theater of war by rapidly moving his men and materiel from place to place before the enemy did likewise.

And Mycenaean fleets were well run indeed. The king's men drafted rowers from the towns of the realm. The rowers were paid, sometimes in land allotments, and their families were looked after while they were at sea. They deserved it, because in addition to rowing, these men also doubled as marines and, once the ships landed, as infantry. If we may judge by Bronze Age Egyptian Nile boats, Greek rowers had to endure harsh discipline: in Egypt, the whip and the stick were routinely used aboard ship.

Greek kingdoms also maintained professional seamen, such as pilots and pipers (who kept time for the rowers), as well as sail weavers and other specialists. Naval architects supervised teams of skilled woodworkers in building and taking care of galleys. It took six months for a team of a dozen carpenters, supervised by an architect, to build a Bronze Age galley, as an expert estimates.

This frenzy of naval activity left the Greeks ship-crazy. They gave their sons names like "Famous Ship" and "Fine Sailing." Linear B tablets record the names of more than five hundred rowers. Idle scribes doodled sketches of ships, while artists created more sophisticated images of the same on gems, pots, and pillars. And then there is Homer. If he composed his poems in the 700s B.C., the maritime world that he describes—and describes in detail—is closer to that of the Bronze Age. The *Iliad* is an epic of land war, but sea power runs through the story like a golden thread: without it, the whole fabric of the poem would unravel.

Without the hollow ships, the Greeks could not have resupplied their army at Troy, nor raided the enemy's cities around the coast of the Troad and on the islands of Tenedos and Lesbos; they never could have gone to war with Troy at all. And the watery truth about Greece, that seafaring land, is brought home again and again by the most humble reminders in the least expected places. Like this ghostly image: one of the men found on Crete, who might have been the victim of human sacrifice, was wearing a seal on a thong around his wrist, and carved into the stone was an illustration—of a ship.

There were a lot of ships and men at Aulis. But were there really 1,186 ships, the huge number cited by Homer? Or 102,000 men aboard, as calculated by Thucydides (ca. 460–397 B.C.), the Athenian historian who was himself an admiral? And did the Trojans and their allies have 50,000 men, as Homer states?

Hardly. The Hittites had 47,500 men at the battle of Qadesh in 1274 B.C., which is one of the largest Bronze Age armies mentioned in historical texts. No such figures for navies survive, but the great naval power of Ugarit was said in 1187 B.C. to have had considerably more than 150 ships. If true, then a Greek coalition around 1200 might well have mustered hundreds of ships at Aulis—but not 100,000 men. Fielding an army that big in a protracted war seems beyond the means of a Bronze Age society.

A more modest figure is in order, and here is a way to an educated guess: Troy's excavators estimate a total population for the city of 5,000–7,500 people. In preindustrial societies, typically a little more than 20 percent of the population is males of military age (18–49): so, 1,125–1,700 Trojans. Combine this with Agamemnon's statement in the *Iliad* that the Greek army greatly outnumbers the Trojan soldiers who lived in the city of Troy—in fact, the ratio is greater than ten to one. The problem is, continues Agamemnon, that the Trojans have allies at their disposal, "who knock me far off my path and keep me from capturing the well-peopled fortress of Ilion, no matter how much I want to." On that reckoning, the Greek army was greater than 11,250–17,000 men. So a conservative estimate might calculate armies of about 15,000 men per side.

To carry 15,000 men to Troy the Greeks would have required three hundred penteconters, assuming every man rowed. Some of the ships might have been smaller than penteconters, that is, twenty-oared ships, and some might have been larger, that is, merchant vessels, so "around 300" is a plausible estimate of the number of Greek ships that left Aulis for Troy.

It is possible that the Greeks had some merchant ships at Aulis, in spite of their apparent willingness to leave trade in the hands of Canaanite ships and captains. The Ulu Burun shipwreck is suggestive of Greek priorities. When the ship sank off the southwest coast of Anatolia around 1300 B.C. it carried everything from copper ingots to hippopotamus teeth, but only one Greek product: weaponry (two sets of spears, swords, and knives). Yet merchant ships were so well suited for transporting men, animals, and supplies that the Greeks may well have bought or built some for the Trojan expedition. A Bronze Age merchant ship could carry as many as 250 men, which is no doubt why Pharaonic Egypt used merchant ships to transport soldiers, horses, and chariots. Homer's Eumelus of Thessaly (in central Greece) brought his peerless mares to Troy, and he would surely have found a merchant ship convenient.

Perhaps merchantmen were also used to carry arms and armor as well as a limited supply of food and water. But no more than a limited supply, because ancient armies expected to live off the enemy's land. The ideal was to fare like the army of Egypt's King Thutmose III (1504–1450 B.C.) in northern Syria. After victory, his men found fruits on the trees, grain on the threshing floors, and vats overflowing with wine. They got as drunk as at a party at home in Egypt.

Whether sobriety reigned or not, the day finally came to leave Aulis. At dawn, a favorable wind was blowing. The pitch-black hulls had been eyed and pawed and checked by hand for any holes. The gear was stowed, the horses brought on board, the fodder was found, and the men were ready. All that remained was for the chiefs to sacrifice to the gods. They set up an altar at a spring under a plane tree and led the bulls to the slaughter.

Then, when everything was done, an ill omen appeared—this one, reported in Homer. A snake crawled up the altar and onto the tree, where it found a sparrow and her eight chicks in a nest on a branch, and killed them. Then the snake turned to stone. A rational explanation of the phenomenon might be that the beast died on the spot. In any case, only Zeus could have done it: everyone knew it, and they were terrified.

It took the seer Calchas, son of Thestor, to break the spell. Imagine him wearing a long robe, with a bay-leaf wreath in his hair, and carrying a staff tied with the ribbons of the god Apollo, whom he served. He carried himself with the dignity of someone close to the gods and with the caution of the man who had given King Agamemnon the bad news that his child would have to be sacrificed.

Divination—predicting the future on the basis of natural phenomena—was common in the Bronze Age. Birds were important omens, especially in Anatolia, and so were snakes. The portent at Aulis meant, Calchas explained, that a long, hard war lay ahead. For nine years they would struggle but in the tenth, absolute victory would be their reward. The chiefs chose to accentuate the positive: final victory.

And so, at last, the chiefs boarded their vessels, and the fleet was off. The size of the expedition was extraordinary, but the act of setting sail was common. Homer describes such a scene well:

> *Then launch, and hoist the mast: indulgent gales,*
> *Supplied by Phoebus, fill the swelling sails;*
> *The milk-white canvas bellying as they blow,*
> *The parted ocean foams and roars below:*
> *Above the bounding billows swift they flew. . . .*

When the wind fell the men would row. They sat on benches in the long ships along two open, well-ventilated galleries, with leather screens to protect their heads, which stuck out over an open bulwark.

They averaged twenty-five men on a side, and each of them pulled an oar. The men's grain was stored in leather bags; their water and wine were in clay jars or skin bottles. Their gear was under the benches. If challenged, the men would have to grab a shield, spear, and sword and take on the enemy's boarding party, but they would not be challenged: they had the greatest navy in the world.

After leaving Aulis, the sleek hulls would have passed through the channel between the Greek coast and the island of Euboea and then turned eastward, island-hopping from the Sporades to Lemnos to Imbros. From there, it took only twenty miles on the bright sea for the black ships to reach Troy.

The Greeks would have a great deal to worry about when they got there: finding the right landing ground; protecting themselves from the slings and spears and arrows of the Trojan army that would surely be there to await them; securing local sources of food, fodder, and water; and winning some easy loot in order to keep the men happy. But there was one thing the Greeks would not have to worry about—the Trojan navy. Amazingly, despite its location by the sea and its economic dependence on maritime trade, Troy had no navy, or at least no significant one.

This was more than a passing weakness; it was a major vulnerability for the Trojans. Because they had command of the sea, the Greeks were able to raid the enemy coast at will. If it had similarly possessed competitive naval power, Troy could have brought the war to the enemy with an offensive across the Aegean Sea into the Greek heartland. Without a fleet, however, the Trojans were continually stuck on the strategic defensive. Agamemnon might have felt like the Hittite King Hattushilish III, who said that he could "cast a glance" at the enemy's country but the enemy could not cast a glance back at him.

Here is a paradox: Troy was a seaport that did not fight at sea. Founded by continentals looking *outward* to the sea, it became rich by offering sailors a foothold in the wind, but without developing its own navy. The Trojans fit the description of Bronze Age peoples of whom Thucydides says "although they inhabited the lowlands they were not sea-goers"—at least not when it came to fighting at sea. The Trojans no doubt had boats but not of the quality of the Greek warships nor in large enough number to compete.

For example, when Paris went to Sparta to bring back Helen, he had ships specially made for the trip. The builder was Phereclus son of Tekton and grandson of Harmon. Phereclus was a superb craftsman, described by Homer as someone who "knew how to make, with his hands, many elaborate and skillfully crafted things." Indeed, his name means Famous, son of the Builder and grandson of the Joiner. Homer says:

> *Thy father's skill, O Phereclus! was thine,*
> *The graceful fabric and the fair design;*
> *For loved by Pallas, Pallas did impart*
> *To him the shipwright's and the builder's art.*
> *Beneath his hand the fleet of Paris rose,*
> *The fatal cause of all his country's woes. . . .*

Phereclus built Paris "well-balanced ships" for his getaway. The implication is that the ships on hand in Troy were no match for Menelaus's fleet.

Troy had little incentive to build a navy. Middlemen have no need to go abroad for plunder. Warships had little appeal to men who could garner wealth, glory, and security by breeding horses.

Archaeology as well as myth makes the Trojans latecomers to the horse. Myth considers Troy's horses a gift from Zeus. Excavation shows that the horse was not native to Troy but arrived around 1700 B.C., late, by Near Eastern standards, after which horse bones abound in the ruins. Trojans took to horses with the zeal of converts. Homer's Priam has royal stables in Troy and a horse farm near the city of Abydos on the Dardanelles. Andromache feeds her husband Hector's horses grain and wine, while Pandarus goes one better, by fighting on foot in order to spare his mounts from missing mealtime.

These were princes who could have rubbed shoulders with any

age's bluebloods, including the horsey Hittites, Troy's powerful ally. And like the Hittites, the Trojans couldn't see beyond a silken mane. Landlocked in central Anatolia, the Hittites tended to imagine the coast as the edge of the world. Hittite kings boasted of extending their realm to "the border of the sea," as if nothing lay beyond. Their treaty with Troy, for example, says nothing about ships, while it specifically mentions Troy's obligation to send infantry and chariotry to Hatti when needed. The horse was king, or so it seemed, but danger came by sea.

According to Homer, a generation before the Trojan War, King Laomedon of Troy promised horses to Heracles in exchange for ridding Troy of a sea monster. Heracles killed the beast but Laomedon reneged. The angry hero attacked the city and "filled the streets with widows."

True, Heracles had only six ships at his disposal, but Heracles's son Tlepolemus brags that his father destroyed Troy, and evidence from Ugarit supports his boasting. In a letter from around 1200 B.C. the last king of Ugarit, Ammurapi, complained that an enemy did serious damage to his country with only seven ships. The crews of Heracles' six ships would have amounted to just several hundred men, and they could not have taken a walled city like Troy, but the harbor town, farmhouses, and other unwalled settlements in the Troad would have all been at their mercy. And who knows? Pushed by Heracles' famous hot temper, they might even have found a weak point in the walls.

Nor should we discount help from their friends within Troy. They needn't have been many; in fact, most Trojans might have winced at the sight of Mycenaean ships, given the tide of violence in Mycenaean culture. How many Mycenaean traders turned into raiders when, like Heracles, they were hoodwinked?

Yet there were indeed Mycenaean merchants at Troy. In fact, the archaeologists have found so much Mycenaean pottery at the site, both imports and imitations made of local clay, that if we didn't know better, we might have thought the place was a Mycenaean colony and not Troy. One of the most eloquent signs of Mycenaean commerce comes from a grave in a cemetery at Troy's harbor: it is a seal stone with a stylized face, mouth open in a wide grin. The style is typically Mycenaean, and perhaps the seal was a trader's device, used to mark his wares. Somebody at Troy did business with men like him. Someone—perhaps a Trojan, perhaps an immigrant—traded with the Mycenaeans for horses or textiles or slaves. And that person might have opened the gates to Heracles' men. Consider the *Iliad*'s Antenor, a Trojan elder who was well-disposed to the Greeks and who proposed that Helen be returned to them. When Troy was sacked, he was spared—some say because he in fact opened the city gate to the enemy.

By developing land power to the exclusion of sea power, the Trojans made the smart choice—or so they thought. It may well be that the Trojans had enough warships to project their power into the nearby islands, but they could not fight off an armada like the Greeks'. Trojan strategists might have reasoned that their land defenses were sufficient to repel any invasion from the sea.

Troy would not be history's only example of a state located on the sea but without a strong navy. Japan, for example, is an island nation that had superb infantry and cavalry but never had a navy before the late 1800s. Japan was not a trading state, but history records commercial powerhouses whose forte was maritime trade and yet had no navy. Consider the cities of the Hanseatic League of the late Middle Ages: at its core about sixty great merchant cities in northern Europe, mainly Germany. They dominated trade in the Baltic Sea but they had no permanent army or navy. Only in the face of a serious threat from Denmark in the 1360s did they put together a fleet, but that lasted only for a few years, until Denmark was defeated. In the 1400s, the new nation-states of northern Europe, such as Sweden and Poland, easily outmatched what little naval power existed in the disorganized League. Another case is the Netherlands: it was a giant of maritime trade in the 1650s, but it had only a small navy, and so it was battered by the English fleet. If the Dutch had strengthened their navy in time, New York might still be New Amsterdam, as it was until the English fleet seized it in 1664.

Like Troy, the Netherlands and the Hanseatic cities were rich and unrealistic. They all faced a similar temptation of putting their resources into productive or prestigious things instead of necessities. They were wrong.

Agamemnon did not make the same mistake. The king of Argos and many an isle built a war machine for all seasons. Argos, a land that Homer calls "horse-nourishing," was a hothouse of chariots, while the islands were guarded by the Greek fleet. The Greek way of war was versatile and it had been for centuries. Now, as Agamemnon sat in his flagship, his fleet of black ships crossed the billowing waves. On every stroke, as we may imagine, calloused hands of rowers strained at the wooden oars, while grooms whispered to the tethered horses not to fear the sea. Slaves checked the chariots against any loosening by the waves, and the surge made one man sick while lifting another to reveries of gold. Warriors missed their wives, seers prayed to Poseidon, and a veteran seaman reached for a goatskin's slug of wine. As the ships advanced, the Harpies of Death flew ahead to scout the plain of Troy.

CHAPTER THREE

OPERATION BEACHHEAD

Helios the Sun, who sees everything and knows the gods, is beginning his ride in his four-horse chariot, turning the sky a gauzy blue and the sea the color of widows' tears. Gulls fly toward the cliffs of the Gallipoli Peninsula across the Dardanelles to the north, framed by the barren peaks of the islands of Imbros and Samothrace. The scene is completed by the brown hills of the island of Tenedos in the west and, in the east, the rolling Trojan Plain, with the long ridge of Mount Ida rising ghostlike in the distance. A pastoral scene, as we might imagine it, then the Greek fleet appears.

The black ships fill the sea like horses at the starting gate. The land, in turn, is unclear at first and as the ships come closer, it reveals fields and scrub. The morning fragrance invigorates the men aboard ship. If they weren't working at the oars, the Greeks might shout, echoing the cry of a Hittite king on the warpath: "Behold, the troops and chariots of the land of Greece are coming!" Across the water, even the toughest Trojan in his bronze armor might shiver at the flutter of the polished firwood oars, driving the armada like birds of prey onto the Anatolian shore. It is the moment of decision.

But not of surprise: the Trojans have had plenty of warning and their troops are poised to stop the enemy from landing on the fertile soil of Ilion. They were waiting, just as a large number of Cypriot troops waited for the seaborne Hittite invaders of King Shuppiluliuma II (1207–? B.C.) when they disembarked on the island. The beach is thick with defenders. What Homer says of a later rallying of the Trojan forces would surely apply that day as well:

Nations on nations fill the dusky plain,
Men, steeds, and chariots, shake the trembling ground:
The tumult thickens, and the skies resound.

Offshore lies part of the small Trojan fleet; the rest is guarding another possible Greek landing ground. The rowers sit ready, while archers and shield-carrying spearmen prepare for the unequal battle ahead. Although they have no hope of defeating the Greek navy they can at least slow it down and ease the task of the Trojan shore defense.

As they watch the enemy ships grow larger on the horizon, the Trojans on shore get ready too. The priests might have been doing what Hittite priests did before battle: hosting the enemy's gods at a ritual meal, of wine and slaughtered sheep, at which they blame the war on enemy aggression. The soldiers no doubt have more mundane tasks. Veterans may be checking their bow or tightening their shield straps while the new men joke as if on an outing. Some might wish that they could reach under their breastplate and wipe off the sweat, while others don't even notice how sore their hands already are from clenching a spear.

The battle of the beach is about to begin. Of this key event, Homer says only that a Trojan killed the first Greek to jump ashore. But the historian Thucydides, writing centuries later, reasoned that the Greeks must have fought and won a battle on their arrival on Trojan territory; otherwise they could not have set up camp. Hector son of Priam struck the first blow, as we learn from the Epic Cycle, those non-Homeric early Greek poems about the Trojan War.

Hector was a great warrior but a mediocre husband. He was strong, agile, fearless, dogged, and by turns self-centered and sensitive. Hector could remember how he had lifted his bride's veil on their wedding night to tenderly offer her a cup of wine but could shrug his shoulders at the thought of the widowhood that awaited her thanks to his aggressive pursuit of glory in battle.

Homer makes Hector an expert spearman who could handle a sword if need be, but he was probably an archer as well. Around 1225 B.C. the ruler of a western Anatolian kingdom not far from Troy had his portrait carved in relief on a cliff. The king strides boldly with a spear in one hand, a bow slung over his shoulder, and a dagger tucked into his belt. What was good enough for him was probably good enough for Hector.

Homer's Hector is tall and imposing, with a streaming mane of black hair and a handsome face, and eyes that no doubt flash from time to time with his reckless and aggressive spirit. He was probably clean-shaven and he might have kept his hair in a ponytail. He probably wore gold earrings, an embroidered kilt, and Hittite-style shoes with upturned toes. If Hector was uncomfortable beneath a bronze breastplate, he lacked the odor of someone permanently stained with sweat since, unlike commoners, royalty took daily baths.

Hector is a type well attested in the ancient Near East, the crown prince burning to prove himself as a warrior. He knew that the only way to show that he was no longer a boy was to lead armies and give commands. A Hittite king told his young Babylonian counterpart that unless he led an armed raid into enemy territory and soon, people would say that, like his father, the Babylonian was all talk and no action. Hector, by contrast, had an old fighter for a father, who advised caution.

Old King Priam, white-haired and scratchy-voiced, confined to the city rather than the battlefield he once strode, still had the power of command. Priam was shrewd, self-controlled, and an old hand at the ways of war as it was waged in the Bronze Age. It was under his leadership, no doubt, that Troy had put together an alliance and a strategy. Priam knew that Troy's best policy was defense and that the farther the Trojans fought from the city's walls the better. Priam might have known the words of the Hittite king who said that the alternative to fighting in the open was risking suffocation in the crushing embrace of an enemy siege. The preferred option was to defeat the enemy on the beach as he tried to land. Should that fail, the Trojans would fight the Greeks on the plain of Troy, keeping them away from the city. If that tactic should not work in turn, then they would fall back to the anti-chariot trenches and palisades that protected the lower city—with the great walls of the citadel themselves as the final refuge. But it would never come to that, not if the gods showed Priam the favor that they always had in the past.

The Storm God—Zeus, to the Greeks—held Priam and his people closer to his divine heart than he did any other king or country on earth. Known in Anatolia by such names as Tarhunt or Teshub, the Storm God was one of the chief deities of the Trojan pantheon. Priam was a favorite of his in no small part because the king knew that the gods help those who help themselves. Priam was not only intelligent but brave out of all proportion to his years. He was so bold and decisive that even an enemy marveled at Priam's "iron heart." No one in the region was more blessed with wealth or sons than Priam. And then the Greeks came.

The Trojans would surely have learned about the Greeks' approach from signal flares sent up by their friends on the nearby islands of Imbros and Tenedos. Allies were expected to serve as "border guards" and "watchmen," as Hittite treaties often state. The use of torches for military signaling goes back at least as far as Mesopotamia in the 1700s B.C. That same era is full of references to the importance of intelligence to warfare. The city of Mari had an intelligence bureau and it may have been headed by an official with the wonderful name of "Little Gnat."

The Trojans may well have taken a leaf from the same book. Homer has the Trojans employ lookouts, perhaps like the "coastal watchers" of the kingdom of Pylos attested in the Linear B tablets. One of the Trojan lookouts was Hector's brother Polites. He was a fast runner and no doubt had excellent vision. Information that he provided would surely have been welcome, even though the Greeks had hardly kept their approach a secret.

On the way to Troy from Aulis, the Greeks seem to have stopped first at the island of Scyros and sacked it. If there is anything to the epic tradition that Achilles' mother had forced him as a boy into a humiliating hiding place on Scyros in girl's clothing in order to dodge the war, which she foresaw, then this would have been sweet revenge for him. When the Greeks attacked en route to Troy, the Scyrians would not have had a chance against so big a force. In addition to settling Achilles' private score, the attack would have been a morale builder for the men, who could thrill to their first victory. It was also an experiment, allowing the generals to see how their untested army might perform.

Then, continuing northeastward, the Greeks landed on Lemnos. The rugged island has unexpected bounties, such as its claylike soil with medicinal properties and its sweet red wine. On Lemnos the Greeks lived like Olympians, feasting on beef and chugging wine by the cupful. The more they drank, the more they boasted: each Greek could take on a hundred Trojans, no, two hundred! It was a last binge for the boys, but the generals had to think about strategy. Lemnos was a stepping stone on the route from northern Greece across the Aegean to Troy and the Dardanelles. Lemnos was also a potentially crucial source of supplies for any Greek camp at Troy as well as a potential market for any captives whom the Greeks would want to sell as slaves. It was essential to secure Lemnos before going on.

But the price of doing business on Lemnos was that it gave the Trojans time to prepare. And then some: the epic tradition outside Homer records that after Lemnos the Greeks took a wrong turn. Instead of landing at Troy they ended up about seventy-five miles to the south on the Aegean coast of the region known as Mysia. Mistakenly thinking they had reached Troy, they attacked the forces of King Telephus. The king's army bloodied the Greeks, but in the end Telephus was wounded by Achilles. Myth says that only a scraping of the wood from Achilles' spear could heal the wound—an unusual example of the herbal medicine practiced by the Greeks. Achilles' gigantic spear was made of ash wood, and boiled ash bark makes a good poultice to apply to a wound. In exchange for the medicine, Telephus showed the Greeks the way to Troy.

Whether or not there is any truth in this story, it underlines the fragility of early navigation—and of early military intelligence. If the tale is true, it means that the Trojans had even more time to prepare. They were indeed ready for the invader.

Troy had assembled a grand coalition. Some of the allies came from Europe—Thrace and Macedonia—but most were Anatolian. Alliances were the bread and butter of Anatolian politics, and many figure in Hittite texts, so Homer's list of Troy's Anatolian partners is historically plausible. First come the Trojans or, more accurately, the Trojans and Dardanians, to refer respectively to the populations of the Trojan Plain and, to its south, the fertile middle valley of the Scamander River—Aeneas's country. Next come men from other places in the Troad, such as Abydos, Arisbe, and Zeleia. Then there are Anatolian regions beyond the Troad, namely Mysia and Phrygia due east; Paphlagonia on the Black Sea; Maeonia to the south, in the Hermus River valley; Caria, farther south, in the Maeander River valley; and Lycia, in the southwestern corner of Anatolia. The allied army might also have included Hittites, perhaps referred to by Homer as Halizones from Halube. So just as they had promised in the Alaksandu Treaty, the Hittites might have sent infantry and chariotry in Troy's moment of need—although surely not as many as Troy would have liked, given the Hittites' bigger problems closer to home.

Still, Troy had assembled a formidable alliance. Putting it together was no doubt a tribute to Priam's diplomacy and his purse, because all business between Bronze Age kings had to be greased with gifts. And they had to be top of the line. For example, in the 1300s B.C. the Amarna Letters are full of such gifts as gold and lapis lazuli jewelry, horses, chariots, pieces of silver, and women. Homer cites gold and silver cups or ingots, bronze tripods, embroidered robes, fine jewelry, weapons, armor, heirlooms, vintage wine, mules, horses, and beautiful women. And it was an ancient custom to repay each gift with another gift, to say nothing of the lavish entertainment that had to be offered to ambassadors. All these benefactions were usually given with elaborate courtesy, but sometimes the veil was dropped, and a king just had to pay up, and pay big. Priam might have remembered, bitterly, the Egyptians' claim that the Hittite king had stripped his kingdom of silver to pay the allied troops who fought at Qadesh (1274 B.C.).

Leading Troy's allied army fell to Hector. On the eve of the Greeks' arrival, he probably mustered the men outside the city, perhaps at the hill of Baitieia, which Homer mentions as a place where the alliance drew up its troops. It was a multiethnic force, so varied in fact, that there was a cacophony of languages. As Homer puts it,

> *Such clamors rose from various nations round,*
> *Mix'd was the murmur, and confused the sound.*

The groups camped separately and no doubt fought by national unit, as the Greeks did. Yet, in order to coordinate operations, Troy's commanders must have came up with a few shared words of command or some sort of lingua franca.

Each nation's army was organized by type of troops, size of units, and hierarchy of commanders, as was standard in the Bronze Age. Some details of military groupings survive in Hittite, Mesopotamian, and Linear B texts, but the clearest picture comes from Egypt. There, the army was divided into infantry units ranging from five-thousand-men divisions to ten-men squads. The basic tactical unit was a platoon of fifty men (five squads), in turn grouped into a company (five platoons) and a host (two or more companies). The chain of command ran down from the pharaoh to generals to combat officers to the ordinary men. Alongside infantry units were chariot units and elite soldiers, as well as, when needed, naval units, garrison commands, and foreign troops.

No more than glimpses survive of the force structure of the armies at Troy. The *Iliad* mentions fifty-men Trojan platoons and hundred-men Greek companies, and the Linear B tablets list what may be military units ranging from ten to seventy men, in multiples of ten. Despite differences, no doubt many differences, these armies and Egypt's probably were similarly composed.

Military logic dictated a number of common practices among Bronze Age armies. For instance, several days before the Battle of Megiddo in 1479 B.C., Pharaoh Thutmose III held a war council with a small group of officers, who then passed on the plan to the entire army. On the day the Greeks came, Hector undoubtedly behaved similarly: he talked over the battle plan with the allied commanders, and they in turn sent the word to their men, each in his own language.

That first day at Troy, each general is likely to have rallied his men with a pre-battle speech, which was already an ancient tradition. King Hammurabi of Babylon (1792–1750 B.C.), for example, knew how important it was before a battle to visit his men in camp and make them "happy with words." Whenever his Hana warriors, tough nomadic tribesmen, marched to Babylon, Hammurabi had them enter the city, where he reviewed them in parade and then ate with them personally. Thutmose III addressed his army before Megiddo. Hector's words on a later occasion are typical of such harangues:

> *Death is the worst; a fate which all must try;*
> *And for our country, 'tis a bliss to die.*
> *The gallant man, though slain in fight he be,*
> *Yet leaves his nation safe, his children free;*
> *Entails a debt on all the grateful state;*
> *His own brave friends shall glory in his fate;*
> *His wife live honour'd, all his race succeed,*
> *And late posterity enjoy the deed!*

Courage was another common theme of these speeches, and honor, and the need to prove oneself as a man. "Be men!" is how Hector and Agamemnon each goads his soldiers. They were speaking a language that would have resonated in Anatolia. Hittite soldiers swore oaths to be loyal to their commander—so help them, gods. Otherwise, they swore, they would dress like women and turn in their arrows for spinning needles. And they often mocked their enemies not only as women but as donkeys, cattle, or dogs.

A good general tailored his talk to the audience. For instance, on the eve of battle, Agamemnon knew whom to compliment and whom to shame. To the first group, he said things like:

Ah! would the gods but breathe in all the rest
Such souls as burn in your exalted breast. . . .

Slackers, on the other hand, were blasted in this manner:

Inglorious Argives! to your race a shame,
And only men in figure and in name!

Bucking up the army was easy. The civilians were another matter. As the soldiers poured out of Troy and gathered on the plain, the news of invasion must have gotten out. The people of Troy no doubt reacted in various ways. Some of them were determined, some of them were terrified, and all of them were suddenly alert because the Greeks were coming. They turned away from their oxen on the plain or from the wool on their loom and they scanned the horizon, waiting for the black ships to appear. Some of them surely cursed Helen for bringing an invasion down on them. And some of them swore by the Storm God of the Army—the first god of Troy, according to a Hittite text—that they would support their troops until they drove the invader back into the sea, they, the Trojan men who served King Priam, who was good at the ashen lance. Others worried that first the Greeks would pen them up like pigs in a sty, then the enemy would take the city, killing the Trojans on the spot or dragging them off as slaves to the islands or to far-off Greece. "Bitter cries" come from the walls of cities when the land is invaded, as a Mesopotamian text sums up civilian morale.

The Greeks would not enjoy the advantage of strategic surprise on their landing, so they had to be certain to choose a good place to land. One of the keys to executing a successful landing is disembarking where the enemy is weak. Geography made this hard to do. There are few beaches on Troy's Aegean shore between Cape Sigeum and the Trojan Harbor at today's Beşik Bay (about seven miles to the south) and those beaches lie under steep cliffs—perfect for defenders. That left the harbor itself and the bay, which, in the Late Bronze Age, stretched southward from the Dardanelles nearly all the way to the city of Troy. Today, that bay no longer exists, having been silted in by the flow of the Scamander and Simoeis Rivers. In the Late Bronze Age the west side of the bay offered a tolerable if not ideal landing ground. The place was marshy and could be reached only by entering the Dardanelles, with its treacherous wind and currents. There was a much better harbor to the south, at Beşik Bay, but it was defended by a fort on an overlooking hill, and surely the Trojans would be dug in there.

Where, then, did the Greeks land? Homer offers no clear answer, but the clues in his text point to the west side of the Bronze Age bay; the best Hellenistic and Roman sources agree; modern experts are divided. Some argue that the Greeks would have gone for the better harbor at Beşik Bay, that is, the Trojan Harbor. But a bloody landing loomed large, and near-term gain usually trumps long-term planning, so the Greek high command is likely to have opted to land at the Bronze Age bay. No matter where they landed, the Greeks surely got command of the Trojan Harbor eventually, and that gave them access to supplies and perhaps income from ships that stopped there, while denying the same to the Trojans.

The Trojans no doubt positioned their army between the two bays and moved when they got the word from their lookouts. If the Greeks were lucky, the Trojans moved slowly. The Greeks sorely needed to be lucky because their leaders had underestimated the enemy. The Greeks so outnumbered the contingent from the city of Troy that Agamemnon was confident of his ability to crush them. But he seems to have grasped neither the size nor the strength of Troy's coalition army, at least to judge by his later complaint about Troy's "unfair" edge in allies. If the dictum is true that in order to win, an attacker needs to outnumber a defender by a ratio of three to one, then the odds favored the Trojans.

But the Greeks had three advantages when it came to grabbing a beachhead. Their ships were, as Homer says, "horses of the sea": fast, mobile, and, even with just their half-decks, serving as raised platforms from which to throw down spears and arrows on the Trojans below. The Greeks were experienced at making fighting runs up onto the beach; the Trojans had little practice in such operations. The Greeks knew how to jump down onto shore rapidly while holding up a shield against enemy arrows, and how to land the ships in a formation that would give their archers maximum protection.

The terror of the ships also gave the Greeks a psychological edge. According to Homer, the unprecedented armada drove Priam's son-in-law Imbrios from his home at Pedaeum back behind the walls of Troy. And, as an ancient Athenian general would note on a later occasion, it was downright terrifying to face the onslaught of enemy ships coming right at you in the surf.

But the most important Greek resource was the quality of their infantry, the backbone of their land power. The spear and the sword were the main weapons. To be sure, Agamemnon was careful to include some contingents of archers and slingers, no doubt remembering Anatolia's reputation as bow country. But his main answer to Anatolian superiority in chariots and archers was the phalanx. It was a primitive phalanx with neither the advanced armor nor the esprit de corps of the classical phalanx. But by the standards of the Bronze Age, it was formidable: in relative terms, cohesive, heavy-armed, and potent.

The Greeks fought in some ways like the Shardana troops whose arresting images stare out at us from Egyptian carved reliefs of the 1200s and early 1100s. The Shardana were foreigners who served in their own units in the Egyptian military—that is, when they weren't busy attacking Egypt in their long ships. As the reliefs show, the Shardana fought with swords and spears but not bows. They wore short kilts, carried round shields, and wore horned helmets—curving horns, sometimes with a disc-topped spike between them. The Shardana served as Rameses II's bodyguard. The Greeks were not Shardana (although just who the Shardana were is unclear), but like them, they were experts in fighting at close range. And it would appear that Greek soldiers too fought in the Egyptian army.

Recently, an exciting discovery was made in the British Museum: a painted Egyptian papyrus from the 1300s B.C. came to light in a storeroom. It had been found in 1936 during the continuing excavations that followed the discovery in 1922 of the tomb of "King Tut" (Pharaoh Tutankhamun, 1334–1325) and then forgotten. Although it is fragmentary and not easy to reconstruct, the painting clearly shows a battle scene. There are at least two Greek warriors fighting, alongside Egyptians, against Libyans. The Greeks can be identified as Greeks because they wear boar's-tusk helmets—a style mentioned in Homer—and because one of them is dressed in an oxhide tunic, a style known to have existed in the Bronze Age Aegean. The Libyans have bows and arrows. We had suspected a Greek presence in Tutankhamun's Egypt because Mycenaean pottery turned up in the 1930s excavation: now we know that it was, at least in part, a military presence.

To speak generally, what Greek infantrymen lacked in chariots and missiles (arrows and slings) they made up for in unit cohesion and speed. Also, unlike the Shardana, the Greeks, or at least some of them, wore heavy armor. They excelled in fighting in thick formation and in letting well-armored champions take the lead.

The Greeks were not deficient in chariot tactics, but their chariotry faced practical limitations. There was little good horse country in Greece, especially compared to Anatolia. There were only so many horses and chariots that could be transported by ship. It would be hard to feed and exercise those horses in the narrow coastal strip of their encampment or to do maintenance on chariots in a camp far from home. Add to this the numerous references in Homer to Greek soldiers like Achilles who were "swift-footed," that is, strong and fast infantrymen who attacked charioteers from the ground with spears and swords, and a picture emerges of a nimble and lethal Greek infantry capable of paying back the Trojans in kind.

The Trojans were great charioteers, which would serve them well on the plain of Troy. The chariot was a multipurpose vehicle, used for transport to, from, and around the battlefield as well as for mobile fire support and for sheer intimidation. The chariot was part tank, part jeep, and part armored personnel carrier. Just as horses were near and dear to the heart of the Hittite Great King—"send me stallions!" writes King Hattushilish III to the king of Babylon—so they were beloved by Priam. In fact, he reared some of his horses with his own hand, just as Pharaoh Amenhotep II (1427–1392 B.C.) did.

But the battle of the beach would not be a chariot battle. It would be a brawl. With ships constantly coming in and men disembarking, with Trojans running forward to stop them and Greeks pushing against the Trojan line, and with missiles flying, neither side could have maintained close order. The result would have been a melee, what Homer calls "a dispersed battle" in which "man took man" and "close combat" was decided by "hand and might."

After all, an amphibious landing on well-defended ground is one of warfare's most difficult maneuvers. The Athenian general Demosthenes reminded his men of this when they had to defend an outnumbered garrison against a Spartan landing by sea. The year was 425 B.C.; the place, an outpost in southwest Greece; and the conflict was the Peloponnesian War. Demosthenes told his men not to fear the Spartans' numbers, because, as experienced seamen, Athenians knew "how impossible it is to drive back an enemy determined enough to stand his ground."

The Spartans failed that day in 425 B.C.; the Athenians pushed them back into the sea. No doubt the Spartans were every bit as tough as Agamemnon's men. But the sandy beach at Troy would be much easier terrain for the invaders than the rocky shore that faced the Spartans. And the Spartans were infamous landlubbers. Seaborne raids, however, were almost run-of-the-mill for Bronze Age Greeks.

Bronze Age galleys could be run right up onto the beach, bow first, and that is surely what the Greeks did at Troy. This procedure generated more speed and power than backing the boat in, stern first. Most defenders would scatter at the sight of a crimson-prowed ship bearing down on them. The discipline of the rowers and the skill of the pilot would be crucial; some ships would hit the target while others would fail. A first-rate pilot, like Phrontis son of One-tor, who served Menelaus, must have been highly prized. Likewise, top-flight rowers, like the Phaeacians of the *Odyssey*, who were strong enough to muscle a ship half its length up onto the beach—perhaps a case of heroic exaggeration.

On each side the commanders would have given the men their orders before battle. Arrows were the best way to cover the distance between ship and shore, so each army would try to get its best archers in position. Slingers could have done damage too, so if possible they would have been positioned within striking distance as well. The Greeks would be particularly vulnerable as they hit the beach, a point the Trojan officers might have emphasized. But Trojans had little experience in the amphibious operations at which the Greeks excelled.

Both sides would have made an effort to get their heroes to the fore: that is, the nobles. This was a sound tactic as well as realistic politics, because the heroes were better armed, better trained, and better fed than the common soldier. On the Trojan side, for example, a man like Euphorbus son of Panthous, whose father was one of Priam's advisors, was taught as a boy the art of fighting from a chariot. The young Achilles, to take another case, was trained (according to Homer) by the hero Phoenix and (according to myth) by the centaur Chiron. The Greek or Trojan infantryman, by contrast, might have been instructed in drill, like the Egyptian conscript, but in combat he might have gotten more use out of what he had learned in scuffles in the barnyard or backstreets.

Before embarking that morning, the Greek chiefs would have had to decide the order in which the ships would come in to shore, because the harbor would be much too small for all the vessels to land at once. The commanders would have wanted elite troops in the first wave, while also saving good men for the later stages of the battle. The Greeks might expect a quick victory over any Trojan ships in their way, but they could count on a tough fight afterward.

As the Greeks jumped off their ships they would have faced what looked like a stockade of spears. The Trojans had the sun in their eyes, but if they could make out the details, they might have seen the images of lions, bulls, or falcons painted on the bows of the Greek ships. They would have heard the thud of timber on the sand and the twang of enemy bows.

Battlefields are rarely quiet as even a king like the Assyrian Shalmaneser I (1274–1245 B.C.) commented. But as he probably knew, noise is a weapon. Homer gives his heroes enormous lung capacities and lionlike roars, and this might not be far from the truth. In the primitive command-and-control conditions of the day, a leader had constantly to think about communicating with his men. The ability to bellow was a practical advantage. And a heroic scream also served as psychological warfare against an impressionable enemy. And so Homer's description of a battle later in the war might be applied to that first day of fighting as well, beginning with Hector:

> *With shouts incessant earth and ocean rung,*
> *Sent from his following host: the Grecian train*
> *With answering thunders fill'd the echoing plain;*
> *A shout that tore heaven's concave, and, above,*
> *Shook the fix'd splendours of the throne of Jove.*

The battle ashore began as the bow of the pine-hulled ship crashed onto the beach and the king of Thessaly leapt down. He turned and faced the enemy. Leadership by personal example is always a key factor in battle but rarely more so than in the hierarchical world of the Bronze Age. If a hero didn't take the lead, no one would. So when Protesilaus son of Iphiclus became the first Greek to set foot on Trojan soil it was not merely a high honor, it was a necessity. But it was a distinction that he had little time to savor, because he was also the first Greek to die. Hector, royal prince and son of King Priam, was waiting for him. He would probably have aimed his spear at a seam in Protesilaus's armor or at his neck or at an unprotected part of his face, all common places for a weapon to penetrate and cause a fatal wound.

The great Achilles had thought about jumping ashore first, but held back because he believed that the first Greek to land at Troy would be killed. He had been warned by his divine mother, Thetis—which may be another way of saying that even tough guys go with their gut feelings sometimes. And so the war had its first combat casualty, which led to the first widow. At home in the city of Phylace, Protesilaus left a wife to tear her cheeks in a sign of mourning.

The men in the Trojan vanguard might have tried to push their way onto the enemy ships or at least to hoist themselves up high enough to grab the ornament off the sternpost as a trophy. Anyone brave enough to try would surely face a rain of enemy arrows and spears and perhaps be hacked at with swords.

It must have been a hard-fought battle and yet we don't hear a word about the role of the ordinary soldier in it. We can be sure that he was in the thick of things. When it comes to the rank and file, the silence of the sources and the clamor of reality are typical of the Bronze Age. Hittite and Egyptian texts, for example, often tell the story of a battle the same way: the Great King or pharaoh single-handedly defeats masses of enemy soldiers. An extreme case is the official Egyptian version of the battle of Qadesh: Pharaoh Rameses II killed so many Hittite soldiers that the plain of Qadesh became impassable from all the blood and corpses. Pharaoh had the help of the gods alone in this victory. In other words, the enemy is a crowd of common soldiers but our side has one divinely inspired hero.

Homer and the other poets of the Epic Cycle take a similar approach. They focus on great warriors and their divine enablers, generally leaving it to the audience to fill in the experience of the masses. Although Homer does little to put a face on the battle experience of the rank and file, other sources of evidence allow educated guesses.

Start with an Egyptian sculpted relief of the early 1100s depicting a sea battle near shore. It shows the damage that could be done by archers, whether aboard ship or posted ashore. The common man in Bronze Age armies was at risk because he had the flimsiest armor or none at all—sometimes he even lacked sandals. The dead fell, as the Egyptians said, as crocodiles fall into the water. Fighting their way ashore, the Greeks would have had to wade through corpses, often their own comrades.

Once he got ashore, the Greek soldier might have aimed at his Trojan counterpart. Well-armored Trojan nobles made poor targets, but a Trojan commoner was a fair foil for the Greek's spear or sword—if the Greek had one, and for his bare fists, if he didn't. If they teamed up, a group of Greek privates might have captured a Trojan hero and held him for ransom, arms tied behind his back, just as one Greek common soldier boasts in one of Homer's rare glimpses of the enlisted men. But surely more ordinary Greek soldiers fell at the hands of Trojan heroes.

The Greeks were not certain of victory until Achilles—by now ashore—killed Cycnus, a Trojan ally who was inflicting big casualties on the Greeks. Cycnus is said to have had the superhuman power of a son of the god Poseidon, to use the Greek name; the Trojans might have known him as the Great Sea God. To declare someone no mere mortal but a god was a Bronze Age gesture of respect to the great and powerful.

Achilles is said to have strangled Cycnus with the leather straps of Cycnus's own helmet. Cycnus appears not in Homer but in the Epic Cycle. It is a less-reliable source, but Cycnus symbolizes both the Bronze Age and the little connection Troy had to the sea.

Cycnus was king of the city of Colonae, located on the Aegean coast of the Troad about fifteen miles south of Troy. The site of Colonae was inhabited during the Bronze Age. It was a maritime location, opposite the island of Tenedos, which, in some myths, was first settled by Cycnus's son. No less intriguing, Cycnus is a Greek word meaning "swan" (compare English "cygnet"), but it also recalls the name Kukkunni, a king of Troy mentioned in a Hittite document. We don't know just when he reigned but Kukkunni was a predecessor of Alaksandu, who sat on the throne ca. 1280 B.C. How appropriate that a name recalling both a Bronze Age Trojan king and the Aegean shore is used for the first man to die for Troy in the war with the Greeks.

Achilles' victory sparked an advance. It encouraged Greece's superb infantry to press forward, while it made the Trojans think about retreating and regrouping. When the Trojans heard their leaders' cry to give up and move back toward the city, the victorious Greeks might have taunted them, calling them weaklings, with legs good for nothing except running away, the kind of men who dropped their bows, their packs, and their water skins for a quick getaway. Then the Greeks would have looted the armor of the enemy corpses.

Meanwhile, the gatekeepers of Troy would have opened the doors wide to let the exhausted soldiers pour back into town. As the news of the dead and missing spread, the sound of wailing would rise. On the citadel, Priam might meet anxiously with his advisors. On the ramparts, the watchmen might anticipate that they would be out that night and for many nights to come. And every time they heard a stranger's voice call out, they would stiffen up.

The Greeks had taken their beachhead. After tending to the wounded, gathering the dead, and praying in thanksgiving to the gods, they would proceed to set up camp. Homer insists that for the next nine years, the camp was left unfortified. The mere presence of heroes such as Achilles and Ajax offered better protection than any wall or trenches could. Only after Achilles quit in a huff did the Greeks get around to fortifying their base. This is implausible but not impossible. For example, encamped before the battle of Qadesh (1274 B.C.), Pharaoh Rameses II's army relied on little more than a barricade of shields for protection. Classical Sparta, to take another case, went without city walls, trusting instead its elite army (and its mountains) to scare off any attacker. But in the Trojan War, the verdict of Thucydides, who knew Sparta, commands respect: after winning a battle upon their arrival, the Greeks fortified their encampment.

Tradition says that the Greeks buried Protesilaus across the straits, near Cape Helles, at the edge of the Gallipoli Peninsula. Excavations at the site find no Bronze Age settlement after 1300 B.C., about a century before the Trojan War, so the authenticity of the tradition is in doubt; the poignancy of the site is not. Looking south from here, the Greeks could have clearly seen the towers of Troy across the straits, crowned by Priam's palace and the temples of the gods, guarded by a double band of walls, all gleaming in the morning light across the blue surface of the Dardanelles.

But long before warlike Protesilaus was turned over to the black earth—wherever he lay—a messenger surely brought word of the battle to Priam. Did the king look his fellow elders in the eye at the news that a hostile army had won a bloody foothold on the Trojan shore? Or was he too ashamed and disappointed to share their judgment of what his family's policy had wrought?

Maybe Priam thought back to his youth, as old men do, to a great battle on the Sangarius River in Phrygia where he fought as an allied soldier. Or maybe he preferred to think ahead, to the idea of a fresh start. In any case, the king would have to face the new facts.

The battle of the beachhead was over. The battle for Troy was about to begin.

(*Above*) THE WINDY DARDANELLES. The north wind whips up whitecaps on the water in summer. The Gallipoli Peninsula is in the foreground and the Asian shore lies across the straits. (*Barry Strauss*)

BOREAS. The north wind is personified as a powerful man, winged, flying, and blowing through a shell, in this sculptured relief on the Tower of the Winds in Athens (150–125 B.C.). (*Barry Strauss*)

THE NARROWS. At Çanakkale (foreground), north of Troy, the Dardanelles narrow to a width of less than a mile. In the center the Koca River (Rhodius in Homer) flows into the straits; the Gallipoli Peninsula stretches on the far shore. *(Murat Kiray)*

KARABEL RELIEF. Carved on a cliff about 200 miles south of Troy, this Late Bronze Age sculpture shows a warrior, possibly a king, armed with bow and spear. Might the Trojan prince Paris have dressed like this? *(Sevim Karabıyık Tokta)*

MYCENAE. With its huge blocks and sculpted lions (or lionesses) the Lion Gate of the citadel symbolizes power. Soldiers manning the walls above would have hemmed in attackers on three sides. *(Barry Strauss)*

(Below) PHTHIA. The olive groves that fill the plain illustrate the fertility of the supposed homeland of Achilles. *(Barry Strauss)*

LEMNOS. The harbor of Mirina, the island's capital, lies on the west coast of Lemnos, near the site of the ancient city of Myrina. *(Barry Strauss)*

KNOSSOS. After the Mycenaean Greeks conquered Crete in the 1400s B.C., they ruled this palace, whose throne room complex (reconstructed) and central court are shown here. *(Barry Strauss)*

LACEDAEMON. The Menelaion, or shrine to Menelaus and Helen, stands on a hill east of the valley of Lacedaemon. In the distance, snow-covered Mount Taygetos rises. *(Barry Strauss)*

MYCENAEAN WOMAN. Fragment of a fresco from a house in Mycenae, 1200s B.C. *(National Archaeological Museum, Athens/ Hellenic Republic, Ministry of Culture)*

HITTITE GODS. This sculptured relief, carved on the side of a cliff near Hattusha, is a detail of a larger work. Note the figures' conical hats and sickle-shaped swords. *(Barry Strauss)*

TROY FROM THE WEST. This aerial view shows the ridge on which Troy stood. The ruins are visible in the foreground, and farmland stretches toward the hills in the distance. *(Hakan Öge)*

TOWARD TROY'S HARBOR. Troy's harbor has been identified as a cove just beyond the Beşik Promontory in the center of the photo. The island of Tenedos lies to the right. *(Barry Strauss)*

GREEK CAMP? A view from Troy toward the ridge on which the Greeks might have camped. At the time of the Trojan War, most of the fields seen here would have been underwater, covered by a bay of the Dardanelles. *(Barry Strauss)*

SEAL FROM TROY. Three views of the only Bronze Age writing found at Troy: a small, double-sided bronze seal, written in Luwian, bearing the names of a scribe and his wife. *(Troia Project Archives)*

BRONZE FIGURINE. This four-inch-high statuette from the Lower City of Troy VIi shows a man standing in a gesture of prayer. The workmanship appears to be Hittite. *(Mehmet Gülbiz/Dogan Burda Magazine)*

CHAPTER FOUR

ASSAULT ON THE WALLS

The bolts are pulled back into their sockets and the double doors—wooden, plated with metal, and tightly fitted together—swing open. The travelers enter the city, passing quickly and quietly through the defenses of Troy. If these walls could talk they would scream. They would cry havoc and let the generals roar for victory and the fugitives shout for ropes to pull them up and the sappers give out war whoops as they hack away with their bronze tools. But today the walls are dead silent: a mass of stone and earth that won't be breached without blood.

The travelers are heading in the opposite direction from the one in which traffic usually moves at this early hour, when the herdsmen head out of town with their goats, sheep, and cattle. But these are unusual times, with an enemy army camped on the rich pastureland of Troy. Homer describes the outcome of the travelers' journey; let us imagine their trip.

Odysseus son of Laertes and king of Ithaca has the build of a boxer and the eyes of a hunter. He wears a trim beard and long hair cut short in front so as not to give the enemy something to grab on to in battle. He is dressed in a glossy tunic beneath a heavy woolen cloak with double folds, colored purple. The folds are clasped by a solid gold brooch incised with an image of a hound killing a fawn. If the expression on his face is a mask, it is no more insincere than the language of brotherhood in which royal scribes couch ultimatums, and no trickier than the nighttime troop movements by which Bronze Age generals steal a march on the enemy. War is deception: no one knows this better than Odysseus. His traveling companion, Menelaus, might dream of avenging his honor, but Odysseus just wants to win.

The expression on his face is a riddle; not so that of Menelaus, whose eyes glow with anger. The two men ride in separate two-horse chariots, driven by trusted friends. They are escorted by a detachment of heavy-armed spearmen but not from their own army. The escorts are Trojans, and they are leading a Greek delegation.

The soldiers are elite troops, wearing bronze armor shining for the parade ground. They are protecting the city from the Greeks and the Greeks from the city. Let the long-haired Greeks see the strength of Troy's walls but not the weak spots in need of repair. And don't let the Trojans and their wives, whose garments sweep the ground, see who is suddenly within reach of vengeance. The Greeks have just arrived in the country, but they have already created refugees and mourners.

The two visiting kings are not likely to have reacted in the same way. Menelaus's blood might have been boiling at the thought that he was in Troy, where his adulterous wife was dishonoring his name and her lover was cuckolding him and defying the gods. Paris had violated the laws of Zeus himself, the god of hospitality and strangers. Odysseus was an accomplished sacker of cities and a born scout, the most cunning man in the Greek army. We may imagine him consumed less by anger than by curiosity. The paved streets, the wide courtyards, the exotic statuettes of the bull that represented the army's god, the veiled women, the wind that blew stronger the higher they climbed on Troy's hill—nothing would have escaped the scrutiny of the man of many ways, as Homer calls him.

Ancient Near Eastern etiquette demanded that a king lay down an official challenge to his opponent. It was unmanly, said a Hittite king, to start a war with a sneak attack. The Greeks came, therefore, to give the Trojans one last chance for peace; the alternative was en-mity and death. Or so they said. A razor-sharp Trojan might have known the Hittite practice of sending an envoy who held two sets of instructions, a "tablet of war" and a "tablet of peace"; one tablet threatened the enemy, but the other proposed a deal, should the enemy refuse to give in. But the Greeks were in no mood for a deal. It was up to the Trojans to back down and restore peace. Was it worth dying for Helen?

Odysseus and Menelaus headed for the home of Antenor, their host. In spite of the circumstances, they would not have forgotten to bring him gifts, perhaps including a statuette of a god, as a Greek king once sent to the Hittite monarch. Antenor might have lived in one of the two-story mansions in a newly fashionable section of the lower city. When Troy was rebuilt after an earthquake around 1300 B.C., the town's strict class segregation came to an end; no longer did wealthy people live just on the citadel, and the citadel was no longer just the preserve of the rich.

Imagine Antenor's house with painted plaster walls and a sep-arate kitchen wing with a dozen large vases sunk into the earth to provide a kind of refrigerated storage. Inside a house like this were imported jewelry and seal stones, delicate pottery and silver bowls, and woven textiles and carved ivories. Perhaps it was even Antenor who owned a bronze figurine of a man standing in a ges-ture of prayer: a wide-eyed, straight-nosed piece, apparently of Hit-tite workmanship. (This figurine has just recently been excavated at Troy.)

Although a Trojan, Antenor was a friend of the Greeks. He was an important person in Troy, an elder statesman, noble, and royal ad-visor. He was married to Theano daughter of Cisseus, who was priestess of Athena, which is a sign of Antenor's social prominence. Antenor always took the Greeks' side in Trojan debates, and we might guess that he had business interests, kinship, and marriage ties that allied him with Greeks. As for Athena, the Trojan equivalent isn't known, but we can assume there was one, because Anatolian cities often had a protector goddess.

Antenor had reason enough to speak for peace without Greek influence: he had many sons whom he no doubt did not wish to sacrifice in war. So when Menelaus and Odysseus spoke up in the Trojan assembly, Antenor supported them. The Greeks demanded that Helen and the stolen treasures of Sparta be returned.

The two Greek speakers made a lasting impression on Antenor. Menelaus was more imposing physically but the lesser speaker. Menelaus said what he had to but he seemed to be in a hurry to get the words out. Just minutes away sat his wife, Helen, under Paris's roof. Menelaus surely knew that every man in the gathering looked at him with scorn. Every word might be taken as a sign of weakness, so no wonder the man kept his speech short.

Odysseus was different. His remarks were delivered with the strategic skill that was his trademark. First, he softened up the audience by playing the hick, too intimidated by the big city to do any more than hold his scepter and look at the ground. But when his turn came, Odysseus let out words that fell on the assembly like a snowstorm. It was a verbal reminder of the man's toughness. War was Odysseus's business. As he reminded Agamemnon when the going got rough:

> *This is what Zeus has given us, from youth to old age:*
> *To fight hard wars to the finish, until we are all dead.*

But the Trojans did not give Odysseus what he wanted. Indeed, things nearly got out of hand in the unruly assembly. The leading hawk was another important Trojan, Antimachus. Like Antenor, he had sons. But the prospect of their corpses on the funeral pyre did not soften his stand: there could be no surrender to the Greeks. Antimachus was a man of fiery temper, but Homer says that something else was afoot: Antimachus had been bought by Paris with especially good gifts, namely, a large amount of gold, no doubt from the hoard brought back from Sparta.

Not only did Antimachus argue against returning Helen or the stolen treasures, he said that the Trojans should kill Menelaus then and there. This would have been "disgraceful" and "an outrage," as Agamemnon later put it. But it would have been a smart move. Killing Menelaus would not only have cost the Greeks a prominent (if not overly effective) leader, but it would also have stripped the war of its logic. The Greeks would have found themselves fighting to return Helen to a dead man and to avenge a murdered king—in fact, two murdered kings, since killing Odysseus would have been a brilliant stroke too. In the long run, no Greek would do more harm to Troy than he did, although the Trojans could not have known that yet.

In the end, the two men were given safe passage back to their camp at the sea. But they returned empty-handed, without Helen or the treasure. And surely Priam approved of that. He had certainly welcomed the adulterous queen to Troy, and he treated her with warmth and chivalry, as Homer shows. While other Trojans blamed the war on Helen, Priam insisted that, as far as he was concerned, it was the gods and not she who were responsible. And he never lifted a finger to return her to the Greeks.

But he couldn't afford to. Priam did not have the luxury of waging war without considering domestic politics. No king did. Civil war lurked in Bronze Age cities, from Canaanite towns to the Hittite capital. One Canaanite mayor confessed his fear of his own peasantry; another was driven into exile by a younger brother who despised him. In Hittite history, a whole population or just part of it could force a city into surrendering. Troy itself had suffered civil war not long before in the 1200s B.C., forcing the exile of King Walmu, a Hittite ally. So Priam and his family had to tread carefully.

Returning Helen would be admitting that it had been a mistake to let her into Troy in the first place. And that admission might well bring the downfall of the house of Priam. It would have been an invitation for a coup by a member of another branch of the royal family, which was not short of pretenders, or even by an outsider like Antenor.

Meanwhile, Priam's supporters in the assembly could argue against appeasement. Give back Helen and the treasures, and the greedy Greeks would ask for more. Accept the ambassadors' demands, and say goodbye to Trojan independence. Let the enemy just try to storm the city: he would stop in frustration soon enough. All that Troy needed was patriotism and patience, the argument might go.

So Priam and his people would face the war and fight to win. That left the Greeks with no choice but to sharpen their spears and wage war with everything they had. Menelaus might have glowed at the thought of vengeance and at the sweet odor of death. But the shadow of Troy's massive walls would have fallen over Odysseus's thoughts, pragmatist that he was.

The question of what the Greeks did next—of how they fought—is much more difficult than it might seem. There is no direct answer in the *Iliad*, focusing as it does on the penultimate part of the war. Another early ancient epic, the *Cypria*, discusses the previous phases of the war. But only a few lines of this poem survive and the *Cypria* is less reliable than Homer. Fortunately, Homer provides clues about the earlier fighting.

The first clue comes from a comment by Poseidon, the god of the sea, horses, and earthquakes. Even mythological figures such as the gods speak to Homer's authenticity. Ancient peoples were deeply religious. In the Bronze Age, for example, Hittite and Egyptian accounts regularly give the gods a role in military campaigns. No Hittite scribe would think of recording a victory without thanking the gods for having marched in front of the army and thereby having granted the king success. No ambassador would swear to abide by a treaty unless an assembly of the various gods had witnessed it. In his poem about the battle of Qadesh (1274 B.C.), Pharaoh Rameses II declares that the god Amun spoke to him and sent him forward.

Even in the rationalistic heyday of classical Greece—and later— gods and heroes were commonly seen in the heat of battle. Sometimes their mere presence provided encouragement to the soldiers. At other times, divinities gave specific military advice. And sometimes they even fought! At the decisive battles of Marathon (490 B.C.), Salamis (480 B.C.), Aegospotami (405 B.C.), and Leuctra (371

B.C.), for example, contemporaries thought that gods and heroes took part.

On the treacherous plain of Troy the only rock of certainty was the gods. Men needed to believe that the deities cared about their fate because the alternative was the loneliness of death. So when Homer sets verse after verse in Olympus, he is not offering mere window-dressing; he is opening a window into the soul of the ancient Greek soldier. And when Homer quotes a god, he may be reporting what men claimed to have heard at the time.

By the ninth year of the war, in an attempt to buck up the Greeks when the battle was going badly, Poseidon cast scorn on the enemy. The ninth year, that is, in Homer's reckoning: we have already seen that the real war was much shorter. How can the Greeks let the Trojans push them back on their ships, he asks, when the Trojans usually behave like frightened deer? The Trojans have been running through the woods as if afraid of the wolves; defenseless creatures without a heart for battle. They were never willing to stand their ground against the armed might of the Greeks.

Achilles makes a similar claim. He says that up to now Hector had never wanted to fight far from the walls, and he would advance no farther than the oak tree near Troy's main or Scaean Gate. There he would have the help of soldiers stationed in the towers at either side of the gate. Even so, the Greek adds, Hector once barely escaped Achilles' charge. And Hera goes one better: she claims that when it came to the Dardanian Gate, Hector wouldn't dare so much as go outside the walls—presumably because this postern gate lacked protective bastions.

This is exaggeration, but the Trojans did indeed spend most of the war on defense, leaving attacks to the Greeks. Perhaps some of the Trojans were cowards, as Poseidon says, but most were sound strategists. Like their brethren elsewhere in the ancient Near East, they knew that coming out and fighting made better rhetoric than strategy.

The Trojans had only limited choices. Tactically, they could have nibbled away at the Greeks with guerrilla raids—and we can fault the Trojans for doing so little of that. But the Trojans were absolutely right to avoid a frontal assault of the Greeks' camp. The Trojans depended on allies and so they had to avoid casualties; high losses would make those allies give up and go home. By staying on the strategic defensive, the Trojans bowed to the realities of warfare at the time.

The Late Bronze Age knew three ways to conquer a fortified city: assault, siege, or ruse. Assault meant either scaling the city walls with ladders, breaking through the walls or through a gate with battering rams or hammers and axes, or tunneling below the walls. Siege meant encircling the city walls, preventing supplies from entering, and starving the defenders into surrender. Ruse meant any trick or tricks, sometimes coordinated with traitors inside the walls, that could gain control of the city.

Each of these tactics was difficult and dangerous. To penetrate the walls at Troy meant you first had to reach them, and that meant either winning a pitched battle against the army that protected Troy or pulling off a surprise attack. During years of intermittent fighting on the plain of Troy, the Greeks reached the walls a few times, but the Trojans always quickly forced them back. The Trojans had taken to heart the Mesopotamian proverb that strong gates alone can't save a city without a strong army to defend them. Chariots were Troy's "secret weapon" and, as Odysseus knew, when men mount swift-footed horses, they could decide the outcome of an equally matched war— and decide it in a flash. No wonder that, when he said goodbye to his wife, Penelope, on the day he left for war, Odysseus told her that he expected many Greeks never to come home.

They had no supply lines from home to sustain them. Instead, large numbers of Greek soldiers had to sail off on food-hunting raids or settle down as farmers on the Gallipoli Peninsula on the other side of the Dardanelles. Thucydides is the source of this insight, and the sober historian may be right because later Greek armies did the same sort of thing when necessary. With the Greeks unable to gather all their men for one big push, the Trojan War could only be bloody and frustrating. No wonder that Odysseus characterized it afterward as "a hateful path decreed by thundering Zeus to lead many men to death."

It is common to speak of the siege of Troy but in fact there was no siege. The Greeks never encircled the city. They built no palisades or ditches to cut off Troy from access to the outside world by land, because they couldn't. They lacked the superiority in numbers to establish a ring around the city without risking an overwhelming Trojan counterattack. The Trojan defenders were, as Odysseus says in another context, "as many as the leaves and flowers that come in spring."

On three occasions before the last phase of the war, the Greeks reached the city walls and nearly took control of them, at a place near the landmark of a particular wild fig tree, near the western gate. If Bronze Age armies had a field manual it would have called for the use of a stratagem to reach the enemy's walls, such as a surprise attack at night or a decoy to lure his army away and leave the walls unprotected. The early Hittite rulers Pithana and his son Anitta (1700s B.C.?) each stormed an enemy city by night. We don't know whether the Greeks used such tactics or took the more direct route of winning a pitched battle and pushing on to Troy. In any case, their probes had found a weak spot in the fortifications, perhaps that point in the northwestern wall where a former gate had been filled in with rubble, a pile that was now sagging. It was there, under the leadership of the two men named Ajax—Ajax son of Telamon and Oilean or "Lesser" Ajax—that Idomeneus, Diomedes, Agamemnon, and Menelaus, the best Greek soldiers, nearly sealed Troy's fate.

The source of this information is not a soldier but a woman: Hector's wife, Andromache. She stood with her husband near the Scaean Gate of the Trojan wall, and the tough-minded lady gave him military advice. If that seems like Josephine telling Napoleon how to invade Russia, it adds to the evidence of the relative freedom of Trojan women. One ancient Greek literary critic even wanted to delete these lines as not really Homer's because he couldn't believe that Andromache would lecture her husband on strategy. But Andromache wasn't Greek. She says:

That quarter most the skilful Greeks annoy,
Where yon wild fig-trees join the wall of Troy;
Thou, from this tower defend the important post;
There Agamemnon points his dreadful host,
That pass Tydides [Diomedes], Ajax, strive to gain,
And there the vengeful Spartan fires his train.
Thrice our bold foes the fierce attack have given,
Or led by hopes, or dictated from heaven.
Let others in the field their arms employ,
But stay my Hector here, and guard his Troy.

A woman like Andromache had perhaps the most to lose in a sack of the city because she would end up a slave and mistress to one of the victors. We can't help but wonder if her statement of three near-breakthroughs isn't another case of heroic exaggeration. But even one attempt to break through the walls would have been frightening enough to the Trojans.

Although the Greeks had much experience storming cities, their forte was attack from the sea. We have to wonder whether they were equal to those experts in land assaults, the Assyrians, Egyptians, and Hittites.

Scaling a city's wall was an elite operation, and Andromache is specific about which Greek champions led the assault. Agamemnon and Menelaus, brothers, kings, and sons of Atreus, have already been introduced. If not the Greeks' greatest warriors, they were nonetheless strong soldiers and key political leaders. Their presence in an attempt to scale Troy's walls is no surprise. The four other attackers (Andromache also mentions Idomeneus and Lesser Ajax as part of the assault), all famous soldiers, represent respectively the Greeks' best hand-to-hand fighter, their most vicious cutthroat, a veteran of their most successful recent assault on a city of the day, and an older man who was as experienced as he was expendable. Surely it also mattered that the latter two had brought the biggest contingents to Troy after Agamemenon and the elderly Nestor. Odysseus, that all-around soldier and well-known sacker of cities, is not recorded as having taken part in the assault on the walls. But the Trojans had a hard time picking Odysseus out of a crowd because he was shorter than some of the other Greek heroes, so perhaps Andromache missed him. Here are the other leaders of the assault team:

Idomeneus was son of Deucalion and king of Crete, the island that, two centuries earlier, had been among the Greeks' first conquests. He was a tough warrior who carried a huge figure-of-eight shield into battle, made of leather, rimmed with bronze, and held together by two rods. Although no longer in the flower of youth, he still loved to fight and was known as a great spearman. Along the wall of his hut stood a barbaric display of spears, shields, helmets, and breastplates stripped from Trojans whom he had killed. It was a modest version of the more than one thousand pieces of arms and armor, including two gilded chariots, that Pharaoh Thutmose III took when he conquered Megiddo in 1479 B.C.

Figure-of-eight shields such as Idomeneus's once seemed anachronistic, since they were thought to have gone out of use around 1500 B.C. But not long ago a painted pottery fragment turned up that shows these shields still in use in the 1300s, so they may well have been a feature of the battlefield at the time of the Trojan War.

Ajax son of Telamon of Salamis was no genius but he was a murderous giant who never passed up a fight. He and Achilles were cousins. Among the Greeks, only Achilles was bigger and stronger than Ajax, and Idomeneus reckoned Ajax could defeat Achilles in a hand-to-hand fight though he could never match Achilles' speed. Ajax would fight Hector, Troy's greatest warrior, to a standstill. Ajax was more like a wall than a man, which is why they called him "the bulwark of the Greeks." He went into battle wearing a full body-suit of armor and carrying a huge, tower-shaped shield made of seven layers of leather and rimmed with bronze. While most tower shields depicted in Mycenaean art are covered with oxhide, some appear to be metallic, so Homer's description might be accurate. Ajax's normal weapon was the spear, but he was strong enough to lift a big piece of marble, swing it above his head, and then bring it down on a Trojan with enough force to smash the man's helmet and crush his skull.

Ajax son of Oïleus of Locris suffered in comparison to the prowess of the comrade whose name he shared, so he was called the Lesser Ajax. But he was in no way deficient when it came to mayhem. He was a foul-mouthed brawler with a short temper and ready fists. He is remembered in the Epic Cycle for dragging Cassandra from the altar of Athena to rape her. Who better than such a brute to lead the first wave over the wall?

Diomedes son of Tydeus was king of Argos. Like Odysseus, with whom he teamed up from time to time, Diomedes was a warrior for all seasons. And, although he was the youngest of the Greek champions in the *Iliad*, Diomedes excelled in pitched battle. Homer details the murderous spree in which Diomedes killed the great Trojan bowman Pandarus son of Lycaon, nearly did the same to Aeneas, and even wounded the gods Ares and Aphrodite—surely a way of saying that he was reckless on the battlefield. Warriors had been wounding goddesses at least since *Gilgamesh*, a Mesopotamian epic with roots in the 2000s B.C.

Diomedes was a favorite of Athena, just as Hattushilish III (1267–1237 B.C.) was a favorite of the goddess Ishtar, whom an Assyrian inscription refers to as the "mistress of strife and battle." In the Hittite king's case, Ishtar was everywhere in battle, now marching in front of Hattushilish, now holding his hand. Diomedes likewise might have felt as if he had Athena's goatskin itself wrapped around his shoulders as he fought.

Diomedes wore a full suit of bronze armor and his helmet was probably bronze with a horsehair plume. His shield was another of the figure-eight style. A combat veteran, he had taken part in the expedition that finally destroyed the city of Thebes; his father, Tydeus, had died trying in an earlier attempt. But he had not died gloriously, as a story in the epic tradition reports. Tydeus killed a Theban warrior, Melanippus, but not without receiving a fatal wound himself. While he lay dying, Tydeus reached over and helped himself to some of Melanippus's brain tissue, which he then ate. The gods approved of warriors who crowed in victory but they drew the line at cannibalism: myth says that Athena punished Tydeus by withdrawing a promise of immortality.

To storm a walled city it was necessary to use ladders, soldiers armed with protective shields, and archers to provide covering fire to the attackers; slingers were also useful. By the Late Bronze Age the art of assault had advanced considerably. Battering rams and siege towers were now common in the ancient Near East. A battering ram was, at its simplest, a long beam tipped with metal. A siege tower allowed the attacker's bowmen to shoot at the defenders on the battlements, thereby protecting the men operating the battering ram below. Another refinement was to put wheels on the scaling ladders, as the Egyptians did. Attackers sometimes built a dirt ramp up to the wall. And it was not unknown to try to tunnel beneath the walls and enter the city from below.

Military architects always tried to keep one step ahead of the latest advance in storming technology, and Troy's walls were up to date. The city had two sets of walls: an outer perimeter protecting the lower town and an inner citadel to which the defenders could retreat. At nearly a mile in circumference, the outer wall was more difficult to defend than the compact circuit of the citadel.

The outer wall consisted of a stone foundation on top of which lay sun-dried mud bricks, better known in North America as adobe. The bricks, made of a mixture of mud, sand, straw, and manure, were cheap and easy to manufacture. Adobe cushions the shock of a battering ram, but unfortunately it is vulnerable to enemy sappers, who can cut right through it; the higher the stone foundation, therefore, the better.

In the *Iliad* the Greeks build a rampart of wood and stone to protect their camp. They surround it with a deep trench, in which they place stakes. Troy's outer wall was similarly surrounded by a wooden palisade and a trench, cut into the bedrock, to eight feet deep and ten to eleven feet wide. At intervals the trench was interrupted for access to the gates. The Greeks' trench was built to stop chariots, and no doubt the Trojan trench was too, but it would also have stopped siege towers and made it difficult to use battering rams anywhere except at the gates.

The trench protected the outer wall before about 1300, but by the 1200s it had been filled with dirt, potsherds, and animal bones. That would have made no military sense except in the unlikely event that the sherds and bones were sharp enough to serve as caltrops (cavalry obstacles). Perhaps the trench was filled in for public-health reasons, since rainwater in it might have represented breeding grounds for mosquitos, leading in turn to outbreaks of malaria. The Trojans would not have known the cause of the illness, but they might have noticed a correlation between the outbreak and the trench. But the likeliest explanation is that the lower town had prospered and grown. A second trench has been discovered, about three hundred feet southeast of the first; it could have replaced the first trench as a defensive barrier.

In any case, the Trojans would not have wanted to concede the lower city without a fight, especially not after the movement of wealthy citizens there in the 1200s B.C. The area could survive attack because of its own fresh water from a well located in the massive Northeast Bastion. Sling stones and metal weapons have been found in the destruction debris around 1200 B.C. of Troy VIi (formerly known as Troy VIIa). All of this may well be evidence of a failed defense. But after breaching the outer wall, the enemy would have to battle through the lower city and its maze of narrow streets. Then would come a bigger challenge: Fortress Troy.

The citadel of Troy, called Pergamos, rose about one hundred feet above the plain, a half-acre stronghold. The defenders could stockpile food and they could also rely on a supply of fresh water from an underground spring, reached via a network of manmade tunnels dug some five hundred feet into the rock.

Pergamos was protected by one of the finest fortifications in the world: a 1,150 foot circuit of walls standing about 33 feet high and more than 16 feet thick. The bottom of the wall was made of stone and stood about 20 feet high with an adobe superstructure about another 13 feet high. A walkway for the defenders crowned the walls, protected by a breastwork. The stone base of the wall sloped outward, thereby denying attackers a blind spot out of reach of a defender's arrow.

The gates were state of the art. The South Gate, probably the main entrance to the city, stood beside an enormous tower built in the 1200s B.C. At a height of more than thirty feet, the tower was a defender's dream. The East Gate had an entrance passage that channeled attackers into a narrow courtyard between two walls and then made them turn a sharp corner before reaching the gate itself. In the 1200s the courtyard was made at least about sixty feet longer and a massive defensive tower and a sort of foregate were added. The imposing Northeast Bastion took advantage of a natural cliff. It stood about forty feet high and was about sixty feet wide. Probably the bastion flanked a gate in the lower town's wall, just as a tower flanked the South Gate in the citadel wall.

Only a punishing and blood-spattered fight could have brought the Greeks over the top at Troy. Imagine, for example, Diomedes in the thick of battle, an angry lion, leading his crack troops in a charge to the ramparts.

The attack on the wall would have been also an assault on the senses: a combination of sights and sounds to terrify defender and attacker alike. We might imagine the twanging of bowstrings, the hum of javelins in motion, the swish of slings, the bang of missiles hitting shields that protected soldiers' backs as they climbed the scaling ladders, the crash of falling ladders, the thud of the battering ram against the doors of the gate, the grunts of the defenders as they tried to absorb the blow and hold the doors in place, the moans of the wounded, the crack of whip on horseflesh and the whinnying of the frightened beasts, the blare of the trumpet ringing out the call to one last charge, and the snapping of the city's standard as it blew in the wind above the walls. Then too, there were surely other sounds that were no less terrifying for their low volume: the pop of a breaking shield strap, the gurgling of a dying man. And imagine, through it all, Diomedes' battle cry, a bellow that came from someplace deep in his heart.

As the Greeks reached for glory and the Trojans made a stand for their homes and families, the cruel war-god, Ares, would have had his fill of victims. A lone Greek warrior might make it up to the battlements, hauling himself up the rungs of the ladder, hand over blistered hand, and then spear a Trojan defender before being stabbed to death himself. Wounded men would tumble down from the ramparts and the scaling ladders. Corpses would lie in heaps of blood, some with their hands cut off, some decapitated, some with their bellies ripped open. Flies would buzz around them in the hot sun and cluster in their mouths and ears.

And yet, the Greeks did not manage to storm the city. Troy stood firm.

CHAPTER FIVE

THE DIRTY WAR

It is probably a sunny day, but then, it usually is a sunny day on the Gulf of Edremit. Imagine the sky and sea as a cascade of light blue wildflowers, crocuses, windflowers, chicory, and bellflowers. The meadow is an ocean of grass punctuated by islands of juniper shrubs and an elm tree for shade. Here in the shadow of woody Mount Plakos, the only sounds are the herdsman's pipe and the occasional bleating of the glossy white sheep. The cattle are too intent on eating to make a sound. There are seven herdsmen, all sons of King Eëtion of Thebes-under-Plakos, a city at the head of the gulf. They were half-brothers whose mothers were Eëtion's wives. They are not quite slumming, these princes tending the animals, since the herds are the wealth of the kingdom, but they are blessedly free of the court and its cares. We might imagine that they have nothing on their minds except horseplay, wine, and how to find willing servant girls—when suddenly, an enraged boar comes running out of the woods.

That is, it seems like a boar but in fact it is a man. Brilliant, swift-footed Achilles, the equal of the war-god Ares, is covered with bronze and carrying a shield and a giant spear of ash tipped with bronze. He is massive too, and he is coming at the boys at what seems like an impossible rate of speed. He screams something in Greek—

the words are foreign but the tone is hair-raising—and throws his javelin into the nearest herdsman's neck, and then he pulls out his sword and starts slashing. It is all over before they can take cover or beg or offer ransom or fight back. Seven unarmed princes, seven corpses, and one giant, sweating and panting and smeared with his victims' blood. And he is richer by a very fine herd of cattle and sheep.

Or so Homer tells the tale. The real Achilles was no doubt accompanied on the raid by a platoon of his men, the Myrmidons, his faithful comrades who loved war and fought ferociously.

We would also expect to find Achilles' right-hand man at his side, Patroclus son of Menoetius. Patroclus played a role in the Myrmidons akin to that in the Egyptian army of the top general Horemheb, who was "Sole Companion, he who is by the feet of the lord on the battlefield on that day of killing Asiatics." In other words, Patroclus was Achilles' chief deputy, and no mean commander in his own right. He was murderous on the battlefield but gentle off it, having learned a thing or two since boyhood, when he killed a playmate in a fit of rage during a game of dice. Later Greek writers made Achilles and Patroclus lovers, and perhaps they were, but Homer doesn't say so.

Achilles is the main character of Homer's *Iliad*. The writer focuses our attention on the alternately brooding and bloodthirsty character of the supposed ninth year of the war. But he also offers glimpses of earlier days when Achilles was less emotional, more pragmatic, and more effective.

Homer says nothing about the notorious heel. He does not mention the tale that Achilles' mother, Thetis, dipped her infant son in the River Styx and made nearly all his body invulnerable, except the heel that she held him by. Those details are probably later additions to the story. Homer's Achilles receives a lot of help from the gods but he is mortal.

Like Greece's other great generals, Achilles had an instinct for asymmetry. The Greeks fought war in two dimensions, land and sea, which encouraged them to think creatively. The Trojans acted as if the aim of their policy should be to destroy the enemy's military power. The Greeks' goal was to destroy *all* sources of support for the hostile state, including its economy and even its prestige. And Achilles was the hammer of destruction.

Achilles came from Phthia, a region in central Greece at the raw edge of Bronze Age Greek civilization. He embodied the best and the worst of the era, its talent and its violence. In all the Greek army no one could match Achilles for his looks or physique. He was tall and striking, and his handsome face was crowned with a mane of long, dirty-blond hair. Modesty was not a heroic virtue, and Achilles would have agreed. He calls himself big and beautiful, and furthermore, he says:

> *None of the bronze-wearing Greeks is my equal*
> *In war, although some are better than me in the assembly.*

Achilles was temperamental, but when he was in the mood he couldn't get enough of battle. Combat was his road to what every hero wanted: fame, glory, and honor.

In what Homer calls the ninth year of the war, Achilles claimed to have destroyed no fewer than twenty-three cities, which comes to about two and one-half attacks annually. If twenty-three is an exaggeration, it is not out of line with Bronze Age hyperbole. For instance, the eastern Anatolian king Anum-Hirbi (ca. 1800 B.C.) claims that the enemy destroyed twelve of his towns and Hittite texts record similar claims. If the Greeks had originally hoped to terrify Troy into surrender when they landed, they failed. But when Troy made its strategy of forward defense work, the Greeks employed a counterstrategy of slow strangulation. They raided Trojan territory, especially beyond the well-defended plain of Troy, and they carried out two sorts of operations: ambushes of civilians outside Troy's walls and assaults on Trojan settlements and nearby cities friendly to Troy.

The Greek camp at Troy had several functions and one of them was that of naval station: it made a convenient jumping-off place for attacks. Because they enjoyed command of the sea, the Greeks could strike the long Trojan coastline virtually at will. So they ransacked cities; carried off Trojan women, treasure, and livestock; killed some leading men, ransomed others, and sold most of the rest as slaves on the islands of Lemnos, Imbros, and Samos.

The Greeks were not the only sea raiders of the era. Pharaoh Amenhotep III (1382–1344 B.C.), for example, had trouble with Shardana pirates. The Lycians of southwestern Anatolia were another group with a reputation for piracy. Amenhotep's son, pharaoh Akhenaten (1350–1334 B.C.) was plagued by Lycian sea raiders who seized Egyptian towns year after year; Akhenaten accused a Cypriot king of providing aid and comfort to the Lycians.

Greek plundering raids, of which the *Iliad* offers many anecdotes, served several purposes. Loot was a morale booster for wavering Greek soldiers. The raids offered a break from the boredom of camp life. More important, the raids secured food and fodder for poorly supplied Greek forces. For example, Odysseus and his men stormed and sacked the city of Ismarus in Thrace, a Trojan ally. And this was just on their way home.

Livestock loomed large in the Late Bronze Age's list of booty. Egyptian, Mesopotamian, and Hittite texts, for instance, often list it as a coveted prize of war. Among the Greeks, raiding cattle, horses, and sheep was honorable, profitable, and violent. When Attarissiya (Atreus?) attacked the kingdom of Madduwatta in southwestern Anatolia around 1400 B.C. he targeted cattle and sheep. Homer mentions various wars in Greece fought over cattle thieving, and it was not unusual for noblemen to die in the process. Helen's brother, for example, the Spartan prince Castor, was killed in one such raid. And cattle raiding could disrupt an enemy's economy and society. For instance, one Melanippus son of Hicetaon was a kinsman of Hector and an important figure in the town of Percote on the Dardanelles. When the Greeks came after his cattle, he prudently moved to Troy and was put up by Priam. Melanippus saved his skin and lived to fight in the Trojan army, but he was no longer a force of law and order in Percote—assuming that the town survived a visit by the Greeks.

Slaving was lucrative as well. Anatolian slaves were prized in Greece, no doubt in part because of stereotypes about slavish easterners that were common in classical Greece. But Anatolians fetched high prices in the Bronze Age for a more practical reason: in general, they were better-educated, more sophisticated, and more highly skilled than ordinary Greeks. Civilization had deeper roots in the East than in Greece; literacy was more widespread, cities more common. Myth records that Greeks imported engineers from Lycia to build the stunning fortification walls of the city of Tiryns in the Peloponnesus.

Achilles once described the attacks on the cities as a matter of "making war on other men over their women." But he was speaking to Agamemnon then and bitter over their quarrel about a woman. Captive women feature prominently on Egyptian and Hittite booty lists as well as on Linear B tablets that inventory the wealth of Greek kings. And yet women were only a small part of the loot that the Greeks amassed.

Finally, the assaults on other cities hurt Troy, which had connections of marriage and presumably of friendship and alliance with at least some of them. Some had given Troy expensive "gifts" of gold and silver and others might have sold supplies to the beleaguered city. Of the towns that Achilles sacked, eleven were in the vicinity of Troy. Greek attacks harassed civilians and insulted Trojan honor, and they picked off vulnerable allies. Unable to lay siege to Troy, the Greeks inflicted an indirect punishment on it.

How many people—like Melanippus of Percote—left the countryside for safety behind the great city's walls? As a practical matter, only those who, like him, had family in Troy to support them, could have afforded food and shelter in the big city. Most people would probably have needed to rely on local strongholds, which lacked the security of Troy's ramparts, hoping that the Greeks did not come to their corner of the Troad. But there were surely some refugees in Troy, an excess population that could only have increased pressure on the infrastructure of the town.

Needless to say, the Greeks considered it fair game to attack any Trojan civilian who ventured out to do business, even women going to the spring to fetch water. Homer mentions two springs of the Scamander River that flowed into basins

> *Where Trojan dames (ere yet alarm'd by Greece)*
> *Wash'd their fair garments in the days of peace.*

This is reminiscent of the Canaanite *Kirta Epic* (1300s B.C.) in which women flee from the woods, threshing floors, springs, and fountains for shelter in the cities and towns when the enemy invades "like locusts."

We hear nothing about Trojan counter-expeditions to defend the cities that the Greeks attacked. Either they lacked the resources to protect any place except their home territory or Homer has left out the details. Archaeology shows that two towns at the southern end of the Trojan Plain were fortified. They were located outside the entrance to a pass that led southward through the hills of the Mount Ida massif. Conceivably, Trojan soldiers manned these forts and sallied out to attack Greeks traveling overland. But the Greeks seem to have had no such worries farther away from Troy, on the periphery of the Troad. Taking Troy was hard work; taking Thebes-under-Plakos was a romp in the meadow.

Years after the war, King Nestor of Pylos remembered Achilles as having shone especially in the sea raids. And well he might have, since Nestor profited from one such raid on the island of Tenedos, from the spoils of which Nestor was awarded the lovely Hecamede, as hostess, servant, and bedmate. She was the daughter of a great man named Arsinous, and she had beautiful hair and divine looks.

A Roman-era collection of myths names seventeen cities that Achilles is supposed to have sacked and adds that there were "many others." But this late source cannot be trusted. Much better to follow the *Iliad*, which specifies six of the cities sacked by Achilles: besides Thebes-under-Plakos, they were Lyrnessus and Pedasus, both in the Troad; and Lesbos, Tenedos, Scyros: all islands, and presumably the main town is meant in each instance, as Homer specifies in the case of Scyros. On the east coast of Lesbos, excavation turned up a Bronze Age city at Thermi that was violently destroyed in the 1200s. Each of the islands supplied a beautiful woman to one of the Greek heroes: in addition to Nestor's Hecamede, there were Iphis, a Scyrian woman who slept with Patroclus, and Diomede daughter of Phorbas of Lesbos, who slept with Achilles (at least in the absence of his favorite female, Briseis). Among the many trophies in Agamemnon's collection were seven beautiful women from Lesbos.

It is a good guess that the weapons used in the attacks on the islands were naval pikes, which the Greeks carried on their ships for sea battles. These were long spears, allegedly forty feet, jointed by iron rings, and tipped with bronze points. Naval battles in the Bronze Age are not well documented, but it is clear that they were mainly attacks on personnel rather than attempts to destroy ships. This is suggested by recently discovered, fragmentary images from Greek vases of the 1100s B.C.

Perhaps the earliest recorded naval battle took place between Hittite and Cypriot ships during the reign of the Hittite King Shuppiluliuma II (1207–? B.C.). But no details survive: around the same time, ca. 1187, there was a battle between Egyptian ships and those of the Sea Peoples and it is well illustrated on a sculpted Egyptian relief. Both sides' vessels carry archers and marines armed with pikes, swords, and shields. The prows of the Sea Peoples' ships have posts ending in duckbill-shaped projections, and these may have served as a kind of ram. The Egyptians are supported by archers on shore as well. A different source, Minoan and Mycenaean images of sieges, shows ships approaching fortified cities and men drowning, presumably battle casualties.

On the mainland, Lyrnessus and Pedasus were taken on the same operation as Thebes-under-Plakos. The order in which the cities were attacked is not known. None of the sites has been securely identified, but Homer does supply some hints, so it is an educated guess that all three cities were on the northern shore of the Gulf of Edremit.

It was no doubt after killing the princes that Achilles led the Greeks to sack Thebes-under-Plakos. In theory the Greeks could have reached the city on foot from their camp at Troy but in between lies rugged country. It would have been easier, faster, and cheaper to go by sea. Safer too, since the Trojans could not stop the Greek navy.

Located in Mysia, the town gave its name to what was then called the Plain of Thebes (today, the Plain of Edremit). Achilles calls the town the "holy city of Eëtion," after the king. Eëtion is probably a non-Greek name; Homer calls the people whom Eëtion rules Cilicians (not to be confused with the better-known Cilicians of southern Anatolia). Plakos, at whose foot Thebes sat, was a wooded mountain, perhaps a spur of Mount Ida.

To conquer Thebes-under-Plakos, Achilles would have needed a detachment of ships and men that was large enough to take on a fair-sized town without depleting Greek forces at their beachhead camp and leaving them vulnerable to attack. The Trojans never took advantage of the enemy's temporary weakness. Whether they missed their chance or whether the Greeks carefully kept troop strength high at their camp by sending out only small groups, we do not know. Another possibility is successful deception: for instance, the Greeks might have lit extra fires at night to hide the raiders' absence.

An educated guess is that Thebes-under-Plakos was a city of one thousand people that could muster around three hundred fighting men. Although described as "high-gated," Thebes-under-Plakos's fortifications are not likely to have presented much of a challenge compared to those of Troy. Imagine that the Greeks enjoyed manpower superiority of three to one: a comfortable if not huge advantage. In that case the Greeks would have needed nine hundred men or eighteen penteconters, assuming the soldiers did their own rowing. In addition to spearmen, the Greek force would have required archers and slingers to provide covering fire for the soldiers assaulting the city. They would also have needed ladders, which would be raised and climbed by veterans of earlier assaults. In the best-case scenario they would also have brought a battering ram. In any case, the mission to Thebes-under-Plakos was a success: "we destroyed it and brought everything here [to the camp at Troy]," said Achilles afterward.

It began with the long ships putting out from the shore at Troy and heading south. They would have rounded the rocky coast of Cape Lekton, oars striking rhythmically. Heading eastward along the southern shore of the Troad, they would have had to their starboard the island of Lesbos, its outline shimmering in the day's heat. They would have passed scrub-covered hills and sheer gray cliffs, and heard the distant braying of donkeys. They would have passed the dry gullies of the summer months, when the snow has long disappeared from the slopes of Mount Ida above. Finally, they would have reached Mysia. The Myrmidons would have leaped off the vessels as they were anchoring, following their chief, Achilles, toward the walled acropolis on the hill above.

When the Greeks took Thebes-under-Plakos, Achilles killed King Eëtion. Achilles is said to have shown respect to the man's corpse, which he cremated along with the king's armor and then buried under a mound of earth. Considering the usual practice of stripping an enemy's armor, this showed high respect. Was Achilles' gesture a nod toward Eëtion's in-laws? The king's son-in-law was Hector, who had married Eëtion's daughter, Andromache, and brought her to Troy. "The distant Trojans never injured me," Achilles said in protest to Agamemnon, later on. He spoke out of anger, but his chivalry to the dead Eëtion suggests that Achilles meant it.

As for the other men of Thebes-under-Plakos who survived the battle, the few wealthiest might be ransomed, some of the others would be sold into slavery, and the rest would be slaughtered. The women and children would be enslaved; the beautiful women from noble houses would become mistresses of the Greek heroes, while others, we might guess, were forced to serve as camp whores.

The Greeks took all of the king's treasures, aside from his armor; we know of two items that Achilles kept: a lyre and an iron weight, used in athletic contests—in the Bronze Age, iron was relatively rare and expensive. As for the lyre, Achilles enjoyed sitting in his hut at Troy and playing the clear-toned instrument:

> *(The well wrought harp from conquered Thebae came;*
> *Of polish'd silver was its costly frame.)*
> *With this he soothes his angry soul, and sings*
> *The immortal deeds of heroes and of kings.*

Achilles also acquired a superb horse named Pedasos. The queen of Thebes-under-Plakos was exchanged for a hefty ransom, no doubt paid by her Trojan in-laws. Andromache and Hector took in the ransomed queen but she died in their house "of Artemis's arrows," that is, perhaps of a heart attack or stroke. The Trojan connection gave the Greeks an additional motive for sacking Thebes-under-Plakos: the city was probably a Trojan ally, supplying "gifts" or intelligence or rendering some other service, although apparently it did not send soldiers. The destruction of Thebes-under-Plakos deprived Troy of logistical support and struck a blow against morale.

One of the captive women was a visitor from a nearby city. Chryseis daughter of Chryses came from the city of Chryse in the southwestern Troad, about twenty-five miles from Thebes-under-Plakos. According to an ancient commentary on Homer, she had come to visit the queen of Thebes-under-Plakos for a religious function, which is appropriate, since her father was an important priest of the god Apollo. The unlucky girl was shipped off to the Greek camp, where she was given to Agamemnon as a mistress. It would prove to be a fatal connection, indirectly responsible for the quarrel between Agamemnon and Achilles and its bloody consequences. But at the time, the Greeks might have looked on the capture of Chryseis as a real coup.

Lyrnessus also fell to the Greeks on the Thebes-under-Plakos campaign. As at Thebes-under-Plakos, the assault began with a cattle raid. Achilles almost caught a very big man among the livestock: Aeneas son of Anchises, prince of the junior branch of the royal house of Troy, and a leader in battle and council. We may imagine the scene:

Aeneas had been standing unarmed in the countryside, checking his cattle, the mainstay of his wealth, when the enemy arrived without warning. Suddenly Aeneas might have envisioned his fat heifers and thick-necked bulls slipping through his fingers as weightlessly as gold dust. But there was no time to cry: unless he leapt down the paths of sacred Mount Ida, his linen tunic fluttering out behind him, his leather sandals flying over rocks and tree roots, the massive Greek warrior behind him would have thrust his bronze-tipped spear into the Trojan's back. Normally Aeneas was a lion in battle who could slice through a man's throat with his spear, but with Achilles after him, he had to race down the hill like a runaway slave girl. Miraculously, he outran Achilles, all the way to Lyrnessus. As Aeneas explained afterward:

> *Zeus*
> *Preserved me, He roused my courage and my nimble knees.*

Aeneas escaped Achilles, but the people of Lyrnessus did not. We can imagine their struggle as well. The arms of the Greeks stretched over the countryside and then fell on the town, not that the men who attacked it knew what Lyrnessus was called—or cared. Chances are that they were drunk, scared, homesick, and eager to take it all out on the enemy. The men of Lyrnessus stood before the gate, more steadfast than a row of bricks. The Greeks unleashed a storm of arrows and sling stones that pushed the defenders back. The Lyrnessians prayed to the god Kurunta, Lord of the Stag and their protector, but he had already abandoned them. They could not stop the enemy from hacking at the town gate or from dragging their ladders up against the walls. A blare of horns, a volley of arrows, a roar as the Greeks topped the battlements, and it was over. The defenders died choking on their own blood or staring with terror at a severed arm or curling up beside a dying horse with a spear-torn belly.

The Greeks surely found killing exhausting work, especially after having rowed to Lyrnessus in the hot sun. They also had their own dead and wounded to look after. Some soldiers tended their comrades' injuries with herbs and bandages. A surgeon operated on a man with a grave head wound. The only hope was to drain the swollen cranium by removing a portion of the skull. Known as trepanning, it was an ancient procedure and a desperate one. It rarely worked.

The other Greeks dealt with the defeated. There was livestock to round up and jewels to loot. Any Lyrnessian males who had survived were sold into slavery on the Aegean islands. Some of the women were raped on the spot, and they all were dragged off as prizes of war. The women's future lay in hauling water jugs from Greek wells, weaving wool on Greek looms, and warming the beds of the Greek warriors who had destroyed their lives. Their last memory of home was the sight of their menfolk's corpses stripped naked by Greek scavengers and already attracting flies.

Achilles killed two princes at Lyrnessus, Mynes and Epistrophus, both of whom died fighting in a battle of spears. Their father, Evenus son of Selipiades and king of Lyrnessus, was presumably killed as well. Achilles also slew three brothers of the noblewoman Briseis, who saw them die, as well as Mynes, who appears to have been her husband.

In Homer, Briseis, Helen, Andromache, and Hecuba all watch battles from the walls. Minoan and Mycenaean art also show women doing so. A relief on a silver drinking cup from Mycenae depicts six women looking out at the fighting, waving and gesturing in excitement to the men below. But would real women in the Bronze Age have played such an assertive role, and such a risky one, where they might have been hit by an enemy arrow? Probably yes. When the Pharaoh Kamose (ca. 1550 B.C.) took a fleet up the Nile to attack the city of Avaris, he saw the enemy's women peering out at him from the walls. Better-documented, later periods of ancient Greek history offer a few examples of women spectators during a siege. Nor should we discount the morale value to the defenders of seeing their women on the walls. Indeed, both sides in Homer evoke the women and families for whom they are fighting. The presence of women also served as a taunt to the enemy.

Briseis was taken captive along with the other women of Lyrnessus. She ended up as Achilles' mistress. As she was led off, Briseis wept. She couldn't get over the horror: having witnessed the deaths of her three brothers and her husband she would have to sleep with their killer. But Patroclus comforted her. As she said to him later:

> *Thy friendly hand uprear'd me from the plain,*
> *And dried my sorrows for a husband slain. . . .*

Patroclus promised Briseis a high status, saying that Achilles would bring her to Greece and marry her. This was generous and no doubt astute since Patroclus knew Achilles well enough to recognize a woman who could win the hero's heart.

Achilles' conduct during these raids says a lot about the laws of war, such as they were, in the Late Bronze Age. Achilles might well have nodded in approval at the Hittite King Hattushilish I's description of a victory: "I trampled the country of Hassuwa like a lion and like a lion I slew [it] and I brought dust [down] upon them and I took all their possessions with me and filled Hattusa [with it]." Or, as Pharaoh Seti I (1294–1279 B.C.) put it, an instant of trampling the foe is better than a day of jubilation. For Seti, "trampling" meant slaughter, annihilation, and filling valleys with corpses stretched out in their own blood. And he specifically singles out for the slaughter heirs as well as their fathers. The troops of Pharaoh Merneptah (1212–1203 B.C.) took more than nine thousand hands and penises as trophies in a battle in 1208 with Libyan aggressors: common practice in Late Bronze Age Egypt. The Assyrian king Shalmaneser I (1274–1245 B.C.) boasted of having 14,400 enemy captives blinded or, as some say, just having their right eye gouged out. Judging by such acts, the Greeks were not especially brutal; they were playing by the rules of the day.

By Seti's rules, killing heirs was common sense, and that was reason enough for Achilles to mow down the seven royal brothers outside Thebes-under-Plakos. But they were hardly an immediate threat. The herdsmen princes might have carried daggers for protection, but as far as we know they were otherwise unarmed. Did Achilles and the Myrmidons deliberately attack and kill civilians? By today's standards, Achilles might be judged a war criminal.

But we must remember that the princes of Thebes-under-Plakos were not civilians but potential soldiers who could have put on their armor in minutes. Achilles had every right to round them up or even to kill them if they continued to resist or if no guards were available. No doubt he would have kept the princes alive if possible, since his usual practice was not to kill his enemies but, rather, to ransom them or to sell them into slavery on one of the Aegean islands. As Achilles explains late in the war, after he had turned more brutal:

> *I used to like to spare Trojans,*
> *And I took many alive and sold them.*

A case in point is the Trojan prince Lycaon, one of Priam's sons. Achilles ambushed the lad one night while Lycaon was in the royal orchard outside Troy, furtively cutting young fig wood to use for chariot rails—in other words, Lycaon was on a military mission. Achilles' operation was a stakeout. It brought little glory but potentially a lot of profit, and the great Achilles did not hesitate to stoop to conquer.

Lycaon was a valuable commodity; Achilles spared the boy and sold him for a good price, one hundred oxen as well as a gift to Patroclus of a Phoenician silver mixing bowl. The buyer was a Greek nobleman, Euneus, on Lemnos, son of the famous Jason the Argonaut. But luckily for Lycaon, a family friend stepped in: Eëtion of the island of Imbros ransomed Lycaon for three hundred oxen—which means that the Lemnian made a hefty profit (assuming that a Phoenician silver bowl cost considerably less than two hundred oxen). Once freed, Lycaon took ship for Arisbe, a city on the Dardanelles, and then made his way home to Troy.

Lycaon was not a civilian and he would not have been better off if he had been, since civilians had few rights in Bronze Age warfare. If his city was conquered and he was caught, a civilian would be lucky to suffer mere slavery and not death. But it was better not to be caught, even if that meant heading for the hills. Consider, for example, the people of Apasa (probably the later Ephesus), capital of the western Anatolian kingdom of Arzawa, when it was conquered by the Hittite King Murshilish II around 1315 B.C. Most of the population fled, many of them to nearby Mount Arinnanda, probably today's Samsun Dağ, the classical Mount Mycale. This is a long and high summit, climbing from sea level to four thousand feet. Murshilish reports that the terrain was too rocky and overgrown for ascending on horseback. So his army went after the refugees on foot—allegedly with the king himself in the lead. It was, says Murshilish, a battle against the mountain, and the king won.

The loser, of course, was not the mountain but the huge mass of Arzawan refugees, the bulk of whom, says Murshilish, were starved out. Before winter came, the Arzawans surrendered, even though they no doubt knew what lay ahead: like other conquered peoples before them, they would be shipped back to Hatti as "deportees," a class of unfree laborers condemned to menial work—they and their children. Murshilish says that the total number of deportees was beyond measure, but the royal share alone came to 6,200 people.

Whatever booty the Greeks grabbed on their raids belonged to the entire army and not to individuals. It was shared according to the number of men who had participated in the action, with the leader entitled to an extra cut. Each man's share was known as his *geras*, his "gift of honor" or "prize." But sometimes it was a poison gift: fights over the division of the spoils are documented in later Greek history, and so were mutinies by sailors over their pay. When, toward the end of the war, a quarrel over plunder broke out in the Greek camp, probably few people were surprised.

Raiding was a mixed blessing for the Greeks. It prolonged the war, and protracted wars are often as hard on the attacker as on the defender. The Greeks may have amassed mountains of loot in their beachhead camp, but the walls of Troy stood as strong as ever. The result would have been frustration, exhaustion, and anger among the attackers. Although he is one of the few who remained optimistic, Agamemnon nicely summarizes the Greek army's gloom:

> *Now shameful flight alone can save the host,*
> *Our blood, our treasure, and our glory lost.*

CITADEL FORTIFICATIONS. Anyone attacking Troy's citadel from the east would be forced into an alley between the citadel's imposing fortifications (left) and an overlapping wall (right). *(Barry Strauss)*

SOUTH GATE. The main entrance to Troy's citadel featured a paved street (center) and a monumental tower, part of whose foundations are seen here (left). Note the stele in front of the tower (front left). The canopy (rear) protects an early Bronze Age mud brick wall. *(Barry Strauss)*

(Above) TROJAN HOUSE. A large and well-built residence just outside the citadel in the north-west of the Lower City, built in Troy VIi. *(Barry Strauss)*

TROJAN DEFENSE. A part of the defensive ditch around the Lower City, interrupted by a causeway that was protected by a wooden palisade. The stone foundations of later structures are visible on the causeway. *(Troia Project Archives)*

SCAMANDER RIVER. In summer the water level is low in the main river of the Trojan Plain. Note the marshy shores. *(Barry Strauss)*

MOUNT IDA. A spring-fed pool on the south slope of the mountain that overlooks the Troad. Note the deciduous trees. *(Barry Strauss)*

CHRYSE. The cove in the center of the photograph may be the harbor of ancient Chryse. Agamemnon's beautiful captive, Chryseis, was brought back here by ship to her father, the priest Chryses. *(Barry Strauss)*

CAPE LEKTON. A rugged headland at the southwestern tip of the Troad. Raiders heading from Troy to the Gulf of Edremit would have sailed past this spot. *(Barry Strauss)*

GULF OF EDREMIT. A view, through olive trees, toward the mountains above Edremit (ancient Adramyttium), taken from near the presumed site of Thebes-under-Plakos. *(Barry Strauss)*

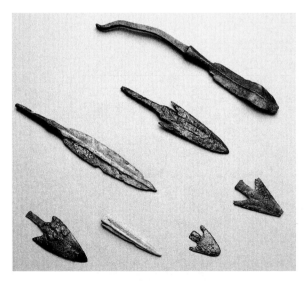

EVIDENCE OF WAR? These arrow- and spearheads were found in the excavations at Troy. *(Troia Project Archives / Dogan Burda Magazine)*

ODYSSEUS. The hero is shown speaking, dressed in a felt cap, cloak, and scabbard, on this chalcedony ring stone from Crete, 400–350 B.C. *(Bildarchiv Preussischer Kulturbesitz / Art Resource, NY)*

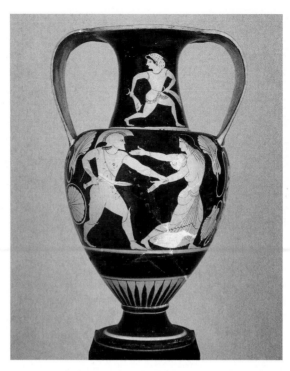

MENELAUS THREATENING HELEN. The king draws a sword on his wayward wife in this red-figure Attic amphora by Oltos, 525–515 B.C. *(Réunion des Musées Nationaux/Art Resource, NY)*

WARRIORS AT REST. Achilles and Ajax play dice in this black-figure vase from the late sixth century B.C. *(Réunion des Musées Nationaux/Art Resource, NY)*

TROY LAID LOW. Achilles drags the body of Hector behind his chariot. Black-figure vase, Diosphos Painter, early fifth century B.C. *(Réunion des Musées Nationaux/Art Resource, NY)*

TROJAN HORSE VASE. Detail of the neck of a Cycladic relief vase, depicting the Greek warriors inside the Horse, 675–650 B.C. *(Mykonos Museum/Hellenic Republic, Ministry of Culture)*

MYCENAEAN ARMOR. This suit of bronze body armor was found in a tomb at Dendra, not far from Mycenae, and is dated to the late 1400s B.C.

MYCENAEAN WARRIORS. This sherd from Tiryns shows parts of two body shields, a spear, and a boar's-tusk helmet.

CHAPTER SIX

AN ARMY IN TROUBLE

Bronze Age soldiers were well-known gripers, and fisticuffs provided an opportunity to let off steam without serious bloodshed. But, as the war dragged on, things were getting out of hand. The supreme commander, Agamemnon son of Atreus, and the best of the Greeks, Achilles son of Peleus, had done something worse than come to blows. They had split the coalition. And the ugliest man who had come to Troy had seen it happen.

So Homer describes him: Thersites was stoop-shouldered, hollow-chested, lame, and his pointy-looking skull was nearly bald—the signs, perhaps, of a congenital disorder in skeletal development. And he had a mouth to match his form. In the manner of a put-down comic, he specialized in insulting men such as Achilles and Odysseus, which was sure to draw a crowd and to make the men laugh.

They needed to laugh, now more than ever. For nine days an epidemic had gripped the camp. It started with the mules and the dogs, then it spread to the men. Infection followed a trajectory like that of anthrax, plague, SARS, avian flu, and the many other diseases spread from animals to human, but no specific illness can be identified from Homer's brief description. It is enough to know that the beach at Troy was crowded with funeral pyres.

When the pyres were lit, smoke billowed out from the softwood used for kindling. It was "evil smelling smoke," as a Bronze Age king put it, because the fumes concentrated the odor of decomposing human flesh. Not until the fire had heated up enough to make the oak logs burn did the billows give way to a red glow and to the aroma of burning meat. Then it was possible to forget that this was a mass cremation in a war zone. But the stink had been unmistakable all the way across the plain, where the wind blew into the city and made the Trojans cry tears of bitter joy.

At the best of times the Greek camp was no rose garden. It smelled of butchered sheep, goats, and cattle; of cooking spices, doused fires, latrines, animal dung, and human sweat. There were flies and mosquitoes, and mice; fleas too. Flea bites became infected from time to time. Lice were everywhere. And there would have been a host of minor illnesses, the sort that always plague travelers (although Homer says nothing of them), from the common cold to diarrhea.

Malaria had been a major problem around Troy until recent years. Did it exist there as early as the Bronze Age? Biomolecular science may one day provide an answer, but we don't yet know. Homer possibly refers to malaria in the *Iliad* when Priam notes how the dog days of summer "bring much fever to wretched mortals." This season was associated with malaria from Roman times on. Imperial Rome managed to achieve grandeur in spite of endemic malaria. Trojans could have survived the disease by adopting so-called avoidance behaviors in malaria season, such as keeping clear of the wet, low-lying areas at night and sleeping with shuttered windows—just as Romans did.

The wind on Troy's hill would have protected the city itself from mosquitoes. But the Greek army, camped in the swampy lowlands, would have been at high risk. The effect on soldiers would have varied widely. For some, malaria would have been devastating, as it frequently was to armies of northerners who attacked Rome. But other Greeks would have shrugged off the illness. Adults who come from areas where malaria is rife are generally immune to the disease, having survived repeated childhood infections.

Whatever the cause of the epidemic, on the tenth day Achilles called an assembly on the beach beside the hollow ships. It was here that the quarrel broke out. The prophet Calchas, no friend of the son of Atreus, made a terrible announcement: Apollo had sent the epidemic to punish the Greeks for having turned a deaf ear to his priest, Chryses, who served at the shrine of Apollo Smintheus in the southern Troad.

Ten days earlier, Chryses had come to the Greek camp to beg for the return of his captured daughter, Chryseis. He offered the Greeks a generous ransom, which would no doubt have been accepted, except that Agamemnon wouldn't give her up. In fact, he threatened to have her father killed if he didn't leave the Greek camp immediately and never return.

The episode typifies Bronze Age religion in western Anatolia, a region with special interest in epidemics and their cure, that is, magical cure. Hittite and other ancient rituals used against disease commonly blame a god, whether local or an enemy's, for making people sick. The Hittites blamed epidemics on the god's anger. Western Anatolians were used to the connection between gods and illness, since the local war-god Iyarri was also the god of pestilence, and he was called "Lord of the Bow"—similar to Apollo "of the glorious bow." In northwestern Anatolia and especially in the Troad, Apollo was worshipped as Apollo Smintheus, a god of mice and plague. A shrine to him stood near the city of Chryse at least as early as 700 B.C. and possibly in the Bronze Age too.

Calchas, backed up by Achilles, put the king on the spot. Bronze Age kings hated bad news and had a tendency to blame the messenger. The Hittite King Hattushilish I, for example, had exploded at the men who reported that their battering ram had broken during a siege: he said he hoped that the Storm God washed them away! Agamemnon in turn snarled at Calchas. But in the end, the king grudgingly agreed to give back Chryseis. Then he upped the ante by demanding compensation with another "prize," that is, another girl. "What girl?" said Achilles, coming right back at him. And with that, the center of gravity moved from the tug-of-war over a woman to the fight between two warrior-kings, a clash that had been a long time coming. The outward problem was the division of loot, but the real issue was honor. Of the various heroes who vied for the right to be called "best of the Greeks," none hated each other more than Achilles and Agamemnon. Achilles found fault with Agamemnon for taking the lion's share of the booty even though Achilles did most of the sacking of cities. Agamemnon found Achilles insolent and uppity. Achilles lacked respect for Agamemnon's preeminence as Greece's leading king, while Agamemnon felt threatened by Achilles' preeminence as a warrior.

So the two men began by calling each other names: Achilles called Agamemnon greedy, shameless, and cowardly. Agamemnon countered by threatening to take Achilles' girl. Then Achilles raised the temperature by threatening to take his ships and men and go home to Phthia, to which Agamemnon responded by making it official: he was coming after Briseis, Achilles' prize girl.

Visibly furious, Achilles gripped the silver hilt of his great sword and started to draw it out of the sheath. For a moment it looked like he was going to rush the king. But after hesitating, he pushed the sword back in again. Out poured another torrent of abuse, and then came an oath. Achilles and his men would not fight for the Greeks any longer. Achilles hurled the speaker's scepter onto the ground.

Agamemnon moved swiftly to return Chryseis. First the whole army had to purify itself by washing and then it had to sacrifice oxen and goats to Apollo. Agamemnon ordered a twenty-oared ship hauled down to the shore to bring Chryseis back to her father. The return of the priest's daughter was a sensitive, high-prestige mission. Agamemnon chose his crew carefully, selecting as captain the shrewd diplomat Odysseus, and picking men, who were, says Homer, "the youths of the Achaeans"—probably, all nobles.

The ship was about thirty-five feet long. Between the two files of rowers, bulls were loaded to be given to Chryses for sacrifice to Apollo. Chryseis sat on the raised quarterdeck, on a chair under a canopy. In addition to her, Odysseus, and the twenty oarsmen, the ship no doubt carried a few seamen, and a herdsman for the cattle; the oarsmen might have stowed their arms below their seats. The mast was up, the sail unfurled, and the ship took advantage of what little breeze there was.

When they reached the harbor of Chryse, the men took down the mast and sail and rowed the ship into a protected corner. Then they moored her, stern first. To hold the ship in place, a pair of stone anchors was dropped from the bows, and stern lines from each quarter were run onto the shore and carefully secured. The crew pulled down a gangplank and disembarked the bulls. Then Chryseis stepped ashore. Escorted by Odysseus she walked to a nearby altar, where she was delivered into the eager hands of her father.

What followed next was, from the Greeks' point of view, the heart of the matter: a sacrifice to Apollo to lift the epidemic that he had called down on them. Archaeology confirms Homer's description, showing that Bronze Age Greeks such as the warriors in the *Iliad* slaughtered bulls as a sacrifice to the gods and then, after cooking the meat, ate most of it in a ceremonial meal. In fact, at Thebes, a sacrifice of about fifty animals—sheep, goats, pigs, and cattle—seems to have been enough to give a taste to each of a thousand people!

Around the altar the men arranged the bulls, a Greek gift that, as a cynic might have noted, had been looted from the people of the Troad. There followed a ritual washing of hands and sprinkling of barley groats on the victims. Then Chryses lifted his hands skyward and prayed to Apollo on behalf of the Greeks. The cattle were slaughtered, flayed, then butchered according to ritual. A fire had been prepared, over which the priest now burned, on a wooden spit, the god's portion—the thighbones plus pieces of raw meat drawn from each leg, all doused with wine. Meanwhile, the innards were roasted and passed around to be eaten by all the worshippers.

So much for the ritual: at this point the rest of the meat was carved up and cooked on five-pronged forks. Wine cups and mixing bowls were brought out. After the wine was mixed with water, every cup was filled to the brim, beginning with a few drops in each cup to be sprinkled on the ground as an offering to the gods.

After feasting, the young Greeks chanted a hymn to Apollo and danced. Homer says they spent the entire day in song and ceremony until night fell. But having traveled about forty nautical miles by ship from Troy to Chryse, after having returned Chryseis, sacrificed oxen, cooked the meat, and having feasted and drunk, they would not have had much daylight left. The song and dance would have lasted an hour or two, until the exhausted men fell asleep beside their ship.

The paean was a prayer for all seasons and occasions, from war to weddings. An appeal for deliverance or a hymn of thanksgiving, a paean could be elaborate or simple but it always included the chant, *Iē Paian, Iē Paian*, which was mysterious and ancient, since the word *Paian* dates back to the Bronze Age.

The paean was no bacchanal; it was meant to be dignified. Perhaps the singing followed the pattern of Hittite music, where singers were divided into two groups, often a soloist and a responding choir. One example is even called "the song of the bulls," which would have fit the scene at Chryse. But twenty-odd tired and drunken young men, deliriously happy at the thought of delivery from an epidemic, were probably not very dignified.

Meanwhile, at the Greek camp, Agamemnon sent two heralds to bring him Briseis from Achilles' hut. Surprisingly, Achilles gave up the girl without a fuss.

But Briseis left Achilles' hut unwillingly. Perhaps she had come to identify with her captor, even to love him, a sort of ancient equivalent of Stockholm Syndrome. Or maybe Briseis simply reasoned that Agamemnon's bed would be worse than Achilles'. Maybe the clear-eyed girl was not a lost soul but a survivor.

Hard-boiled Greek warriors speak of their women as prizes of war. But we might suspect that they formed genuine attachments. Agamemnon says that he prefers Chryseis to his own wife. Among the cattle, cauldrons, and gold, she was flesh. She represented to the son of Atreus the world he missed.

After Briseis left him, Achilles sat on the beach and cried like a baby: tears of rage, to be sure, but perhaps of loss as well. He was not a happy man. Then again, who could be happy knowing as Achilles did that he was fated to die young? Like many other men in the epics, Achilles weeps freely and regularly.

Some philosophers and critics, beginning with Plato, censured Homer for making his heroes crybabies. But in doing so, Homer was following both Bronze Age poetry and Bronze Age life. For example, both the Mesopotamian (and Hittite) hero Gilgamesh and the Anatolian storm god Teshub cry in their respective poems; so does the Canaanite epic hero Kirta (1300s B.C.); so do the Egyptian Wenamun and the Philistine prince Beder of Dor in the Egyptian tale of Wenamun (eleventh century B.C.). And the Hittite king Hattushilish I (1650–1620 B.C.) disinherited his nephew and designated heir because the man failed to cry when Hattushilish lay sick and was expected to die.

Homer describes how Achilles appeals through the tears to his divine mother, Thetis, to have mighty Zeus himself intervene and bring ruin to the Greeks who had dishonored him. Whether or not they believed that divine blood flowed in the veins of the mighty, Bronze Age people expected that great men could lobby the gods for help. After all, a king was the favorite of the gods, as the Assyrian Tukulti-Ninurta asserted. He was a god and the sun, as Abi-Milki of Tyre told Pharaoh. He was the child of heaven and a guardian angel, as the mere governor of the Mesopotamian city of Nippur was addressed by one of his underlings.

Back in the Greek camp, the epidemic ended, but the military situation was worse than ever for the Greeks. The disease had caused a significant number of casualties, and Achilles had withdrawn from the fight. His men muttered about sailing home. The Myrmidons made up about 5 percent of the Greek force. And an oracle had said that the Greeks would not take Troy without Achilles. But we may posit a more practical concern, and that is, the Myrmidons were elite troops. Arguably, their specialty was the same as their leader's: speed. Homer frequently calls Achilles "fast runner." Achilles' strength was multiplied by his ability to outrun others. He was one of those rare warriors who on foot could kill a man on a chariot. Every hero worth his salt was expected to be able to fight both on foot and from a chariot. But few could overwhelm a chariot from the ground: Diomedes, on foot, knocks Phegeus off his chariot; Menelaus and Antilochus son of Nestor, working as a team, pick off a Trojan and his charioteer; Hector and Aeneas planned to overwhelm a Greek pair on a chariot but other Greeks showed up in time to stop them. Old Nestor as a young foot soldier had killed the enemy's best chariot-fighter.

We should expect that in each of these cases the hero(es) received help from his men. Not even swift-footed godlike Achilles could run down a chariot by himself. But ordinary soldiers would not be much help unless they were well equipped and well trained. Leadership was key. Homer notes that the Myrmidons were divided into five battalions and the roll call of their five leaders was: two sons of gods, the third-best spearman among the Myrmidons, a minor king who had taught Achilles the art of war, and a warrior knowledgeable enough to give tips in tactics to Achilles' charioteer. They were a cut above the mere mortals named in the Linear B tablets as commanding companies of soldiers or rowers at Pylos. Unit cohesion mattered as well, and the Myrmidons were solidity itself when they took the field:

> *Ranks wedged in ranks; of arms a steely ring*
> *Still grows, and spreads, and thickens round the king.*
> *As when a circling wall the builder forms,*
> *Of strength defensive against wind and storms,*
> *Compacted stones the thickening work compose,*
> *And round him wide the rising structure grows:*
> *So helm to helm, and crest to crest they throng,*
> *Shield urged on shield, and man drove man along;*
> *Thick, undistinguish'd plumes, together join'd,*
> *Float in one sea, and wave before the wind.*

The withdrawal of such an elite group might have demoralized the rest of the Greek army. Nearly two weeks had passed since Achilles had withdrawn from the war. But Agamemnon had dreamed that Zeus had decided to give the Greeks victory. Bronze Age peoples took dreams seriously as messages from the gods, as did their descendants in the Iron Age. King Naramsin of the Sumerian epic *The Curse of Agade* (ca. 2200–2000 B.C.), for example, saw the ruin of his city in a dream. A thousand years later, Hittite King Hattushilish III (1267–1237 B.C.) had a dream in which the goddess Ishtar promised success in a dangerous court case, and Pharaoh Merneptah (1213–1203 B.C.) received the sword of victory from the god Ptah in a dream. Seven hundred years after that, Herodotus reports how the Persian Emperor Xerxes dreamed during war councils over the planned invasion of Greece in 480 B.C. Agamemnon was so excited that he called a council of his generals to pass on the news. They agreed that it was time to get the men into their armor and onto the field. But Agamemnon suggested a slight delay: he would call an assembly first to test the men's morale.

The men, says Homer, thronged out to assembly like a swarm of insects. The massive gathering required nine heralds to obtain quiet so that the king could speak. Agamemnon stood up. Instead of telling the army the truth, which was that he had dreamt of victory, he pretended that the game was over: Zeus had decided for defeat. The boats were in poor shape, Agamemnon said:

> *Our cordage torn, decay'd our vessels lie,*
> *And scarce insure the wretched power to fly.*

This sad assessment recalls the lament of a Syrian general around 1340 B.C., writing to his overlord, the Hittite king, from a frontier outpost on the border with Egypt:

> *Now, for five months the cold has been gnawing me,*
> *my chariots are broken, my horses are dead, and my troops are lost.*

Agamemnon pretended that the war was lost and the only sensible thing to do was to go home:

> *Fly, Grecians, fly, your sails and oars employ,*
> *And dream no more of heaven-defended Troy.*

Agamemnon hoped to hear the men shout "No!" Instead, the men took him at his word and stampeded for the ships, behaving like conscripts running for their lives at the first sound of the enemy. Every army has its breaking point. The Greeks had turned into a mob—and not just the ordinary Greeks: heroes and kings ran too.

Odysseus's quick thinking saved the day. Borrowing Agamemnon's royal scepter, he ran into the multitude and restored order.

The scepter was part escutcheon and part relic. An ancient symbol, the scepter denoted kingship throughout the ancient world, for the Assyrian King Tukulti-Ninurta (1244–1208 B.C.) as well as for Agamemnon. The scepter stood for divine approval, as Odysseus put it:

> *To one sole monarch Jove commits the sway;*
> *His are the laws, and him let all obey.*

The Greeks did not make a good revolutionary mob, not least because they didn't believe in revolution. They wanted to trust their king.

Homer's account of what follows is amusing, but mutiny was serious business to Bronze Age commanders. With vicious wit Thersites expressed the misgivings that many must have felt about the king who had dishonored Greece's greatest fighting man. Thersites sneered at Agamemnon's arrogance and mocked his fellow soldiers' willingness to tolerate it:

> *Whate'er our master craves, submit we must,*
> *Plagued with his pride, or punish'ed for his lust.*
> *Oh women of Achaia; men no more!*
> *Hence let us fly, and let him waste his store*
> *In loves and pleasures on the Phrygian shore.*

Whether Thersites was a renegade noble, as some think, or simply a common man who was allowed to speak in the assembly, or even a traitor fomenting discontent to help the enemy, he gave voice to the longing for home felt by the ordinary Greeks at Troy. They were the ones who never got the best cuts of meat, if they got meat at all; the ones who never tasted fish; the ones who lived mainly on a diet of beans and barley, which surely left the air thick with foul odor. They washed down the food with young, unseasoned wine, rather than the fine Thracian vintages brought by ship to Agamemnon daily; they mixed their wine and water in wooden rather than silver bowls, and drank from plain pottery cups. They were usually short and wiry, often round-shouldered with bad teeth. They received less care than champion horses. No rubdowns with olive oil after a hot bath for them, no bronze tubs and no soft female hands to wash their backs. Most of their baths were in the salt sea, and they no doubt treasured the occasions when they got to take a dip in a river or a clear mountain spring. They had no perfume to offset the odors of sweat and sheepskin. They did not live in huts made of hewn fir and thatch roofs, as the heroes did. They slept in tents or in the hollow ships or outside on the shore, making it through winter as best they could by huddling around communal fires. The kings had rugs for pillows, the soldiers had leather shields. Their chairs were piles of brush and twigs covered with a goatskin throw, which did double duty as a bed—no lamb's wool rugs for them. They had no beautiful, enslaved princesses as bedmates, only quick trips to the camp whores.

They had come to Troy with one tunic each, as well as a homespun cloak and a pair of rawhide sandals—a basic pair, without the laces that made sandals fit comfortably to the foot. That is, if they were free: slaves were dressed in rags and went barefoot. And once the heroes had taken the pick of the booty, they had whatever was left along with whatever they could steal. Even so this was more than they could ever have hoped to put aside from a lifetime working the thin soil of Greece or herding another man's sheep or goats or cleaning out his pigsty.

They were oarsmen, stewards, cooks, grooms, and perhaps even farmers. They were the men who pulled the wooden chocks out from under the long ships at the moment of departure, the men who cast off the cables and hoisted the pinewood masts. They trooped into the hills to cut oak with axes made of dull bronze rather than sharp iron, gathered firewood, split kindling neatly, built and tended fires, stuffed goat intestines with blood and fat and then roasted them until they were sausage; carved meat; poured wine; gathered jugs of water from the river for drinking, for hand-washing before prayer or sacrifice and for heroes' bathing (loading them onto mules, if they were lucky, but otherwise toting the jugs themselves back to camp). They groomed the horses, dug defensive ditches, cut posts for palisades and hammered them into the ground, repitched the ships, dug trenches for latrines, cleaned the camp of animal dung. They picked up corpses, from which they had to shoo away swarms of flies, and hauled them onto the funeral pyres. They were indispensable to the expedition, but they counted for nothing in battle or council, as their betters were in the habit of telling them.

Some days they fasted until dusk because they worked so hard. A few of them talked back to their lords, like Thersites or the unnamed Trojan commoners who gainsaid Hector in the Trojan assembly, much to his annoyance. But most of them, we may suspect, were more likely to take their lord by the wrist and kiss his hand, whether out of devotion or fear. Agamemnon expected the common people to honor him like a god. Even a high-status noncombatant like Eurybates, Odysseus's herald, had to spend his days following the king and picking up the royal cloak when Odysseus dropped it. Do their job well and the men who counted for nothing could expect a pat on the back. If they were caught misbehaving they could expect a sharp blow, on the back or shoulders, with a stick.

Sometimes in the distance the Greeks could hear the sound of the dogs fighting. The wind carried the insistent, rhythmic, alternating barks and yelps of those bony beasts as they brawled over a bone, perhaps a man's bone that had been left out in the sun from some earlier engagement, or a human limb hacked off in battle. Other times, at night, when they sneaked up in a raid on a Trojan town, the men could hear the sound of prayers to the local god to deliver them from the "visitation of foreign dogs."

Odysseus needed to turn the tide. He said to Thersites,

Have we not known thee, slave! Of all our host,
The man who acts the least, upbraids the most?
Think not the Greeks to shameful flight to bring,
Nor let those lips profane the name of king.

Odysseus showed that Thersites was not the only Greek to know how to work an audience. He threatened that if he ever again heard such cheap sniping at Agamemnon from Thersites, he would strip off Thersites' clothes. He even refers disparagingly to the sight of Thersites' genitals, which strikes a rare and vulgar note for Homer. But soldiers are not known for their delicacy, and what soldier doesn't love to see that the general is just as rough as the next fellow? To finish Thersites off, Odysseus smashed his scepter down on Thersites' back hard enough to raise a welt and to reduce the man to tears.

The audience cracked up. Better to laugh at Thersites as a buffoon than to cry at their own spinelessness. The Hittites knew the value of slapstick humor: they had festivals in which one man hit another over the head three times with a club and another where one man poured hot coals over somebody's head, all for a laugh.

Now that Odysseus had broken the mutiny with some sharp, well-chosen words, it was time to rekindle the men's bellicosity. He had the herald quiet the crowd so he could speak again. The message was brisk and simple. Honor demanded that the Greeks stay and fight. He reminded the men of Calchas's prophecy at Aulis: the war would be long but they would emerge victorious.

Stately, patriarchal Nestor had a smooth voice but when it came to war, he didn't hesitate to pour oil on a fire. He spoke next. Like Odysseus, he pointed out the favor of the gods, in the form of an omen: lightning on the right as the ships first landed at Troy, a sign of Zeus's approval of their mission. Nestor showed that he too understood psychology by offering another answer to the implicit question of "why do we fight?" He said:

Encouraged hence, maintain the glorious strife,
Till every soldier grasp a Phrygian wife,

Till Helen's woes at full revenged appear,
And Troy's proud matrons render tear for tear.

Nestor also offered Agamemnon advice: he should call a muster of the entire army with the men arranged "by peoples and groups." This as a way of judging the quality of the army. Agamemnon got up and readily agreed. He told the men to fill their bellies, sharpen their swords, prepare their armor, feed their horses, and check their chariots: they were going to war.

There was a roar of approval from the men, a rush to the huts, a series of sacrifices to the gods, and the troops got ready for the muster. Agamemnon called his most trusted lieutenants to the ritual: Nestor, Idomeneus, the two Ajaxes, Diomedes, and Odysseus; Menelaus joined them on his own initiative. After the ceremony, these leading commanders fanned out across the camp to supervise, while heralds cried for the men to muster.

They came from their huts and shelters and ships: their polished shields gleamed, their marching shook the ground, and their numbers filled the plain like flocks of cranes or swans. The Greeks rallied, which leads to a famous moment in the *Iliad*, the so-called Catalog of Ships, in which the poet lists all the captains, kings, and countries who took part in the war.

Homer is not, as some critics think, merely exploiting the occasion to roll the credits, as it were. Instead, he is describing sound, simple, and standard military policy. For example, the conquering Hittite King Shuppiluliuma I (1344–1322 B.C.) stopped in southeastern Anatolia to review his troops and chariots before continuing onward to his goal, the siege of the city of Carchemish. From Pharaonic Egypt to Pennsylvania Avenue, parading the troops in review, unit by unit, has been a basic way of building morale. And if there was ever a force that needed its morale reestablished, it was the Greek army at Troy.

No general could have been dressed with more spit and polish, no titan could have bestrode the earth with greater satisfaction than royal Agamemnon did as he moved among his men,

Like some proud bull, that round the pastures leads
His subject herds. . . .

But Agamemnon was not overconfident. He knew that on the far side of the plain, Hector would be mustering his troops.

A smart general knows you cannot suppress a wartime mutiny without shedding blood. Nothing wipes the slate clean like a corpse. Not having executed anyone for the wild dash to the ships, Agamemnon did the only sensible thing he could do: he sent his men out to die.

CHAPTER SEVEN

THE KILLING FIELDS

When the Hittites went to war, they sang hymns to the war-god. Before battle, they would chant an old poem whose refrain asks that they be buried at home with their mothers. When, in the *Iliad*, the Trojans and their allies rush out against an unexpected Greek attack, they shout battle cries to steel themselves. The Greeks are as silent as a boxer conserving his energy for a knockout punch. Two armies approach each other on the Trojan Plain, barely visible through the dust raised by their marching feet.

Suddenly one man steps forward through the ranks on the Trojan side; another man dismounts from his chariot on the Greek side, which makes the Trojans retreat. Then, a third man, a huge figure, appears in the middle of the Trojan ranks and gestures with his long spear. All around him the soldiers sit down, and soon he is the only Trojan standing.

The long-haired Greeks begin to shoot at this perfect target with arrows and slings. The Persians called arrow feathers "messengers of death," and Bronze Age archers could hit a target at 300–400 yards. Estimates are that a top slinger could reach a speed of 100–150 miles per hour and hit a target 150 feet away.

Homer identifies the Locrians and some of the Thessalians as great bowmen among the Greeks. The Cretans were also famous as archers. The Locrians included slingers as well. Most archers and slingers fought without armor or shield and were stationed behind the lines of heavy-armed spearmen. Some were outfitted with composite bows, made of wooden staves reinforced with horn and sinew, much more powerful than the simple wooden bows.

But Agamemnon called for his men to cease their fire. It was clear that Hector wanted a parley. The Trojan proposed that, instead of a general engagement, there be a battle between two champions: none other than Paris and Menelaus, the originators of the war, as it were, and, in fact, the two men who had just stepped forward on each side (it was Paris who had then quickly retreated). If Menelaus killed Paris, the Trojans would return Helen and the Spartan treasure; if Paris killed Menelaus, the Greeks would allow Helen and the treasure to remain in Troy. In either case, the two sides would swear friendship and the Greeks would go home. The Greeks agreed, with the proviso that the Trojans show their good faith by having Priam ride out to the field and sacrifice two lambs while he swore an oath to abide by the outcome of the duel. The Trojans accepted this condition.

Homer shows Paris under pressure from his hard-as-nails older brother, Hector, to prove himself in combat. Hector insults Paris by calling Paris "girl crazy": real men think about war not women. The rebuke was an old one in the Near East. Consider a case around 1800 B.C. involving two Mesopotamian princes, Yashmah-Addu and his older brother, Ishme-Dagan, both sons of King Shamsi-Adad of Ekallatum (1814–1781 B.C.). Ishme-Dagan was the favorite, and chosen to succeed his father, while Yashmah-Addu was made king of nearby Mari.

Shamsi-Adad writes to his younger son with the good news that Ishme-Dagan has triumphed in battle and won a name for himself as a great general. Then comes the kicker: "Here your brother has killed the [enemy] general," writes the old king, "while there you lie about among the women." He then tells Yasmah-Addu to be a man and lead an army against his enemies. Yasmah-Addu might have sympathized with Paris's predicament.

A contest between champions was standard procedure in the

Bronze Age. Two kings could fight it out, or two corporals—a low-risk alternative chosen when the Greek Attarissiya invaded southwestern Anatolia around 1400 B.C. Now, at Troy, champion battle suited both sides' needs. The Greeks had suffered significant manpower losses as a result of disease and defection, and their morale was shaky. The Trojans had hurried out to battle from an assembly, with little time to spare for buckling their war belts.

Priam, accompanied by Antenor, rode out of the city and sacrificed as required. The duelists stepped forward onto a measured field. They would fight with long spears. It was the hero's weapon of choice. The shaft was sometimes ash, sometimes olivewood, and the spearhead was bronze.

Paris drew the right to throw first but his spear broke on Menelaus's shield. Menelaus had better luck on his turn because his spear went clear through Paris's shield and breastplate. But the nimble Paris twisted away and received only a nick to his ribs. Menelaus followed up with a sword blow to Paris's helmet, but the sword shattered. In frustration, Menelaus manhandled Paris by the plume of his helmet and began dragging him back to the Greek ranks. But the leather chinstrap snapped and Paris broke free. It was the work of his patron goddess, who now whisked him to safety in his home in Troy. So Homer says, and no Bronze Age soldier would have reason to doubt it, since every king claimed to have a patron god or goddess on the battlefield.

Then one of the Trojan commanders broke the truce. According to Homer, the gods persuaded Pandarus son of Lycaon, one of Troy's leading allies, to shoot an arrow that wounded Menelaus. Now both sides reached for their weapons. As has often happened in the history of war, a rogue soldier upset the generals' plans.

Pandarus used his magnificent composite bow, which was made from the horns of a wild ibex—presumably set over wooden staves and reinforced with sinew—and tipped with gold. He braced the bow on the ground, took an arrow from his case, and fitted it to the string. Hiding for safety behind his men's shields, he drew the string and the arrow butt to his chest and shot. Pandarus's feathered arrow was tipped with an iron arrowhead, unlike the bronze arrowhead used by the Greeks. Iron weapons existed in Bronze Age Anatolia. But Menelaus escaped with only a flesh wound, because he was protected by his golden belt and his corselet.

But the wound bled enough to worry Agamemnon, who called for the doctor Machaon. In the Bronze Age, medics doubled as veterinarians, so between one thing and another, their linen tunics were usually clotted with blood. Machaon pulled out the arrow, sucked out the blood from the wound, and applied an ointment. It might have been a bitter root, such as Patroclus later used on a similar wound; an ancient commentator suggested Achillea (woundwort) or Aristolochia (birthwort). Or it might have been honey, a natural antibiotic used to dress wounds. A salve of one part honey and two parts grease (either animal fat or olive oil) appears on the Linear B tablets as antiseptic, fungicidal, and antibiotic.

Menelaus did not require surgery, but if he had, a Bronze Age practitioner had cutting tools made of obsidian or bronze as well as such bronze instruments as forceps, probes, spoon, razor, and saw. Opium was available to ease the pain. Linen bandages were known in Egypt, but the only bandage in Homer is a woolen sling doing double duty as a dressing. An unbandaged wound might have been a common sight in the Greek camp.

An expert treated Menelaus's injury, but Menelaus was the supreme leader's brother and so had special access to the scarce supply of physicians. Often in Homer even a champion settles for a companion to remove a spear or arrow, as both the Greek Diomedes and the Trojan ally Sarpedon do later that same day.

Because Pandarus had broken the truce to which Priam had solemnly sworn, a pitched battle ensued. It was unplanned, and yet Agamemnon could not have arranged things better:

> *No rest, no respite, till the shades descend;*
> *Till darkness, or till death, shall cover all:*
> *Let the war bleed, and let the mighty fall;*
> *Till bathed in sweat be every manly breast,*

With the huge shield each brawny arm depress'd,
Each aching nerve refuse the lance to throw,
And each spent courser at the chariot blow.

Agamemnon may emerge as an unappealing personality in Homer, but he could be a good general. He did make a number of mistakes, but he knew how to admit errors and switch course—fast. He gave up Chryseis, for example. He let his colleagues Odysseus and Nestor quell the troops' mutiny. He reviewed the troops and then led them into battle. And he would soon eat his words by apologizing to Achilles and offering him a king's ransom, including the return of Briseis, to rejoin the fight.

One of the strengths of the Greek army was the collective experience of its leaders, from Ajax to Odysseus. Call them an army of forty kings, like the force from the Armenian Plateau that faced the Assyrians under King Tukulti-Ninurta (1244–1208 B.C.). And call them an army of forty counselors, none more impressive than Homer's Nestor. Although he was too old to fight, he had not stayed at home; he was on hand to offer invaluable advice. The Trojan army had no counterpart. Priam stayed on the sidelines and was rarely listened to. Except when he let his emotions get the better of him, as he did with Chryses and Achilles, Agamemnon was careful to consult his colleagues. And he was able to judge who offered the best counsel.

Like modern battle, a Bronze Age engagement was complex. To orchestrate it required accurate information, which made scouts and spies essential. Before clashing, the two sides pushed, tricked, and feinted for the best ground. A Bronze Age army was a combined-arms force of foot soldiers and chariots, skirmishers and linemen, bowmen and spearmen. Each army would try to maximize the deployment of its strengths against the enemy's weaknesses: for example, by raining a cloud of arrows on light-armed troops. If the armies were coalitions, each side had the opportunity to sow discontent in the other by concentrating its attack on the allies while leaving the leader of the alliance relatively untouched.

We can grasp the outline of pitched battle from the daylong engagement that followed Pandarus's bow shot. At a signal the two armies, both thickly massed, marched toward each other. Now came a bombardment of arrows and slings, although archers and slingers are the forgotten men of the *Iliad*. Arrow wounds were frequent and often fatal; merely removing a barbed arrowhead could kill, because of shock or infection, and the pain could be agonizing.

The two phalanxes advanced, perhaps in a crooked line. But advance the Greeks and Trojans did, in close order, and with discipline and speed before coming to blows. Meanwhile, the chariots were coming.

Chariots carried leaders to and around the battlefield. They were light wooden carts, covered with either oxhide or wicker work. Sometimes they were inlaid with ivory and gold, and sometimes they were painted crimson both to stand out and to hide the color of blood. The wheels were also wooden. Each chariot was drawn by a team of two horses, and its crew consisted of a driver and a warrior. The warrior might fight from his chariot but it was more usual for him to dismount and exchange blows on foot. The main advantage conferred by chariots was mobility. Secondarily the chariot was a psychological weapon, since the noise of the wheels and the sight of the horses may have frightened some of the enemy. The tanklike charge of a mass of chariots in order to break the enemy's line may have played a big role in Egyptian and Hittite warfare—the experts disagree—but it was not to be found at Troy. For most of the year the terrain was too wet for that and, besides, neither side had enough chariots for a mass charge: Troy lacked the imperial wealth and Greeks lacked the horse power!

When the infantrymen clashed, the best fighters stood in the front lines, unless the commander had thrown ordinary troops before them to prevent those troops from fleeing. Homer refers to the best soldiers as "fore-fighters" *(promachoi)* or simply "the first men." Elite troops, they inhabited a different world from ordinary soldiers. The elite were professionals, well armed, well trained, and well prepared for the shock of battle. Ordinary soldiers were conscripts, lightly armed, poorly trained, and ill-prepared for bloody combat. It was bad luck for them if they had to step up and replace their comrades, both the fallen and those who simply went to the rear to rest.

The men in the front lines, especially the champions, had a full set of arms and armor. The complete warrior wore bronze greaves (shin guards), a leather kilt, and a crested helmet. He may have worn a loose-fitting bronze breastplate and back plate, which could be extended with pieces to cover his neck, lower face, shoulders, and thighs. An alternative was a linen tunic with bronze scales to serve as a breastplate. An elaborate belt, perhaps red or purple and decorated with gold or silver, would be worn over the tunic or breastplate. The front line fighter carried a big, heavy shield, shaped either like a figure-of-eight or a tower, and composed of multiple layers of leather on a bronze rim. It hung from his shoulder on a strap that may have passed diagonally over his torso. The shield was meant to offer full protection, which is why very few warriors in Homer are described as wearing both a metal breastplate and holding a shield. A scabbard, holding a bronze double-edged sword, lay along his right thigh, suspended by a strap from his left shoulder.

The ordinary soldiers, the majority in either army, consisted of various kinds of light-armed troops. We can imagine them in a linen tunic without armor, leather helmet and kilt, and linen greaves. Most men did not carry a body shield but had to make do with a small, light, round shield. Some men might have had to manage by holding up, as some kind of protection, a simple, unfinished piece of leather without a bronze rim.

When the two phalanxes clashed, the men brought their oxhide shields together and attacked with their spears. The spear was the main close-range weapon at Troy. Swords were only second best because of their tendency to break at the hilt. A few of the heroes may have wielded a type of sword that was new in the Aegean, bronze and about two and a half feet long, much more efficient at inflicting slashing wounds than its predecessors. Because the blade had roughly parallel edges for most of its length, rather than the tapered edges of a dagger, this sword was good at cutting. And with a single piece of metal for both blade and hilt, it was less likely to break than its predecessors. This so-called Naue II sword was of central European origin, and it began to appear in Greece shortly before 1200 B.C. But it was probably a rare import. We hear in the *Iliad* of a few Greeks and virtually no Trojans who wield slashing swords. In any case, a man could do a lot of damage with an ash-wood spear tipped with a six-inch bronze head, its sides bulging outwards like a leaf's—especially if he put his legs and back into thrusting it into the enemy.

Men on each side proceeded to try to slaughter each other by thrusting with a lance or throwing a javelin. When a man went down his comrades tried to drag his corpse back to safety, but the enemy would contest that. Stripping an enemy's corpse gave a man both loot and bragging rights. So a kill was usually followed by knots of men tussling ferociously over the corpse and its armor. Because of encounters like this, however tightly packed the unit had been when it reached the enemy, it could not have stayed that way.

Duels were probably not unusual on the Bronze Age battlefield. But surely they were not nearly as prominent as they are in Homer. Bronze Age battle poetry exaggerates heroic individualism and downplays group effort. Homer's emphasis on duels between heroes is more likely to reflect Bronze Age literary style than actual Bronze Age warfare.

At this point in the encounter, the Trojans gave ground, but they did not flee the field. As was typical, they regrouped for another stand. Meanwhile, the Greeks were not pressing their advantage. In fact, here and there they were slackening: Homer has the goddess Athena buck them up, just as he has Apollo—the war-god Iyarri, no doubt—put some backbone in the Trojans. With the two armies relatively evenly matched, the battle followed a rhythm, with each side taking turns in gaining ground on the other.

But with the Greeks still holding a slight advantage, Homer's attention now shifts to their champion Diomedes. Efficient killer that he was, Diomedes could have accomplished little without the help of his men, but the poet leaves them in the background. First Diomedes defeats, on foot, two noble Trojan brothers in their chariot, killing one and so terrifying the other that he leaves behind both chariot and his brother's corpse. Then Diomedes goes on to slaughter twelve named warriors, including Pandarus, whose arrow started the battle. He nearly kills Aeneas, the Trojans' best warrior after Hector, and he wounds the gods Aphrodite and Ares. He makes most of his kills with lance and javelin, but he also takes out his sword and slashes a man's shoulder off. Apparently, Diomedes is one of the men lucky enough to have a Naue II sword. His squire and charioteer, Sthenelus, followed behind. It was his job to haul away the booty as well as to be ready to give Diomedes a ride to the next target.

Diomedes would have won more booty by taking Pandarus alive and ransoming him. But his comrades had no cause to complain about Diomedes, whose vigorous leadership caused the Trojans to retreat back to the Scamander River. And the Greek offensive inflicted terrible casualties on the allies. Whether the Greeks had purposely targeted them or not, their plight was enough to cause Sarpedon, commander of the key allied division from Lycia, to send a message to Hector: rally the Trojan troops or face a big problem.

Hector responded quickly. He stepped down from his chariot and exhorted the Trojans on foot. They roared their enthusiasm and turned back to give battle. Meanwhile, the Greeks were remobilized by their leaders in turn and they fought fearlessly. But the Trojans steadily pushed them back.

Aeneas then makes a miraculous return to the field. Diomedes had hit him on the hip joint with a huge rock, which tore Aeneas's tendons and broke his socket. But the gods whisked him off to Troy, cured him, and arranged for his wondrous comeback—a case of heroic exaggeration at its finest. In real life, Aeneas would probably have gone into shock. A less serious fracture would not have presented a problem to Bronze Age physicians, because they could set bones so that a fracture healed perfectly.

Directed by Diomedes, the Greeks rediscovered their fighting spirit. They broke through the Trojan ranks and began driving them back toward Troy. But once again, Hector saved the day by rallying the troops. The Greeks pulled back. It was an opportunity for Hector to take the advice of his brother Helenus, Troy's best seer, and dart back into the city where he could have Queen Hecuba organize a special women's appeal to the goddess whom Homer calls Athena. Whether she was worshipped at Troy—ancient peoples often borrowed each other's gods—or whether Athena was actually an Eastern goddess, a prayer to a goddess for military success was not unusual in Anatolia. Hittite King Tudhaliya IV (1237–1209 B.C.), for example, prayed to the Sun-Goddess of Arinna for victory against an unnamed enemy, possibly the Assyrians. We can assume that Troy had a protector goddess even if she cannot be identified.

This religious mission, in the heat of combat, speaks volumes about the nature of this battle. Either Hector was superstitious himself or he knew that his men were. The story demonstrates the awareness that battle would be intermittent. It also underlines the reality that even the doughtiest champion needed to take a break from time to time.

Homer reports how thirsty warriors were after battle. Mesopotamian war poetry called for mind over matter: a soldier needs strength, vigor, and speed; he has to make his mind command his body.

Hector returned to the field with his brother Paris in tow, which gave the Trojans a second wind. Soon it became clear that, far from wanting to continue to fight, Hector sought a graceful way of calling it off. Homer says that Apollo had changed Hector's mind, but the Trojan had good reason to have reached his conclusion without any help from the gods. He needed a respite; he needed time to meet with his commanders and hammer out a fresh plan, as well as to rest the men and to brief them anew. For Hector had received a key piece of intelligence:

The great, the fierce Achilles fights no more.

The best and most honorable way to achieve his goal was for Hector to issue a challenge. Single combat at this point served several purposes. It was a chivalrous way of ending a long day of fighting that had bloodied both sides without a clear outcome. It would strengthen the Trojans' standing in their allies' eyes by showing

Hector's courage. And it would earn Hector political capital in the debate that lay ahead. Before taking his army back to war Hector would have to deal with an urgent issue of morale. As an assembly that very night would show, the nation's will to fight was at question.

Hector was careful not to put as much at stake in this latest duel. When Menelaus fought Paris, Helen and the Spartan treasures were on the line. Hector offered only an honorable funeral for the loser. But he did not have to offer much because the Greeks were equally glad to leave the field.

Ajax won the lottery among the eager Greek champions and he faced Hector with swords. By now it was night. The two champions fought an inconclusive duel. The judges declared a draw, the combatants accepted, and the two made a gallant exchange of gifts. The weary men in each army withdrew.

The long day of battle had rebuilt the morale of the Greeks. Menelaus disgraced Paris, Ajax beat back Hector's challenge, while notable kills were scored by Agamemnon; Idomeneus; Odysseus; the Thessalian leader, Eurypylus; Idomeneus's second-in-command, Meriones; and Antilochus son of Nestor, who teamed up with Menelaus (apparently recovered from his wound in record time). And who could forget Diomedes' bloody rampage through the Trojan ranks? Yet Nestor knew the price of success:

> *How dear, O kings! This fatal day has cost,*
> *What Greeks are perish'd! and what people lost*
> *What tides of blood have drench'd Scamander's shore!*
> *What crowds of heroes sunk to rise no more!*

The Greek dead included many prominent men, most notably Tlepolemus son of Heracles, leader of the Rhodian troops.

Meanwhile, the Trojans and their allies held a stormy assembly outside Priam's palace on the citadel. Antenor proposed the return of Helen and the Spartan treasures. After the day's bloodshed, he would have had plenty of supporters. Antenor was speaking from the heart, and he reminded his audience that they had broken an oath today. By shooting Menelaus after having sworn to resolve the war through a duel of champions, Pandarus had put the Trojans in the wrong. No good could come from this.

Paris responded vigorously by saying the gods must have made Antenor mad. But then he more or less admitted his own failure in the duel with Menelaus that day by offering a major concession: he would give back the Spartan treasures and even add a little extra from his own riches. But Paris refused to return Helen. Then Priam rose to support Paris's plan. He was not optimistic about Greek agreement, and he warned the men to expect no more than a cease-fire for burying the dead. The assembly approved Paris's offer: return of the Spartan treasure and then some, but Helen would stay where she was.

The men dispersed, the soldiers returned to their units. They took their evening meal by companies. After the battle they were ex-hausted, but they may have had to settle for sleeping in shifts because the watch had to be maintained at all times.

At dawn, the Trojan herald Idaeus delivered the assembly's mes-sage to the Greeks. He found the chiefs gathered around Agamem-non's ship. At first, his words were greeted with silence. Then Diomedes spoke for the whole leadership:

> *Oh, take not, friends! defrauded of your fame,*
> *Their proffer'd wealth, nor even the Spartan dame.*
> *Let conquest make them ours: fate shakes their wall,*
> *And Troy already totters to her fall.*

Idaeus returned and reported the defiant rebuff. But the Greeks had at least agreed to a temporary cessation of hostilities.

The Trojans wasted no time sending out cremation parties. One detail went into the hills to gather wood for the pyres while another walked the battlefield to pick up the fallen. Since anything of value had probably already been stripped, the bodies had to be identified by their faces, on which the process of disfiguration would have already begun, since they had been left out overnight on the hot, damp plain.

Whenever they found remains that they recognized, the Trojans washed off the dried blood and lifted the corpse onto a cart. They shed tears but otherwise displayed no emotion, because Priam had forbidden lamenting. This might say something about the shaky state of Trojan morale or it might reveal Priam's determination that the Trojans not show weakness to the enemy.

At the day's end, two sets of pyres were lit at opposite ends of the Trojan Plain. The Trojans returned to town, the Greeks to their ships. Early the next morning, just before the first light of dawn, a battalion of specially picked Greek troops went back to the pyre to heap up a burial mound around it. This work was more than a gesture of respect, for the men immediately built their camp's palisade and trench alongside. If they were taking advantage of the armistice they were surely stretching its spirit, but they might have figured that the enemy's exhaustion guaranteed their safety. According to Homer, the entire defensive work was completed in one day. This would have been a tall order. It is probably more realistic to imagine that the Greeks had already fortified their camp, and now they were strengthening its lines.

In either case, Trojan scouts would surely have seen what the Greeks were now up to. That night, while both armies feasted, Hector and his high command would have time to contemplate yet another change in the balance of power and to make new plans. They might have been forgiven for thinking that they faced a whole new war.

CHAPTER EIGHT

NIGHT MOVES

Kings of the Bronze Age dreamed many dreams, none greater than the hope of undying glory. Only the gods could grant such a wish, and the gods would not be forced. But they did appreciate gifts, so the prudent monarch would cap off his reign with a suitable offering of thanks—an imposing monument, perhaps with an inscription expressing gratitude to heaven for success, long life, prosperity, children, and, of course, victory. Victory was the seed of immortality, and victory was granted by the gods in many ways, from the delivery of a king's enemies into his hands to their destruction beneath his feet. But no victory was sweeter than one that reversed imminent defeat. With the gods' help, he would force the enemy chiefs to stop their boasting.

So Hector might have dreamed that night as the funeral pyres blazed on the Trojan Plain. The Greeks had lost some of their best men and had retreated behind weak walls. If the Trojan prince led his armies out now, they might ride a tide of flames to the Greek ships. Hector might have imagined that long after he had replaced Priam on the throne, and in turn been replaced by his own son Astyanax, he would be remembered by the poets as the king who had saved Troy.

So, when the sun rose the next morning, Hector was on fire. He was at the head of an army that charged out the gates of the city, some on foot and some in chariots, all hungry for a fight. The Greeks had little choice but to leave their camp and meet the Trojans on the plain.

For several hours the battle was evenly balanced, but shortly after noon, in the unforgiving brightness of a sky that stretched from Mount Ida to Samothrace, the tide turned in Troy's favor. The Greeks began to run. Diomedes, however, had the courage to turn his chariot toward the enemy and to hurl a javelin that killed Hector's charioteer.

But the gods were on Troy's side. Homer envisions Zeus himself on Gargaros, the highest peak of Mount Ida, looking down on the battle from the gusty summit. The god thundered against the Greeks, then struck the ground in front of Diomedes' horses with a lightning bolt. Not even the courageous son of Tydeus could resist divine displeasure, so he too turned and fled. The Hittite King Murshilish II had likewise been helped by a divine lightning bolt around 1316 B.C. in his battle against Arzawa, about two hundred miles south of Troy. And a Babylonian prayer to the god of the thunderstorm, found preserved in the Hittite capital of Hattusha, shudders at the god's intervention in combat.

Hector now indulged in one of the oldest traditions of Bronze Age warfare. When they weren't spinning tales about the greatness of the man they had defeated, Bronze Age commanders would demean the enemy as a dog, as the "son of a nobody" or as someone whom the gods should turn into a woman. As Diomedes retreated, Hector shouted after him:

Go less than woman, in the form of man!

Then Hector turned to his own troops:

Trojans and Lycians and Dardanians who fight hand to hand:
Be men, my friends, and remember your valor and might.

Feminization was a threat readily brandished by a Bronze Age commander. Assyrian King Tukulti-Ninurta (1244–1208 B.C.), for example, menaced any man who desecrated his new temple to Ishtar with the curse that "his manhood dwindle away."

Homer does not state exactly where the battle had begun, but by now it had moved far away from Troy. Hector had found a new charioteer and his men surged across the Scamander River and pushed the Greeks all the way back to their camp, a distance across the plain of about two miles from the walls of the city. They had the Greeks penned in behind their ditch and palisade.

Suddenly, inspired by Hera and wrapped in a purple cloak, Agamemnon rallied his men. Purple was the royal color of the Late Bronze Age; the color of the wool, for example, in which Ugarit paid its tribute to the Hittite king and queen. Purple-clad Agamemnon stood on Odysseus's flagship, at the center of the camp, and shouted loudly enough to be heard from one end of the ships to another— from the flank guarded by Ajax's vessels to the ships of Achilles at the other flank (not that *he* was listening).

Roused to action, the Greek champions counterattacked. Teucer's arrows killed ten Trojans, including both a son of Priam and Hector's second charioteer. But the one man whom Teucer could not manage to hit was Hector. He was moving, Teucer complained, like a rabid dog, not knowing where to bite next, as a Mesopotamian saying had it—dogs were the favorite animal for insults in Bronze Age invective. Having found another new charioteer, Hector leaped to the ground and took off with a loud yell after Teucer, throwing a stone that nearly killed him. The Greeks began to fall back once again, to take cover behind their fortifications. Hector's men might have pressed their advantage all the way to the ships but night was now falling. Cursing their luck, they had to give up.

But they were not prepared to fall back tamely behind the city walls. For the first time during the war, they pitched their camp on the Trojan Plain, in an open space free of the bodies of the fallen. By camping on the west bank of the Scamander River, the Trojan army took a calculated risk, but it kept the pressure on the Greeks. Homer calls the place "the bridges of war." The Trojan Plain was marshy, especially in its northern end, and "bridges" possibly refers to an area of solid ground for chariots to cross.

The army was deployed in a line stretching northwest to southeast, which protected the city and covered any retreat. The northern end was anchored by the Carians of Anatolia and the Paeonians of Macedonia, while the Lycians secured the southern tip. In between were various other Anatolian contingents as well as the Trojans and their near neighbors. And a new detachment of Thracians under King Rhesus had just arrived.

The Trojans were busy in the dark. Some companies of men were delegated to feed the horses, others to go back to town to bring sheep, cattle, bread, and wine for the soldiers' meal—more or less the same food served by Syrian towns to Egyptian soldiers in the 1300s B.C. Other companies of Trojans went into the hills to gather firewood. The Trojans would keep their fires burning all night long in order to be able to see any attempt by the enemy to load their ships and sail away. Meanwhile, Hector wasn't taking any chances on the home front, and he put into effect a few simple measures of deception. He sent heralds around the street to order out boys and old men onto the walls and women to light the town with a fire in every house. No doubt he also ordered a herald to be ready to sound the alarm in case of sudden attack.

After sacrificing bulls to the gods and feeding barley to the horses, the Trojans themselves chowed down, a company of fifty men at each fire. Then, away from the city for the first time in years, they fell asleep under the stars. The Greeks, meanwhile, were in a panic.

Agamemnon had ordered a teary-eyed abandonment of the expedition. Diomedes responded with a reckless pledge to stand, conquer, or die, and the men cheered. Nestor came to the rescue with a levelheaded plan: post sentries along the wall and call the chiefs to a council of war. The stakes couldn't have been higher. As Nestor said:

This night will either destroy the encampment or save it.

The Greeks now placed seven hundred spearmen between the wall and the trench, in seven companies of one hundred men each, one of which was led by Nestor's son Thrasymedes. They were sentinels, playing a role well attested in Hittite and other Bronze Age armies. The top commanders gathered in Agamemnon's hut, where the best imported Thracian wine was on offer, along with superb food. This was only the first of many sumptuous spreads for the heroes that night. Even one dinner would be out of place in a modern staff conference, and the whole thing might be a case of epic exaggeration. Or maybe not, since in the Bronze Age Near East, hospitality was standard at *any* gathering under another man's roof. Besides, in the Aegean, then as now, meals were as much a social as a nutritional occasion, and there would have been no need to gorge at any one meal.

Nestor spoke frankly. They were ruined, he said, unless they got Achilles and the Myrmidons back, and that would happen only if Agamemnon returned Briseis to Achilles. Nestor might have saved his words because Agamemnon had already reached the same conclusion. He claimed the gods had blinded him when he offended Achilles. Now that he had his wits about him once more, he would make amends not merely by returning the young woman (untouched by him), but by adding gifts worthy of a king whose property was as wide as the sea: seven women captured when Achilles took Lesbos, seven tripods, ten talents of gold, twenty cauldrons, and twelve prizewinning horses. On top of that, Agamemnon offered to Achilles the lion's share of booty from Troy, including gold, bronze, and the twenty most beautiful women besides Helen, as well as marriage back in Greece to one of Agamemnon's daughters, with a huge dowry, plus a kingdom made up of seven prosperous cities in the western Peloponnese.

It was palm-greasing diplomacy at its finest. Nestor was impressed. Protocol demanded that an ambassador bring the news to Achilles, and the old politician had a three-man team in mind: Ajax, Odysseus, and Phoenix. Ajax was the Greeks' greatest warrior after Achilles, while Odysseus was the Greeks' canniest diplomat. Phoenix was a lesser soul, but he came from the household of Achilles' father

Peleus, where he had tutored the young prince. If anyone could pull at Achilles' heartstrings, it was Phoenix.

Although he welcomed the nighttime ambassadors with all the hospitality that a hut in the field allowed, with wine and meat and seats on couches covered with purple throws, Achilles did not budge an inch. They warned him that Hector planned to burn the ships and kill the Greeks come morning, and they emphasized Agamemnon's enormous generosity. But Achilles wasn't interested. The insult had been too great to forgive. Besides, talk of loot from Troy was just empty words, since Zeus clearly now had decided for the enemy. The Greeks would never take the city. So, if they looked out to sea in the first, gray light of morning, they would see Achilles and all his men sailing home.

The ambassadors tried to reason with the great warrior but the best they could get from him was this: a promise to fight if Hector was foolish enough to attack his huts and ships and the Myrmidons. Otherwise, Achilles would do nothing to help save the camp. Despondently, they trudged back to Agamemnon's hut and relayed the bad news. After a long silence, Diomedes called on them all to eat and drink (again) and to get some rest so that, at dawn, they could fight to save their ships.

The wine helped most of them to sleep. But Agamemnon and Menelaus were kept awake by worry. The supreme warlord was stunned by the sight of so many Trojan fires on the plain. The sound of pipes and whistles rose above the general din. The two sons of Atreus decided that a scouting mission might save the army. They hurried off in separate directions to rouse the commanders, beginning with Nestor.

Agamemnon and a small party then checked that the guards had not dozed off before calling a council of war. Agamemnon needed to instill a sense of urgency in his fellow commanders, who had been awakened from sleep and who did not understand that the army was, as Nestor put it, poised on "a razor's edge." Having galvanized them, Agamemnon needed one or more volunteers for an assignment richer in danger than in glory.

This would be no heroic battlefield performance before a crowd.

The mission was to discover the enemy's battle plans, either by capturing a Trojan straggler or by sneaking around and eavesdropping. The stars had shifted westward in the sky, marking the passage of two of the three "watches" into which the ancients divided the night. The men would have to move fast to enjoy the cover of darkness.

Diomedes volunteered and requested Odysseus as a partner. They were so pressed for time that they borrowed their arms and armor from other men who had come better prepared. Both men took swords, while Odysseus also grabbed a bow and Diomedes a shield. Diomedes wore a plain leather helmet, Odysseus an elaborate, antique, and expensive boar's-tusk helmet. As they made their way toward the enemy lines in the black night, they had to step over corpses, abandoned weapons, and pools of blood.

Unbeknownst to them, the Trojans were organizing a scouting party of their own. But what was serious business for the Greeks was almost comedy for the Trojans. Instead of receiving the service of an Aeneas or Paris, Hector had to settle for the son of a herald, who, like Thersites, was rich but ignoble. Dolon—the name is derived from the Greek *dolos*, trick—was the only boy among his father Eumedes' six children. Although he was outfitted for spying, wearing a wolf skin and carrying a javelin and a curved bow slung from his shoulders, the material of his cap was weasel, which strikes a comic note. When Hector promised the spy a reward of a chariot and two horses from the Greek spoils, Dolon made him swear an oath as a guarantee—as if the commander's word wasn't his bond. Then Dolon claimed the horses and chariots of none other than the great Achilles. When the Greeks ran into Dolon just beyond the Trojan lines, they thought at first that he was a scavenger, stripping the corpses. The one thing in Dolon's favor was his speed, which almost allowed him to escape Diomedes.

Men stripped corpses for many reasons, not all of them reprehensible. Some wanted trophies but others had a practical need for arms and armor. They sought spare parts, extra, better, or new pieces of equipment. Some soldiers might have come to Troy without any weapons at all, advised by their commanders that they would have to pick them up from the battlefield. And then, of course, there were profiteers who stripped corpses out of pure greed.

When Dolon was captured, he begged to be ransomed and readily told the Greeks everything they wanted to know. He was a "man of tongue," as informers were called in a letter of around 1800 B.C. from the city of Mari on the Euphrates. Dolon revealed the disposition of the Trojan and allied troops, the absence of guards around the camp, and the presence of Hector in a war council. He divulged new details about the Thracian reinforcements under their king Rhesus son of Eïoneus, with his magnificent team of white horses (a color especially valued in horses in the Late Bronze Age), as well as his chariot with its gold and silver decoration, and armor with gold details. This last piece of intelligence caught the interrogators' interest, since it offered a chance to add loot and glory to their already successful intelligence-gathering. Dolon's reward was death. Diomedes decapitated him in the act of begging for his life on his knees. Diomedes was not generous, but neither was he entirely wrong. Even nowadays it is no war crime to kill a spy, although today a hearing before a military tribunal is general practice first.

The Greeks stripped Dolon's arms and clothing and hid them under a tamarisk, with a vow to dedicate this booty to Athena. They made no attempt to conceal his body. It was just another corpse in the open. Armed with this latest intelligence, the two Greeks were able to head straight for the Thracians. Undetected, they snuck into camp. Diomedes slaughtered twelve sleeping men in a row, and Odysseus dragged away the bodies in order not to risk frightening horses. There was nothing he could do to mop up the pools of blood. While Odysseus untied the horses, Diomedes killed one last Thracian, King Rhesus himself. With the risk of capture mounting every second they hurried off with the horses, leaving the chariot and the armor behind. By the time the enemy woke up and discovered what had happened, the Greeks had reached the tamarisk where they had stashed Dolon's booty. Then they raced back to their comrades, who welcomed Odysseus and Diomedes with handshakes and honeyed words. After the debriefing, the two heroes washed off their sweat in the sea and each returned to his hut for a proper bath and an oil rub-down.

The account of this expedition is marked in Homer by odd vocabulary, unusual weapons, Greek behavior bordering on the most savage inhumanity, and by more-than-usual bias against the Trojans. Homer lays it on so thick that some scholars see the work of another, lesser poet in this chapter. Maybe—or maybe the episode is remarkable for the insight it offers into another side of the conflict, the Trojan guerrilla war.

Unlike regular warfare, which combines mass, force, and speed, guerrilla warfare consists of dispersed, small-scale operations usually over extended periods of time. Although guerrillas cannot defeat a regular army without a regular army of their own, they can weaken the enemy's will so that the regular army can deliver the knockout blow.

The story of Dolon reveals the road not taken, the road that might have led Troy to victory. Although they were dealt a poor hand the Trojans could have played it better by displaying creativity and adaptability. Instead, they were all frontal assault, focused on a war of attrition, revealing a ponderous lack of maneuverability.

The Trojans should have fought what has been called the "the war of the flea," harassing the Greeks by taking a nip here, a bite there. They were right to stay on the strategic defensive, but they should have engaged in opportunistic tactical offensives. They ought to have used their strength, which was an intimate knowledge of the terrain, to exploit the Greeks' weakness, which was their insecurity in a hostile, foreign land. It would have been easy to use light, agile forces for the continual harassment both of the Greek camp and of parties foraging for supplies.

With their knowledge of the Greek language and Greek mores, the Trojans might also have even been able to infiltrate men into the enemy camp or to feed disinformation. They might have been able to assassinate one or more Greek generals. Infiltration, espionage, and assassination were all staple techniques of Mesopotamian warfare. But the Trojans failed to exploit this guerrilla tactic.

At least, they failed according to Homer. In the epics it is the Greeks who harass Trojan stragglers, murder Trojan allies asleep in camp, carry out reconnaissance, capture enemy propaganda resources, and patiently lie in ambush in spite of miserable weather. The Trojans send out one spy and he is captured almost immediately.

Is Homer playing fair? No doubt the Trojans made more use of guerrilla tactics than he allows, and yet Homer convincingly portrays Hector as a man addicted to a heroic illusion of a decisive victory. That is his tragedy—and Troy's.

Bronze Age propagandists were not subtle. Images of chariot charges, reports of battles involving tens of thousands of infantrymen, royalty holding taut bows, perseverance in single combat, assaulting a fortified city with shock troops mounting ladders and wielding battering rams: these were the stuff of victory monuments and poetry. Commando raids, sabotage, kidnapping, theft, spying, throat-slitting in the dark, and ambushes at the stable door all made poor propaganda, however effective they may really have been. So whatever references to such practices survive may be only the tip of the iceberg.

Homer mentions a number of ambushes, covert operations, raids, sorties, and scouting expeditions in and around Troy, almost all carried out by Greeks. In the *Odyssey* all of Odysseus's actions from his return to Ithaca until the slaughter of the suitors and the maids may be seen as one big exercise in irregular warfare, an armed uprising without an army. The chronicles, law codes, poetry, and art of Egypt and southwest Asia before ca. 1100 B.C. record such low-intensity warfare.

Hittite laws document ingenious and active thieves who make off with slaves and every kind of animal, from bulls to pigs, as well as bees, birds, household goods, grain, plaster, a grapevine's tendrils, plows, carts, chariot wheels, water troughs, lashes, whips, reins, spears, knives, nails, curtains, doors, bricks, and foundation stones. The Sumerians write about breaking and entering, the Babylonians about raids on merchant caravans, while the Egyptians decry those who pilfer a loaf of bread or a pair of sandals from a traveler. Sheep-stealing was a way of life in the Levant and the merchant counted himself lucky if his caravan wasn't picked off.

Near Eastern societies were familiar with personal violence of every sort, from tearing off ears and biting off noses to knocking out teeth and breaking bones, to blinding, rape, and murder. They knew every weapon of interpersonal violence, from fists to clubs, from daggers to bows. Here are three examples: A king of the city of Byblos (in today's Lebanon) in the 1300s B.C. foiled an assassin who came at him with a bronze dagger. An Egyptian tale from before 1200 B.C. involves an elder brother who falsely believed that his younger brother had tried to seduce his wife. Imagine him sharpening his spear and standing behind the stable door, waiting to ambush his younger brother when he returned with the cattle in the evening. A macehead was dedicated to the god Asshur by the Assyrian King Shalmaneser I (1274–1245 B.C.).

Just as coastal dwellers had to deal with pirates, people who lived inland struggled with less civilized raiders from across the border. The farmers of Late Bronze Age Ugarit suffered raids by the men of neighboring Siyannu, who cut their vines. In Egypt during the reign of King Merikare (ca. 2100 B.C.), there was continual trouble from the "miserable Asiatic," that is, Canaanite nomads, who moved their flocks with the seasons and raided the locals wherever they went. One text refers to Canaanites as constantly moving in search of food, constantly fighting, never formally declaring war, and behaving like thieves. Though troublesome, the author says, the group could do only limited damage: like crocodiles, they can grab someone on a lonely road but they are not capable of attacking a town. In short, they fought like guerrillas.

There is less evidence for irregular warfare or covert operations, but there is some. Scouting patrols were a regular feature of Bronze Age warfare, from Mesopotamia in the 1700s B.C. to Hatti in the 1200s B.C. The Hittites sent out spies to gather information about enemy towns. They also employed allies to spread disinformation: on the eve of the Battle of Qadesh, for example, they had two Bedouin purposely captured by the Egyptian enemy who then fed the enemy lies. Meanwhile, concealment of their chariots was the key to Hittite strategy against Egypt in the battle that followed. And as early as around 2000 B.C. a Sumerian poem about a war has one king send out his bodyguard to the enemy in order to confuse and mislead the other king.

If the Trojans had wanted to steal Greek livestock, supplies, and slaves, if they had wanted to waylay individual soldiers and kill or capture them, if they had wanted to send out spies to learn what the Greeks were up to or discharge double agents to spread disinformation, if they wanted to leave the enemy jumpy and worn out, they would have had plenty of contemporary models.

But low-intensity warfare requires tremendous patience, and waiting could not have been easy for the Trojans after all they had endured. Their wealth was dwindling after years of feeding the allies at their own expense and showering the allied leaders with gifts. The mansions of Troy had been emptied of the gold and bronze that once filled them. The people were tired of being shut up inside their walls. And the Greeks were stripping their hinterland of its livestock and luxuries, its field hands and finery, just as they were preventing new wealth from flowing in from the ships of the Trojan Harbor.

Hunger was a by-product of invasion. Describing the situation in the city of Ur besieged by the Elamites around 2100 B.C., a poet said that "hunger contorts [people's] faces, it twists their muscles." Troy was not cut off from the world, but Greek raiders probably took a toll on the food supply. Like the chief magistrate of the Bronze Age city of Byblos when his town came under attack, a Trojan might have bewailed the lack of grain and the loss of livestock. The mayor of Byblos claimed that his citizens had to sell their furniture abroad and sell their children into slavery in order to obtain food when under siege.

Hector had no interest in a victory won by sneaking out of ditches or crawling through the mud; he wanted nothing less than glory "beyond measure, rivaling in height heaven and earth." As he once put it:

My early youth was bred to martial pains,
My soul impels me to the embattled plains!
Let me be foremost to defend the throne,
And guard my father's glories, and my own.

But glory did not come without a price.

CHAPTER NINE

HECTOR'S CHARGE

She had begged him not to go. Having climbed up to the windy battlements of Troy, where islands glistened in distant outline, her eyes were focused on the figures on the plain below. She scanned the battlefield, searching for her husband, unable to stop herself from weeping like a widow. And then, suddenly, there he was, right beneath her in the paved streets of Troy, beside the Scaean Gate. He had made a quick trip to town to organize a last-ditch appeal to the gods. She ran down the steps of the tower, followed by a wet nurse, whom she had ordered to bring the baby.

Andromache, daughter of the late King Eëtion of Thebes-under-Plakos, did not want to lose another man to Achilles' bronze spearhead, no matter how much her husband, Hector, was determined to prove himself in battle. She took their infant son from the nurse and held him against her breasts, which were perfumed with oil of iris, tincture of rose or sage or some other aromatic. Wordlessly, Hector smiled at the boy. His tearful wife grasped the warrior's arm, and begged him to take pity on her and their child. She spoke wise words, telling Hector to stay on the defensive and guard the walls. But the prince paid no attention. For a moment he held the baby tenderly in his arms and prayed for the boy's future prowess, then returned him to Andromache. He stroked her cheek and promised he would hold his own in combat. Then he sent her back to what he considered women's work. "All males are concerned with war," he said pointedly, "and me most of all."

Two days had passed since that farewell. Hector had returned to battle. At home Andromache worked at her loom, embroidering a purple cloak with flowers, an ancient talisman for bringing back a man. She had the servant women put a cauldron of water on the fire ready to give Hector a warm bath after the battle. But she had already led those same servants in a ceremony of ritual mourning for the man she never expected to see alive again.

Hector had first brought his troops to the gates of the wall in front of the Greeks' ships. Then came the night when the Trojans camped out on the plain. Now, on the second day of battle and at dawn, they would begin the drive that Hector expected would bring them, torches in hand, to the Greek ships.

The events of these second and third days of pitched battle take up fully one-half of the *Iliad*. And that is only right, because they represent high noon in the lives of the poem's two chief protagonists. But when it came to the fate of Troy these two days were almost a sideshow, and so the military story is related more quickly than the personal drama. In Homer, the Olympians play an especially prominent role in these events. We might dismiss this as epic convention but in fact it reflects the psychology of the Bronze Age battlefield. The harder the fighting, the more religious ancient soldiers became.

A direct attack against a well-defended position is never easy, even when the defender is on the ropes. The war in these books of the *Iliad* is bloody and no-holds-barred. The Greeks were determined to defend every inch of ground, and they were disciplined enough to carry out a series of fighting retreats. Although most Greeks were war weary, the Myrmidons were a strong and rested reserve force that would go into action upon the activation of a trip wire. The Trojan commander ignored warnings of the danger because he hungered for glory and shrank from disgrace. Hector's frontal assault on the Greeks was questionable from the military point of view but it did what Bronze Age culture demanded of a king: to throw his army into battle and smash the enemy, as an Assyrian text put it.

The fight began at dawn. The two sides were evenly matched throughout the morning but in the midday heat the Greeks broke through. They pushed the Trojans all the way back across the Scamander to the walls of Troy, only to be repulsed themselves. One by one, many of the best Greek warriors were wounded: Agamemnon, Diomedes, Odysseus, and the lesser but still important Eurypylus and Machaon. The Greeks were driven behind their trench and wall.

Hector wanted to dispatch the chariots across the trench but he was dissuaded by the Trojan seer Polydamas son of Panthous. Reading the omens was standard practice in Bronze Age warfare. Hammurabi of Babylon (1792–1750 B.C.), for example, announced that he would not have launched a major offensive without first consulting the gods. The details of an operation were also matters for consultation. If a seer turned out to be a judicious tactician, as Polydamas did, then all the better. On his advice, the Trojan attack was carried out on foot. Hector divided his men into five battalions and ordered them to breach the Greeks' rampart. In furious fighting the Lycians under Sarpedon and his lieutenant Glaucus almost broke through a gate, but the Greeks under Ajax and his brother Teucer held them off. Then, thanks to what seemed like divine intervention, Hector is alleged to have hurled a huge stone at the gate and smashed an opening through which his men poured. Repair the gate or suffer a heap of corpses, a Mesopotamian priest had advised a city governor—and the Greeks would have known just what he meant.

The Greeks retreated in good order, adopting a tight defensive formation. Men said that Zeus's brother Poseidon had saved them by breathing confidence into the discouraged troops. They regrouped and, with the two Ajaxes as leaders, they demonstrated the Greeks' disciplined excellence:

A chosen phalanx, firm, resolved as fate,
Descending Hector and his battle wait.

An iron scene gleams dreadful o'er the fields,
Armour in armour lock'd, and shields in shields,
Spears lean on spears, on targets targets throng,
Helms stuck to helms, and man drove man along.

    . . .

Thus breathing death, in terrible array,
The close compacted legions urged their way. . . .

The phalanx stopped the Trojans. Furious hand-to-hand fighting ensued, in which the Greeks got the better of things, especially
against the third Trojan battalion. Its leaders, Priam's sons Helenus
and Deïphobus, were both wounded and obliged to retreat to Troy,
while the third in command, Asius, was killed, as was his son
Adamas. Following Polydamas's advice once again, Hector pulled his
troops back to regroup. But earlier he had brushed off Polydamas's
interpretation of an omen as cautioning against a Trojan attack on
the ships. Nor did Hector really take seriously the seer's warning
about Achilles:

    a man insatiable for war waits
Beside the ships, and I don't think he will hold back for the whole battle.

Hector was at his best and worst that day. He was as reckless as
he was courageous, as arrogant as he was proud, as principled as he
was selfish, as intractable as he was firm. Hector was more consistent than the Greek commanders, who so lost their nerve that it
seemed miraculous when they regained it, but ultimately he was less
effective. When he rallied his men for a new charge Hector succeeded
only in taking a direct hit on the chest from a stone hurled by Tela-
monian Ajax. He blacked out but was saved by a crowd of Trojan
champions, who carried him off the field and had him brought
quickly to the rear by chariot. Water from the Scamander revived
him long enough for him to vomit but then Hector lost conscious-
ness again. It was a decisively bad break for Troy.

The resurgent Greeks forced the Trojans into retreat beyond

the wall and trench and followed them out onto the plain. By this time Hector had recovered and rallied the army. In real life, no man could have bounced back so quickly from a thoracic contusion, not to mention a concussion suffered early in the day. But Hector seemed to enjoy the miraculous intervention of Zeus; as Homer has it, Zeus had discovered the other gods' tricks and now intervened on the Trojan side. He even had Apollo (perhaps Iyarri to the Trojans) smooth the ground for an advance by the Trojan chariots. Seeing the Trojans regroup, the Greeks began an orderly retreat, with the mass of men falling back to the ships and an elite of champions and their best followers out in front. But once the attack began and the gods gave glory to the Trojans, the Greeks ran in panic like frightened cattle or sheep.

Scattered duels did little to slow the Trojans' steady advance, killing Greeks until they had reached the ships again. This time, the Trojans drove their chariots into the camp. They needed them as platforms from which to fight those Greeks who took to the ships' decks and brandished long naval pikes. Meanwhile, on the ground between the ships, other Greeks formed a solid wall.

The Trojans smelled victory; the Greeks knew that the war could be lost in an hour. Both sides fought with the ferocity of fresh troops. This was no long-distance exchange of arrows and javelins but rather a ferocious brawl where the weapons were swords, pikes, battle-axes, and everyday hatchets. The earth flowed black with blood. Ajax refused to give up: he leaped from ship to ship with his pike. But little by little, Hector's inspired leadership drove the Greeks back from the first row of ships to the huts that lay beyond.

As Hector grabbed hold of a ship's sternpost he issued a simple command: "Bring fire!" Could these thrilling words have been spoken without a shiver? Could they have been followed by any prouder shout than the battle cry that Hector now commanded his men to raise in unison? He called out:

Zeus has granted us today, as recompense for everything,
The chance to take the ships that came here against the god's will
And brought us much suffering....

The Trojans pressed forward with renewed force while Ajax lunged with his spear and bellowed to his men to stand and die. Sweating, breathless, and sore from holding up his shield, his ears ringing from the clash of spears against his helmet, Ajax held his ground. But then Hector reached him and sliced through the ash wood of Ajax's spear with his great sword. Ajax was forced to retreat as the Trojan torches began to burn the ship. It was, says Homer, none other than the vessel that had once carried Protesilaus, the first man to fall at Troy.

The long day's battle was a confusion of sounds: human, animal, avian, inanimate, and meteorological (or, as the ancients would have said, divine); a dying cry or the roar of a group of men; piercing or roaring, whistling or thwacking, clanging or thudding, laughing or fulminating; verbal or grunted; shrill or subdued; commanded or uttered in lamentation; words honeyed or harsh, exhortatory or terrified. The field echoed with the thunder of horses' hooves as they drew two-men chariots into battle and, if the driver and warrior fell, rattled with the eerie sound of empty chariots, horses fleeing.

The sights of battle were terrible. As men hacked and lunged at each other, there were lightning-like flashes of bronze. At the Greek ramparts, a storm of stones rained down on the Trojans, followed by a hail of splinters where the wall was breached. The two armies fought in the soft light of dawn, under the hot, midday sun, and in the evening; through clouds of dust, up hills and down muddy river banks, past windy trees and ancient tombs. At the battle's start Zeus sent a rainstorm of blood, which might refer to the real-life phenomenon of showers that deposit red dust carried from the Sahara Desert, still seen in the Aegean today.

The seesaw of battle was dizzying. Soldiers massed and scattered, advanced and retreated as if in some mad dance. The battle raged back and forth half a dozen times over the two-mile-wide plain, forcing the men to cover an exhausting distance. The many ascents and descents of the swale leading up from the plain to the Greek camp would have left men with sore calves and aching lungs. Those who had chariots must have been grateful for the ride.

Between Troy and the Greeks' ship station lay heaps of corpses, horse and human, both fresh corpses and the victims of the fighting the day before, since there had been no truce to retrieve the dead. Many of the human bodies, stripped naked, were covered only by encrusted blood. Some were missing limbs, others had been crushed under chariot wheels. Within twenty-four hours the cadavers would have exuded the pungent odor of death, sweet and sharp. But it would have been a matter only of minutes after death before insects attacked the corpses, and birds and dogs would have followed shortly thereafter. The Trojan Plain would have been thick with vultures and crows, scattering when men approached and returning when they left. Dogs would have grown fat on the abundance of fresh human meat. Swarms of flesh flies would have accompanied the armies on their march. Butterflies and eagles would have fed on the carrion as well. No one on either side would have had any excuse not to know what awaited the fallen.

The Trojans were fighting for their homes, but the Greeks were free to load their ships and leave. No wonder Homer has the day's fighting begin with a visitation to the Greek camp by Eris, the goddess of strife. She emitted such a loud and shrill cry that it goaded the men to think

> *that war was sweeter than sailing*
> *In their hollow ships to their dear fatherland.*

That was an encouraging start but not enough to maintain fighting spirit for the whole long and bloody day. Neither side could have kept going without continual exhortations from the leadership. Battles such as this are won not by materiel but by men. Hector, Agamemnon, Sarpedon, both Ajaxes, Odysseus, Diomedes, and others each addressed the troops from time to time, alternately scolding and encouraging them.

It was vital too for orders to be given clearly. These leaders told the men when to fan out, when to form tight masses, when to attack, and when to fall back. Command and control on the Late Bronze Age battlefield was primitive, depending on speeches from the top, on trumpet calls and hoisted banners. A booming voice was no small advantage; small wonder that the intensity of a man's battle cry was taken as a sign of warrior prowess. Less dramatic but equally important were the subordinate officers who spread the word, especially in the Trojan army, where orders had to be given in a number of different languages.

But all the speeches in the world could not have driven one particular emotion from the soldiers' hearts—and that was fear. The favorable omen of eagle's flight on the right, the feeling of a comrade standing close by, the sound of an enemy in flight: all provided temporary relief. Even so, no one from the sword-bearers to Agamemnon escaped without a moment of terror that day. As a Babylonian hymn says, the war-god shines with a frightening gleam.

The flames of Protesilaus's ship fired Hector's imagination but they also marked the beginning of his end. With an almost mathematical logic, his success entailed his failure because it reawakened Achilles. As the tide began to turn against the Greeks, Nestor planted an idea in the mind of Patroclus: although Achilles had sworn off battle, he, Patroclus, could fight in his behalf. Nestor said:

> *If thou but lead the Myrmidonian line;*
> *Clad in Achilles' arms, if thou appear,*
> *Proud Troy may tremble, and desist from war.*

After the briefest of hesitations Achilles agreed to let Patroclus wear his armor, lead his Myrmidons, and save the ships. In fact, Achilles was so concerned that, as soon as he saw the flames of the burning ship, he told Patroclus to hurry up. The only condition Achilles placed was that he conduct a limited operation. Patroclus could drive the enemy out of the Greek camp but under no circumstances was he to press on to Troy. That might anger some god, Achilles said, and besides, it would diminish Achilles' honor. Patroclus agreed to these terms.

Achilles did everything he could to help his men, except fight. He toured the huts and roused the Myrmidons to arms; he sent them off with a rousing prebattle speech; and he took the precaution of pouring a libation to Zeus. Patroclus also added his own words about the men's glorious reputation and their even more glorious commander, not forgetting to dishonor Agamemnon—not for nothing was Patroclus the perfect second in command:

> *Think your Achilles sees you fight: be brave,*
> *And humble the proud monarch whom you save.*

The Myrmidons attacked the Trojans like ravenous wolves. They drove the enemy back from the burning ship of Protesilaus and put out the fire, but it was a harder fight to clear them from the camp. The Trojans held their ground inside the wall; only after fierce hand-to-hand combat did the Greeks prevail. The Trojans were propelled into a pell-mell flight that left a number of chariots stuck in the trench, the horses having broken free, but the men sitting ducks for Greek bronze.

Back on the plain, Patroclus cut off the Trojans' leading battalions in their retreat to Troy and forced them to stand and fight. The result was bloody but triumphant for the Greeks. Of the many Trojan casualties the most important by far was Sarpedon: a man who claimed to be son of Zeus or the Storm God, king of Lycia, and one of Troy's main allies. His lieutenant, Glaucus, suffered from a hand wound, having been hit by one of Teucer's arrows during the Trojan attack on the walls. But Glaucus knew that his honor depended on the recovery of Sarpedon's body, so nothing could have held him back. He made a blunt approach to Hector: the allies felt abandoned, so he had better help fight for the corpse. And he did. Hector's men engaged in a bitter hand-to-hand battle but the Greeks won. Accepting failure, Hector remounted his chariot and called a retreat. The Greeks stripped Sarpedon's armor while even the heavens sighed; as Homer says, Apollo spirited his corpse back home to Lycia. It was a total triumph for the Myrmidons. In a moment of inspiration, the Trojans had recognized Patroclus's identity, but that wasn't enough to help them stop him.

Then Patroclus got carried away. He disobeyed Achilles' orders and went in thunderous pursuit across the plain to the walls of Troy. There he made three assaults on the wall. Homer says that he climbed the parapet and was pushed back three times before giving up. Presumably a support company had brought ladders with them.

Homer has Apollo call Patroclus down from the walls, just as he talks Hector into rejoining the battle instead of bringing his men to safety behind the walls. Hector ordered his chariot to go after Patroclus, but the Greek was ready. Patroclus killed Hector's latest charioteer, Cebriones. The two men dismounted and fought over the body, joined by their followers. Again, the Greeks won.

By now it was late afternoon. There was still time for Patroclus to make three charges into the Trojan ranks, on which Homer has him kill no fewer than twenty-seven men. Homer mentions by name another twenty-seven Trojans whom Patroclus slew that day, as well as an indeterminate number of others, for a total of more than fifty-four! No single warrior could have carried out all the killing that Homer attributes to Patroclus on his vengeful spree. But with Patroclus at their head, fresh troops like the Myrmidons would have ripped a bloody hole in the Trojan lines.

But now Patroclus's luck had run out. Divine intervention (or a loose strap) caused him to lose his armor, and a young Trojan named Euphorbus son of Panthous took advantage by hurling his spear into Patroclus's back. Seeing his chance for glory, after Euphorbus had removed his javelin, Hector forced his way through the ranks and speared Patroclus in the belly. This was the most vulnerable part of the trunk and a favorite spot in Homer's epic, along with the neck, for administering the death blow. No wonder a Syrian general referred to annihilating an enemy as "smashing his belly"!

The fight for Patroclus's body raged until sunset. Hector had mixed success. He had to suffer charges of cowardice from Glaucus for not having recovered Sarpedon's corpse. He also lost his close friend Podes son of Eëtion, a regular guest at Hector's table. And Hector failed to secure the ultimate prize of Achilles' horses, which had pulled Patroclus's chariot. They escaped. But Hector did manage to claim Achilles' armor and to drive the enemy back across the plain to their camp.

The news of Patroclus's death was a bitter blow to Achilles, but he recovered sufficiently to go to the Greek trench where he boomed in a voice that, like pharaoh's war cry, frightened all the land. According to Homer, Achilles had only to roar three times and the Trojans retreated far enough for the Greeks to retrieve Patroclus's body. By now it was too dark to continue the fight.

The Trojans held an assembly. Once again, Polydamas gave the soundest advice: go back to Troy, camp in the marketplace, and, at dawn, man the walls. They were impregnable, even to Achilles. As Polydamas put it:

> So may his rage be tired, and labour'd down!
> And dogs shall tear him ere he sack the town.

It was good advice, but Hector rejected it. He scorned retreating now that Zeus or the Storm God had decided to give him glory. Not for the last time in history, a general would claim to have god on his side. The Trojans were convinced; rapturously they cheered Hector's speech and put his plan into effect. They would camp out again on the plain and, at dawn, return to battle, Achilles or not.

Now comes one of the most memorable parts of the *Iliad*. The death of Patroclus gives birth to a new Achilles. Older and wiser, Achilles confesses the error of his past ways and decides to return to battle, although not before accepting the gifts that Agamemnon had offered. The next day, presented by the gods with matchless new armor and a marvelous shield, the hero slaughters a crowd of Trojans. He fights even the Scamander River in a display of the sort of superhuman power attributed to pharaohs. Finally, Achilles hunts down Hector.

The tragic education of an arrogant young hero is one of literature's oldest themes, antique already in Homer's day, and dating back to Mesopotamia's *Epic of Gilgamesh* around 2000 B.C. Could anyone tell the tale more eloquently than Homer does in the latter books of

the *Iliad*? Literature aside, in military terms these scenes are important mainly in the negative. With the deaths of Hector and then
Achilles, the Trojan War would continue in a different form, with
new leaders and new tactics.

Homer narrates a double tragedy: Achilles versus Hector, with
Patroclus triangulated between the two. The reality was probably
more prosaic. Achilles says that he is avenging Patroclus out of loyalty to a friend who was his soulmate, his very life, and out of shame
also for having let him down. However, if Achilles did not kill Hector, he would have been finished as warlord. As even Achilles admits,
while Patroclus and many of his other companions had been slaughtered during Hector's offensive, Achilles had sat out the war by the
ships, a "useless weight on the ground." The Myrmidons would not
long have tolerated a leader who was unable to make good on this
failure.

Achilles protests that he knows that by killing Hector he is sign-
ing his own death warrant. The fates had decreed that his death
would follow fast on Hector's. What else could he have said, given
the prophecy? Besides, he loved war; the odor of death was in his
nostrils. Achilles had no other way of salvaging his reputation except
by killing Hector. He said this clearly to his divine mother—or, as we
might put it today, he said it in a moment of honesty:

> Let me this instant, rush into the fields,
> And reap what glory [kleos] life's short harvest yields.

Friendship was fleeting but fame was immortal. Achilles had his priorities clear.

Achilles would have preferred to begin his fight at dawn the
next day but the preliminaries could not be overlooked. There had to
be a formal reconciliation with Agamemnon, and, afterward, Odysseus
prevailed upon Achilles that there be sacrifice and rest before going
into battle. War booty also had to be displayed to the men in order
to stir up their lust for battle. Then Achilles led them out. The
Greeks struck so hard and the enemy ran so fast that after it was

over, as soon as a Trojan found safety behind the walls, his first thought was not relief but quenching his thirst.

The old Achilles had disappeared. The amiable buccaneer who preferred ransoming an enemy to slaughtering him was now a killing machine. His victims included two more sons of Priam, Polydorus and his brother Lycaon, a man whom Achilles had earlier spared and sold into slavery. Achilles ignored his pleas for mercy. Most Trojans ran at the mere sight of Achilles; of those who stood their ground, only a rare few, like Aeneas, lived to tell the tale, and then only thanks to divine intervention.

What made Achilles such a successful warrior was that he had strength and speed and superb soldiers to support him. His reputation alone was enough to panic most enemies, which gave him a huge psychological advantage. In an afternoon on the battlefield the *Iliad*'s Achilles kills at least thirty-six Trojans. It was a smaller tally of victims than Patroclus's but it is no less a reminder that the Bronze Age liked its heroes hot.

Achilles' final victim was Hector. Courageous enough to stand and face him when he might have retreated behind his city's walls, Hector nonetheless had second thoughts. But then he thought of the shame that he would face. Hector had to admit that Polydamas had been right about the danger of an enemy led by Achilles. He himself had been a fool, and the Trojan army had paid a terrible price.

In spite of his fears about public dishonor, in the end, Hector ran. Panicked by Achilles' approach, he sprinted off, only to be followed by the great runner. They circled the city three times; indeed, there are indications in Homer that the poet thought of them as circling the entire Trojan Plain three times, a distance of thirty-six miles or more. Finally recovering his courage, Hector stood and fought. Achilles threw his javelin and missed, but recovered it through divine intervention (or a dash to retrieve it). Hector struck Achilles' shield with his javelin. Then he drew his sword and rushed Achilles, but the Greek was ready and drove his spear into Hector's neck. The Trojan fell to the ground, and, with a prophecy of Achilles' approaching doom, he died.

The thrust to the Greek ships was the high-water mark of the Trojan army's resistance. Never again would it pose such a threat. The Trojans followed the wrong strategy. They should have let the Greeks tire themselves out. (In recent times Muhammad Ali brought such a tactic to boxing, the rope-a-dope.) Impatient, arrogant, and hungry for glory, Hector could not accept low-intensity tactics in a defensive strategy; he went after a decisive battle.

The withdrawal of Achilles and the Myrmidons had marked the breakdown of the Greek coalition. Hector should have taken advantage of it by doing precisely nothing. A good rule of warfare is never stop an enemy from trying to withdraw. Instead, Hector did the worst possible thing by launching a frontal attack on the Greek camp. He drove Achilles and company right back into the other Greeks' arms.

The death of Hector might have been a turning point but it did not mean that the war was lost. On the contrary, it might have worked to Troy's advantage. The Trojans still had a lot of fight in them and, what is more, they had a real chance of putting that spirit to good use. They could still inflict casualties on the enemy; they still defended an impregnable fortress; and they still enjoyed the comparative advantage of an urban base. The Greeks were stuck in their wretched camp. The Trojans could wait them out, especially if they replenished their ranks with new allies.

But Hector's family did not see things that way. King Priam and Queen Hecuba watched their son's death from the battlements, where they had earlier called down and pleaded with him not to risk battle with Achilles. Now they were inconsolable in their grief.

Hector's wife, Andromache, was at home, preparing the house for her husband's return when she heard the cries of lamentation. Fearing the worst, Andromache took two servants as escorts and ran to the city walls. From a high tower, she scanned the battlefield for Hector. Achilles had attached Hector's naked body to a chariot by leather thongs cinched through holes in Hector's tendons. Hector's long hair streamed in the dust as Achilles whipped his horses across the plain, dragging the cadaver behind him in triumph.

CHAPTER TEN

ACHILLES' HEEL

Sweet as it was to drive his spearhead through Hector's neck, to spit out taunts—no fewer than three times—about the dogs and birds that would soon eat the dying man's corpse, to strip off his stolen armor from the Trojan's body, to see his comrades poke the still-warm flesh with their spears, and to raise the victory paean among the Greeks, it was not enough for Achilles. Achilles brought the corpse back to his camp and dumped it before Patroclus's bier. It lay there until after his friend's funeral, when Achilles hitched up his chariot and dragged the cadaver around Patroclus's tomb three times. Like Hittite and Egyptian generals, the Greek leader mistreated his enemy's corpse.

At first the gods displayed no objection; presumably they communicated through their priests. In fact, Zeus allowed Hector to be dishonored in his native land. But after nine days, enough was enough, and Zeus insisted that Achilles return the corpse to Troy for burial or suffer divine retribution. Hector's corpse had not begun to rot and the dogs had kept their distance—miracles both, unless "nine days" merely means a long time.

Achilles' behavior shocks us, but perhaps not as much as his cold-blooded slaughter of twelve noble Trojan youths before Patroclus's pyre. The great hero himself had captured them in battle expressly for this purpose.

Meanwhile, a revisionist version of Hector's story began circulating. The real Hector was a self-absorbed, often sharp-tongued martinet whose honor was more important to him than his country's safety; a man who imagined his wife's suffering in captivity but hastened it by his actions; a man who rejected the prudence that would have saved his own life and that of many of his comrades. Now he became a selfless martyr for his homeland.

The *Iliad* tells how Priam journeyed courageously at night across the plain to the Greek camp and, at the risk of his own life, begged Achilles for Hector's corpse. The old man fell to his knees before Achilles and kissed the Greek's murderous hands. It was humiliating, but Priam was engaging in a classic gesture of prostration and self-abasement. And just as an enemy of the Hittite king might signal his surrender by offering valuable gifts (in one example, a throne and scepter, both made of iron), so Priam came laden with treasures. In all of these cases a tit-for-tat exchange was understood on the part of the winner.

The Greeks granted a truce of eleven days so that Hector's funeral could take place; afterward, the war continued. Only a few details of what followed are found in Homer and mainly in the *Odyssey* rather than the *Iliad*. For more the reader has to turn to what is left of the other poems of the Epic Cycle. Only sketchy summaries and a few quotations survive from the *Cypria, Aethiopis, Little Iliad, Sack of Ilium*, and *The Returns*. These accounts were embroidered by such later writers of antiquity as Pindar, the Attic tragedians, Vergil, Statius, Dictys of Crete, Quintus Smyrnaeus, and Apollodorus—not to mention Herodotus and Thucydides. Where Homer is severe and restrained, some of these other authors revel in gossipy details.

The Greek and Trojan generals took the path of least resistance. Each side having failed thus far in its objectives, the generals' recipe, on both sides, was more pitched battle.

The *Aethiopis* tells the story of a woman warrior named Penthesilea. She was an Amazon, a Thracian, and a so-called daughter of

Ares, who came to help the Trojans fight. Penthesilea enjoyed a day of glory on the battlefield until she confronted Achilles, who killed her. Homer does not mention Penthesilea but he offers a few other details about the Amazons. He refers to them as "women who are equivalent to men" and he names two heroes who fought them in battle: King Priam in his younger days and a certain Bellerophontes, who was the grandfather of the Lycian warrior Glaucus, comrade of Sarpedon. These clashes took place years before the Trojan War. Although "Penthesilea" is a Greek name, "Amazon" itself is probably not a Greek word. Priam is said to have fought the Amazons on the Sangarius River in Phrygia, about 350 miles east of Troy. This is far from modern Thrace, which is in southeastern Europe, but the ancients sometimes imagined Thrace as including northwest Anatolia.

It was left to later writers of antiquity to elaborate other details about Amazons: making them man-haters who killed their own husbands, placing them geographically in Anatolia's Black Sea region, having them attack Athens, and pitting them against such Greek heroes as Heracles and Theseus. Penthesilea is said to have come to Troy with twelve other Amazon warriors and to have distinguished herself in action. She is also supposed to have been so beautiful that, after Achilles took off the dead woman's helmet and saw her face, he fell in love.

Women warriors may have seemed outlandish in much of history but not so today when, for example, several hundred thousand women serve in the U.S. military. Nor are women soldiers unknown historically. The best-documented case may be that of the corps of women archers and spear-fighters in eighteenth- and nineteenth-century Dahomey. Good soldiers, they also were trusted as royal bodyguards, and they had a propaganda value to boot, because alpha males felt insulted to be matched in battle with women.

No other all-female units are known in the ancient world, but there were several Joans of Arc, from Artemisia of Halicarnassus, in 480 B.C. the first recorded female admiral, to Boudicca, the British queen who commanded troops against a Roman army in A.D. 61. At sites in southern Russia and Ukraine, archaeologists have found dozens of graves of women buried with weapons. Swords, daggers, bows, quivers, arrowheads, spearheads, horse trappings, and jewelry as well as household objects are among the objects discovered. In some cases, the women's bones demonstrate that they were accustomed to horse riding, heavy use of the bow, and possibly even that they died in battle.

The earliest of such graves dates to around 600 B.C., the latest to about four hundred years afterward. The skeletons represent three Iron Age cultures: Scythian, Sauromatian, and Sarmatian. No archaeological evidence of women warriors has been found for the Bronze Age, but the Iron Age discoveries raise at least the possibility that they did exist.

Thersites resurfaces in the *Aethiopis* to rebuke Achilles for allegedly having fallen in love with Penthesilea. Achilles did not respond well to criticism, and Thersites paid with his life. Later writers claim that Thersites was Diomedes' cousin; but no army could tolerate a warrior who killed one of its own men for so flimsy an offense. Achilles is supposed to have had to make a short trip to the nearby island of Lesbos to be purified before he could fight again. When he did, he found a new enemy.

Memnon, king of the Aethiopians, came to Troy's aid late in the war, perhaps, as Roman-era sources have it, bringing a large contingent of soldiers with him. If so, they surely were not cheap, to judge from one Anatolian ruler under siege who paid up to seven times the normal wage to hire mercenaries. Although Memnon does not appear in the *Iliad*, he is remembered in the *Odyssey* as a great hero. Among other feats, Memnon killed Nestor's son Antilochus before being killed by Achilles in turn. In Homer, Memnon is son of the legendary Tithonus and the goddess Dawn. Other sources claim a marriage tie between Memnon's family and Priam's.

Memnon is too obscure a character for us to be sure that he existed, but it is worth speculating that he might have been black. Memnon came from Aethiopia, a place thought of by the Greeks in various and sometimes vague ways. The term could refer to modern

Ethiopia, to any land south of Egypt—especially Sudan—to any land with dark-skinned inhabitants, or to the East, that is, the land of the morning. But one thing is clear: to the Greeks, Aethiopians had skin burned by the sun. So, to a Greek, an Aethiopian might have been black.

In the late Bronze Age, Nubia, which is roughly today's northern Sudan, was conquered and annexed by Egypt. Nubian mercenaries fought in the pharaoh's army, and sons of Nubian princes were brought northward to be Egyptianized, alongside the sons of Canaanite princes. Some Nubians rose to high positions in Egypt. Nubian nobles began depicting themselves as Egyptians in their tombs and sometimes assumed Egyptian names.

Egypt was no stranger to the politics of western Anatolia. Pharaoh Amenhotep III (1382–1344) had sought an alliance with the kingdom of Arzawa in western Anatolia by marrying an Arzawan royal princess. More recently, Rameses II (1279–1213) corresponded with the king of Mira, a successor state of Arzawa.

But in spite of Memnon's support for Troy, the Greek army led by Achilles routed the Trojans, who streamed back to the city. And Achilles was on the verge of forcing his way into Troy when he was struck down by Paris.

The surviving bits of the Epic Cycle do not specify how Paris killed Achilles but the presence of Apollo (who was lending divine support) points to archery. The heel was supposed to be the only place where Achilles was vulnerable. Another tradition has him shot in the ankle. If either of these stories were true, and since Achilles died right away, it would point to a poison-tipped arrow. An ordinary arrow that penetrated the ankle or heel should not have been instantly fatal; it might have led to a mortal infection, but then Achilles should have lingered for several days before succumbing.

According to the *Aethiopis*, Achilles was shot at Troy's Scaean Gate. The gate was a potentially weak point in the walls, so the attack was usually pressed hard there. Troy's architects compensated by channeling the enemy into a narrow space at the gate where they could be attacked from above by defenders on the battlements or in a tower. All of the surviving gates of Troy have designs of deadly sophistication, so the challenge facing Achilles is clear (even if the identification of the Scaean Gate is not).

The Trojan gatekeepers had opened the double doors to let the men back in, which was dangerous with Achilles and his men hot on their heels. Priam had coached Troy's gatekeepers, on the day of Hector's last battle, to close the doors in the nick of time, so that Achilles could not follow the fleeing Trojans back into town. On this latest occasion Achilles managed to break in, just as the king had feared. Flung open to let the men stream back to safety, the gates were not closed until it was too late. Achilles had penetrated the city's defenses. But not for long. Paris was waiting and with the help of the god Apollo or Iyarri, he killed Achilles, just as Hector had foretold with his dying breath.

Paris must have taken up a position on the walls. At an elevation of twenty-five feet or more, there were few reference points to judge the distance accurately, which was critical because arrows shot from a compound bow follow an arched trajectory in flight. The ground was also packed with soldiers, so Paris pulled off an extraordinarily lucky shot.

A battle now raged over Achilles' corpse, as the *Aethiopis* reports. Ajax eventually saved the body and brought it back to the Greek camp, while Odysseus played the leading role in holding back the enemy. According to the *Odyssey*, the mourning for Achilles lasted seventeen days. The *Aethiopis* brings in divine mourners and funeral games. And the *Little Iliad* mentions a deadly contest over Achilles' arms, which had been saved along with his body.

As with Hector, the revisionists were not slow to emerge. If Achilles had been so glorious, then why did the gods give him such an ugly, almost random death? Two years after the end of the war, the ghost of Achilles confessed to Odysseus that he, Achilles, had made the wrong choice by opting for an early but glorious death instead of a long, dull life. But, Odysseus protested, isn't Achilles honored as a king in Hades? The ghost replied:

Talk not of ruling in this dolorous gloom,
Nor think vain words (he cried) can ease my doom.
Rather I'd choose laboriously to bear
A weight of woes, and breathe the vital air,
A slave to some poor hind that toils for bread,
Than reign the sceptred monarch of the dead.

Reality was rapidly rejecting the heroic ideal. Nothing was sacred, not even Achilles' arms, at least if the epic tradition is to be trusted. These arms were supposed to go to the Greeks' best remaining warrior, but it would take a contest to choose him. Ajax and Odysseus were the two main contenders; Ajax was all muscle, Odysseus fought with his wits.

The poets agreed that the decision was entrusted to the Trojans, surely a way of avoiding civil war among the Greeks. Homer claims that the "children of the Trojans" made the choice, while the *Little Iliad* offers a delicious if perhaps incredible scheme. Nestor proposed that the Greeks choose the winner by sending eavesdroppers to the walls of Troy. There, they could overhear the enemy discussing the courage and manliness of the Greek heroes. The spies were dispatched and they did indeed hear a conversation but not by Trojan warriors: the speakers were unmarried girls. The first girl sang the praises of Ajax because he had saved Achilles' body, which was more than could be said of Odysseus. The second girl overruled her, arguing that even a woman could drag a corpse to safety, but only a man would have the courage to stand and guard the rear, as Odysseus had. This response was so clever that the poets saw it as the work of Athena.

Indeed, epic sees divine handiwork in the whole affair. The Bronze Age liked to believe that prowess wins battles, but seasoned warriors know that cunning trumps brute force. The best way to state this unpleasant truth was to bring in the gods. According to the *Little Iliad*, Athena willed the outcome.

The Trojan girls' verdict was reported to the Greeks, and Odysseus was declared the victor. Ajax, the original sore loser, went completely mad. Eventually he committed suicide, but not before destroying the cattle of the Greeks. Killing the animals was no small thing, since the cattle represented all the effort that had gone into many raids, usually led by Achilles, and they represented wealth to bring home, sacrifices to the gods, and food for the troops. The *Little Iliad* says that Ajax so angered "the king" (Agamemnon?) that he was denied the usual funeral pyre, and consigned instead to a funerary urn or coffin. Among the Greeks, unlike the Romans, suicide was not considered to be an honorable end.

As for Ajax's burial, cremation was not the norm for Bronze Age kings in Greece but it was for Hittite royalty. And it was obviously an option at Troy. In a cemetery of the 1300s B.C. at the Trojan Harbor, excavators found both cremation burials (that is, the bones and teeth left after cremation) and simple internments (that is, the skeletons left from the burial of unburned bodies). Some of these included Greek artifacts.

Neither side had achieved its objective in the pitched battles that followed the deaths of Hector and Achilles. But it would not be true to say that these battles accomplished nothing. In fact, they were without a doubt the most important confrontations of the war because they were nearly the last. They cleared the decks for one final attempt at an indirect, low-intensity strategy.

From the strategic point of view, the story of the Trojan girls, Ajax's suicide, and Odysseus's triumph sets the stage for the new phase of war. Odysseus was the apostle of unconventional warfare. His moment had finally come. Earlier, Agamemnon had shown good sense by listening to Nestor when it came to the toughest decisions; now, he listened to Odysseus.

Odysseus's first act was to lay an ambush for Helenus, Priam's seer son. Once caught, the seer told the Greeks what he considered to be the secret to success: bring Philoctetes and his bow, which had once belonged to Heracles, and Troy would fall. Philoctetes was a Thessalian warrior who had sailed with the Greeks from Aulis but never reached Troy. He had been bitten by a snake on an Aegean island, either on Lemnos (according to Homer) or Tenedos (according to the *Cypria*) and the venom had left him with a disgusting wound. As a result, the Greeks abandoned him on the island. Now, Odysseus sent Diomedes on a mission to bring Philoctetes.

The physician Machaon was able to heal Philoctetes. Why he was successful this time but not earlier is unclear. But war is often a spur for technology, including the technology of healing, and a process of trial and error on all too many patients might have taught the physician a new herbal recipe or two.

With the bow of Heracles, Philoctetes avenged Achilles by killing Paris. The triumphant Greeks took the body and Menelaus wasted no time in showing his anger by treating the corpse with complete contempt. But the Trojans fought back and recovered what was left of Paris. He was given a decent burial. Trojan custom required that his widow cut short the time spent wearing mournful black. And shortly afterward Helen married his brother Deïphobus. This "levirate marriage" was common ancient Near Eastern practice, found in Ugarit and among the Hittites as well as in the Hebrew Bible. But it was not practiced in Iron Age Greece, which points to the poet's knowledge of non-Greek mores. In levirate marriage a brother is required to marry the widow of his deceased brother. The custom is a reminder that ancient marriage was less about romance than about cementing family alliances and securing male protectors for women.

In Helen's case, her third marriage was either forced on her by the Trojans or it was a sign that she had no desire to return home to face Menelaus—or both. And Helen was still an exceptionally beautiful woman. Ten years later, in the *Odyssey*, she still could be described as looking "like Artemis with her golden arrows."

The generals continued to pay more attention to Ares than to Aphrodite. Both sides were eager for new allies. Homer and the Epic Cycle agree that both parties turned to a new generation of warriors, the sons of the men who had started the conflict. That would have been possible if the Trojan War had really lasted ten years but since it was a much shorter conflict, this detail will have to be ascribed to myth. In any case, the epic tradition says that Odysseus went to the island of Scyros, where he found Achilles' son, Neoptolemus. Having handed over his father's armor, Odysseus convinced the young man to come to Troy to fight in his father's cause. Meanwhile, Priam secured the son of Telephus of Mysia, Eurypylus, as well as the troops under his command. This brought public-relations as well as practical benefit because, like Philoctetes, Eurypylus had a connection to Heracles, who was his paternal grandfather. Priam is also said to have given Eurypylus's mother an exceptionally large gift to win her permission.

Like Neoptolemus, Eurypylus was evidently a very young man, or he would not have required his mother's consent. Such reinforcements came at a very heavy price, since Priam could hardly have been in a mood for largesse at this point in the war, while Odysseus could not have relished giving up the armor that he had competed so hard for. But the stakes were too high to hesitate.

Eurypylus came to Troy and deployed his men on the battlefield, where—naturally—he is said to have fought with distinction. But he was soon to fall to Neoptolemus's spear.

Odysseus was on the verge of a propaganda coup. He sneaked into Troy on what turned out to be the first of two secret missions. The *Odyssey* reports that Odysseus took great pains to camouflage himself, not only exchanging his armor for rags but changing his appearance by striking his face with a whip or a stick until it swelled up. Nobody recognized him in Troy except Helen. Years later, telling the story back in Sparta, she claimed to have helped Odysseus with no less than a bath, a rubdown, and a fresh set of clothes. But she badgered him until he revealed his strategy. As usual, Helen wanted something in return for her attention.

Helen also alleges that, in part thanks to her help, Odysseus killed many Trojans before slipping back out of town. But what was he doing in Troy? Possibly scouting out the target for his second mission. Some sources say Diomedes went along too. Their object was the Trojans' holiest of holies, the Palladium.

In classical Athens, armed Athena was known as Pallas Athena.

Roman-era sources usually describe the Palladium as a wooden statuette of the goddess Athena in arms. Whether the Trojans worshipped Athena is unclear, but the mother goddess was venerated everywhere in Anatolia, so an image of some female divinity might well indeed have held a central place in the Trojan pantheon. Stealing the Palladium was a coup that surely gave a lift to the Greeks while devastating Trojan morale.

In classical times, Greek gods and goddesses commonly had larger-than-life-size statues. But in Late Bronze Age Anatolia and Greece, figurines were a familiar way of representing a deity. The wealthy Hittite capitals had monumental sculptures of the gods, but figurines made of wood and plated with precious metal were more common. Or perhaps the Palladium was just a simple pillar or a stele such as those outside Troy's city gates. Like the sacred medicine bundles carried in animal skins by certain Native American peoples, the Palladium was considered to contain a power beyond its size.

Stealing the enemy's god could be very successful psychological warfare. But for some ancient peoples, it was even more: the Hittites and, many centuries later, the Romans, believed that they could actually bring a particular god over to their side.

The Greeks had tried everything, to no avail. Many of them might have felt as frustrated as the Hittite commanders who, in spite of every effort, despaired of having to leave an enemy town unscathed. But rather than despair, Odysseus sought a war-winning "wonder weapon," to use a modern term of art. Heracles' bow and Achilles' armor were miraculous objects that led to the deaths of Paris and Eurypylus; it was thought that the theft of the Palladium would weaken Troy. That is, if the thieves had been successful: the *Sack of Ilium* says that Odysseus did not seize the real Palladium but rather a fake, set up long before to trick thieves. That would have been a good story for Priam to put out to steady the Trojans' morale.

The walls of Troy stood firm. But were the Trojans still as committed to defending them? Achilles and Ajax were dead, but Odysseus had gone from strength to strength, with Philoctetes and Neoptole mus now at his side. Meanwhile, Eurypylus, Memnon, and Penthe-silea had all come and gone, Hector and Paris were dead, Priam had demeaned himself before Achilles, Helenus had been captured by the enemy and had given up state secrets, and Helen was treating with the enemy. It was time for the Trojans to pray that Boreas would blow the Greek ships back home.

CHAPTER ELEVEN

THE NIGHT OF THE HORSE

He is the last Greek at Troy. Pale in morning's light, he looks like a weak and ragged runaway. But looks can deceive. Sinon, as he is called, claims to be a deserter—the only Greek remaining when the entire enemy and its cursed fleet had suddenly departed. But can he be trusted? His name, Sinon, means "pest," "bane," or "misfortune" in Greek, leading some historians to consider it a nickname, like "the Desert Fox" for German general Ernst Rommel, or a generic name, like "Bones" for a military doctor. Sinon played a key role in the plot to take Troy, although he is often forgotten, overshadowed by the most famous trick in Western civilization.

The famous horse may be imagined as a tall and well-crafted wooden structure, towering over the wildflowers of the Scamander River plain. Its body is made of the pine of Mount Ida, a tree known today as *Pinus equi troiani*, "Trojan Horse Pine," and renowned since antiquity as a material for shipbuilding. The horse's eyes are obsidian and amber, its teeth ivory. Its crest, made of real horsehair, streams in the breeze. Its hooves shine like polished marble. And hidden inside are nine Greek warriors.

Everyone knows the story. The Greeks are said to have packed up their men, horses, weapons, and booty, set fire to their huts, and departed at night for the nearby island of Tenedos, where they hid their ships. All that they left behind was the Trojan Horse and a spy, Sinon, pretending to be a deserter.

The Trojans were amazed to discover that after all these years, the enemy had slunk home. But what were they to do with the Horse? After a fierce debate, they brought it into the city as an offering to Athena. There were wild celebrations. The Trojans underestimated the cunning of their adversaries. That night, the men inside the horse sneaked out and opened the city's gates to the men of the Greek fleet, who had taken advantage of Troy's drunken distraction to sail back from Tenedos. They proceeded to sack the city and win the war.

Everyone knows the story but nobody loves the Trojan Horse. Although scholars disagree about much of the Trojan War, they nearly all share the conviction that the Trojan Horse is a fiction. From Roman times on, there have been theories that the Trojan Horse was really a siege tower, or an image of a horse on a city gate left unlocked by pro-Greek Antenor, or a metaphor for a new Greek fleet because Homer calls ships "horses of the sea," or a symbol of the god Poseidon, who destroyed Troy in an earthquake, or a folktale similar to those found in Egyptian literature and the Hebrew Bible. There has been every sort of theory about the Trojan Horse except that it really existed.

Many of these theories sound convincing, particularly the horse-as-siege engine, since Bronze Age Assyrians named their siege towers after horses, among other animals. But sometimes a horse is just a horse. Although epic tradition might exaggerate the details of the Trojan Horse and misunderstand its purpose, that the object existed and that it played a role in tricking the Trojans into leaving their city without defenses might just be true.

More about the Horse presently: in the meantime, let us return to the spy whom the Greeks had left behind. Although Sinon is less dramatic than the famous Horse, he was no less effective as an agent of subversion, and he inspires far more confidence as a genuine historical figure. The Trojan Horse is unique and improbable, although not impossible. But Sinon plays a well-attested role in unconventional warfare as it was waged in the Bronze Age.

In Vergil's retelling in the *Aeneid*, Sinon pretends to be a deserter in order to work his way into Troy. He testifies that the Greeks have left for good and argues that the Trojan Horse is a genuine gift and not some trick. Eventually, after a stormy debate, the Trojans decide to bring the Horse into the city.

Deceit is not unique to the Trojan saga; it was a fundamental ingredient in Hittite military doctrine. Consider some examples: A king broke off the siege of a fortress with the approach of winter, only to send his general back to storm the unsuspecting city after it had gone off alert. A general sent agents into the opposing camp before battle, where they pretended to be deserters and tricked the enemy into letting down his guard. Another king attacked a neighbor via a roundabout route to avoid enemy scouts. Nor were the Hittites alone in their use of trickery. For example, the siege of one Mesopotamian city by another involved sneak attacks at night and the impersonation of an allied unit of soldiers in an attempt to lull the besieged into opening their gates. (It failed.)

Think of the fall of Troy not as a myth about a Horse but as an example of unconventional warfare, Bronze Age style. The Trojan Horse might be better known as the Trojan Red Herring. Everyone focuses on the Horse but the real story lies elsewhere. In fact, it would be possible to leave out the Trojan Horse and yet tell a credible and coherent narrative of the capture of Troy much as the ancients told it.

Without the Trojan Horse, the story might go like this: The Greeks decided to trick the Trojans into thinking they had gone home when, in fact, they had merely retreated to Tenedos. Once they had lulled the enemy into dropping his guard, they planned to return in a surprise attack—at night. To know when to move, the Greeks would look for a lighted-torch signal, to be given by a Greek in Troy who had pretended to turn traitor and desert. Signals were used often in ancient battles, most famously at Marathon (490 B.C.), when a Greek traitor in the hills flashed a shield in the sunlight to communicate with the Persians. In the clear skies of the Mediterranean, fire signals could be seen from far off. They were visible as smoke signals during the day and as beacons at night. Tests show that the signals were visible between mountaintops up to a distance of two hundred miles.

At the sign, the Greeks would row back rapidly to Troy. The final part of the plan required a few men inside Troy to open the city gate. These men might either have been Trojan traitors or Greeks who had sneaked into the city. With the emergency supposedly over, Troy's gatekeepers would not have proved difficult to overcome.

Compare the set of tricks by which the south Italian port city of Tarentum was betrayed in turn to Hannibal and then to the Romans. In 213 B.C. a pro-Carthaginian citizen of Tarentum arranged for Carthaginian soldiers to come back with him from a nighttime hunting expedition. The soldiers wore breastplates and held swords under their buckskins; they even carried a wild boar in front, to appear authentic. Once the city gate was opened to them, they slaughtered the guards, and Hannibal's army rushed in. Four years later, the Romans under Fabius Maximus recaptured the city by having a local girl seduce the commander of Hannibal's garrison. He agreed to guide Roman troops over the walls at night while Fabius's ships created a distraction at the harbor wall on the other side of town. Although these events took place a thousand years after the Trojan War, they could easily have been carried out with Bronze Age technology.

The Greek plan at Troy was to trick the enemy into dropping his guard. It worked: the Trojans relaxed. At that point, one Greek inside the city lit a signal fire to bring the Greek fleet back and then others opened a gate.

The island of Tenedos lies about seven miles (six nautical miles) from the Trojan Harbor. The Greeks might have moored their ships in one of the sheltered coves on the island's east coast, near Troy but out of sight. At a rate of about five knots (about that of a thirty-two-oared Scandinavian longship traveling one hundred miles) they could have covered the distance in little more than an hour. That is, in daylight; the trip would no doubt have taken longer at night. But the *Sack of Ilium* claims it was a moonlit night and, anyhow, Bronze Age armies knew how to march by night. So the trip from Tenedos took perhaps no more than two hours. From the Trojan Harbor it was another five miles by land to Troy. It was nighttime and the road was primitive but the Greeks knew it well. They could have covered the distance in three hours. Athenian sources claim the month was Thargelion, roughly modern May. At that time of year, sunrise at Troy is 5:30–6 A.M., sunset 8–8:30 P.M. If the Greeks left Tenedos at, say, 9 P.M., and if everything went without a hitch, they would have arrived at Troy between 2 and 3 A.M., that is, about three hours before sunrise. A forced march may have gotten the Greeks to Troy an hour or so earlier.

To carry out their plan, the Greeks had had to infiltrate a small group of soldiers into the city. But they did not need the Trojan Horse to do so. Odysseus had already sneaked in and out of the city on two separate occasions shortly before. People came and went through the gates of Troy throughout the period of the war, making it all the easier now to trick the gatekeepers into letting in a handful of disguised Greek warriors.

Once inside the city, all the Greeks needed was arms, which a determined man would not have found difficult to get. Hardened commandos could easily have overpowered a few Trojan soldiers and taken their shields and spears.

Ancient cities under attack were also often betrayed from within. Not even weapons could stand up to "dissatisfaction and treachery," says an Akkadian poem. Troy too no doubt had its share of people who preferred dealing with the Greeks to prolonging the misery of war.

But if the Trojan Horse was not strictly necessary to the Greek's plan, it might well nonetheless have been part of it. The Trojan Horse would certainly inspire more confidence if ancient history recorded another occasion on which a similar ruse was employed. But how could it? The Trojan Horse was such a famous trick that it could be used only once.

According to Homer, it was Odysseus who conceived of the idea and Epeius, known otherwise as the champion boxer at the funeral games of Patroclus, who built the Horse. Certainly, the Greeks had the technology to build it. Ancient fleets usually sailed with shipwrights because wooden ships constantly need repairs, and Linear B texts refer both to shipwrights and carpenters as professions. There would have been no shortage of men in the Greek camp to do the job.

And there would have been no question about whether a statue of an animal would catch the Trojan king's fancy. Bronze Age monarchs liked animal imagery. A Babylonian king of the 1300s B.C., for example, had specifically asked the pharaoh for a gift of realistic figures of wild animals, with lifelike hides, made by Egyptian carpenters. But which animal should the Greeks build at Troy? A Trojan Dog would have been insulting; a Trojan Lion, frightening; a Trojan Bull or Cow would have thrown Greek cattle-raids in the enemy's teeth. But a horse symbolized war, privilege, piety, popularity, and Troy itself.

Horses are expensive, and in the Bronze Age they were usually used in military context, rarely as farm animals. Rulers of the era often sent horses as a gift between kings, while ordinary Trojans might cherish a figure of a horse. In the Late Bronze Age, horse figurines, made of baked clay, were collected throughout the Near East. Excavators recently found a clay model of a horse in Troy of the 1200s B.C. Finally, there was the religious connotation: as a votive offering, the Horse was all but an admission of Greek war guilt, a symbolic submission to the gods of the horse-taming Trojans.

The Horse would have been used to smuggle a small number of Greek soldiers into the city, but the chances of detection were very high. Although the traditional story of the Trojan Horse cannot be ruled out, it seems more probable that, if the Horse did exist, it was empty. There were simpler and less dangerous ways of smuggling soldiers into the city. The horse's main value to the Greeks was not as a transport but as a decoy, a low-tech ancestor of the phantom army under General Patton that the Allies used in 1944 to trick the Germans into expecting the D-day invasion in the area of Pas de Calais instead of Normandy.

Epic tradition has some Trojans accepting the Horse as a genuine sign that the Greeks had given up while others remain skeptical. The debate lasted all day, according to Vergil, or three days, according to Homer. The *Sack of Ilium* identifies three camps: those who wanted to burn the Horse, those who wanted to throw it down from the walls, and those who wanted to consecrate it to Athena. The length of the debate was in direct proportion to the stakes. The safety of the city as well as individual careers were hanging on the decision.

Vergil makes much of Priam's daughter Cassandra, an opponent of the Horse who enjoyed the gift of prophecy but suffered the curse of being ignored. This story does not appear in Homer or what we have of the Epic Cycle. One person who does feature in the tradition is the Trojan priest Laocöon, a staunch opponent of the Greeks who wanted to destroy the Horse. In Vergil, the debate over the Horse comes to an end when Laocöon and his sons are strangled by two snakes from the sea. The *Sack of Ilium* apparently places this event after the Horse had already been brought into town. Surely the snakes are symbolic; surely Laocöon and his boys were killed not by a sea-snake but by a member of the pro-Greek faction, and so, therefore, by someone perceived as a tool of a signifier of evil like a snake.

Laocöon's snakes may well be rooted in Anatolian Bronze Age religion, local lore of the Troad, or both. Hittite literature made the snake a symbol of chaos and the archenemy of the Storm God. It makes sense for a snake to foil the Storm God's servant, the Trojan priest who was trying to save his city. The Troad, meanwhile, is rich in fossil remains of Miocene animals such as mastodons and pygmy giraffes, and these objects might have made their way into myth. For example, an Iron Age Greek painter probably used a fossilized animal skull as a model for a monster whom Heracles is supposed to have defeated on the shore of Troy. So the story of Laocöon's murder by monsters from the sea may well have Trojan roots.

Laocöon's fate convinced Aeneas and his followers to leave town; they withdrew to Mount Ida in time to escape the Greek onslaught. Vergil famously tells a different story, in which Aeneas stays in Troy, fights the Greeks, and then at last escapes the burning city while carrying his elderly father, Anchises, on his back. But the account in the *Sack of Ilium*, which records Aeneas's departure, strikes a more credible note. Aeneas would not have been eager to die for Priam, a king who had never given Aeneas the honor that he felt he was due. His homeland was south of the city, in the valley of Dardania beside the northern slopes of Mount Ida. What better place to regroup if Aeneas believed that Troy was doomed?

Helen played a double game. She had helped Odysseus on his mission to Troy and learned of his plan of the Horse. Now she tried to coax the Greeks out of the Horse, but Odysseus kept them silent—or perhaps the Horse was empty. Helen is supposed to have gone back home that night and prepared herself for the inevitable. She had her maids arrange her clothes and cosmetics for her reunion with Menelaus.

Whether or not there was a Trojan Horse and whether or not the Trojans brought it into town and dedicated it to Athena, it is easy to imagine them celebrating the end of the war. They treated themselves to a night of partying, according to the *Sack of Ilium*. It was now, when the Trojans were occupied, that Sinon supposedly gave the prearranged torch signal. Once watchers on Tenedos saw it, the expedition to take Troy rowed rapidly back to the mainland.

Surprise, night, and Trojan drunkenness would have given the Greeks substantial advantages, but taking Troy would require hard fighting nonetheless. Experienced warriors, the Trojans would have scrambled quickly after their initial shock. If the battle began in darkness, it no doubt would have continued well into the daylight hours. The epic tradition offers a few details of Trojan resistance. The Greek Meges, leader of the Epeans of Elis, was wounded in the arm by Admetus son of Augeias. Another Greek, Lycomedes, took a wound in the wrist from the Trojan Agenor son of Antenor.

But what the tradition highlights, of course, is Greek victory. Admetus and Agenor, for instance, did not savor their successes, because that same night one was killed by Philoctetes and the other by Neoptolemus. A Greek named Eurypylus son of Euaemon killed

Priam's son Axion. Menelaus began his revenge by killing Helen's new husband, Deïphobus, brother of Paris and son of Priam. But the Greek known for scoring the most kills in the sack of Troy is Achilles' son, Neoptolemus. Among his victims, besides Agenor, were Astynous, Eion, and Priam himself, either at the altar of Zeus—no doubt the Storm God, where the Trojan king had sought shelter—or, as some say, at the doors of the palace because, not wanting to violate a god's altar, Neoptolemus was careful to drag his victim away first.

As for the Trojan women, tradition assigns Andromache to Neoptolemus and Cassandra to Agamemnon. Locrian Ajax had attempted to seize Cassandra but violated the altar of Athena or a Trojan goddess, which made the Greeks loath to reward him and thereby earn divine enmity. Prudent Bronze Age warriors knew better than to insult an enemy's god. For example, when Hittite King Shuppiluliuma I conquered the city of Carchemish around 1325 B.C. he sacked the town but kept all his troops away from the temples of Kubaba and Lamma. He bowed to the goddesses instead.

Priam's daughter Polyxena was, according to the *Sack of Ilium*, slaughtered at the tomb of Achilles as an offering to the hero's ghost. Little Astyanax, Hector's son, was murdered by Odysseus— thrown from the walls, in one version—lest he grow up and seek vengeance.

And then there was Helen. The *Little Iliad* states that Menelaus found her at home, in the house of Deïphobus. Menelaus's sword was drawn to seek vengeance on the agent of his humiliation and suffering, but Helen had merely to undrape her breasts to change his mind. It is the sort of story that we can only wish is true.

So much for the epic tradition. What do other Bronze Age texts and the archaeological excavations tell us about the sack of Troy? Bronze Age documents show that however brutal the sack of Troy may have been, it would have conformed to the laws of war. Cities that did not surrender would, if they were captured, be destroyed. This rule goes as far back as the first well-documented interstate conflict, the border wars between the two Sumerian city-states of Lagash and Umma between 2500 and 2350 B.C.

When the Greeks sacked the city, they put Troy to the torch. Archaeology discloses that a savage fire destroyed the settlement level known as Troy VIi (formerly called Troy VIIa). Blackened wood, white calcined stone, and heaps of fallen building material were found in a thick destruction layer of ash and dirt about twenty inches to six feet deep. The inferno can be dated, according to the best estimate, sometime between 1230 and 1180 B.C., more likely between 1210 and 1180.

The flames must have spread fast. One house in the lower city tells the story: a bronze figurine, as well as some gold and silver jewelry, was left abandoned on the floor of a room. The inhabitants had fled in panic.

Imagine Troy's narrow streets clogged, and imagine the rolling cries of disoriented refugees, the wailing of children; the growls and snorts, bleating, high-pitched squeals, and relentless howls and barks of terrified barnyard animals (in the Bronze Age, typically kept within the town walls at night). Imagine too the clatter of arms, the clang and whistle of cold bronze, the soft sound of blood squirting onto paving stones, the cheers of the avengers, the whiz of javelins in flight, the reverberation of a spear that has found its mark, the holler and thud of street fighting, the surge of wails and curses, the gush and choking of pain, and much of it muffled by a fire burning fast enough to sound like a downpour.

Archaeology draws a picture that is consistent with a sack of Troy. Outside the doorway of a house on the citadel, for example, a partial human male skeleton was discovered. Was he a householder, killed defending his property? Other human bones have been found in the citadel, scattered and unburied. There is also a fifteen-year-old girl buried in the lower town; the ancients rarely buried people within the city limits unless an attack was preventing them from going to a cemetery outside town. It was even rarer to leave human skeletons unburied—another sign of the disaster that had struck Troy.

Two bronze spear points, three bronze arrowheads, and two partially preserved bronze knives have been found in the citadel and lower town. One of the arrowheads is of a type known only in the Greek mainland in the Late Bronze Age. The lower town has also yielded a cache of 157 sling stones in three piles. Another supply of a dozen smooth stones, possibly sling stones, was found on the citadel, in a building beside the south gate that looked to the excavators like a possible arsenal or guardhouse.

None of this evidence proves beyond doubt that Troy was destroyed in a sack. The fire that ravaged the city could have been caused by accident and then been stoked by high winds. If Troy was destroyed by armed violence, were the Greeks responsible? The archaeological evidence is consistent with that explanation but does not prove it.

CONCLUSION

On the mountaintop, where the goats forage in the crevices between the rocks and the only sound beside their bleating is a sudden burst of wind in the wildflowers, the sky is the same shade of pale blue and gray as the eyes of the goddess Athena. That's when it happens: not during an afternoon plunge into one of the chilly pools of Ida, the mountain rich in springs, nor in the thickening darkness when the owls appear and the night's first bats take wing. Only here, on the heights, where the light rakes the treeless ridge, does he let the truth come out, and the truth is that he is no herdsman. Only then, when he relaxes his guard, does he remember that he is a soldier who knows the sound of javelins whirring through the air and the sight of the wounded men crawling on the plain.

Aeneas, son of Anchises, would surely like to stay on the mountain. The mountain is his mother. It was here long ago that Anchises slept with the luminous goddess of love. Aeneas grew up on Ida's slopes, hunting deer in the woods and careening down its trails on wild horses. He takes his bearings by the bees that pollinate its flowers and by the star that rises above it, by the Evening Star, Aphrodite herself, or Ishtar, as she was more likely known in the Troad. If anyone can lead him back, the goddess can, since she was a deity not only of love but of war.

If he must come down from Ida, Aeneas would choose to live in the Dardanian Valley that lies in its lap below. The mountain-sheltered valley is as rich as it is wide and well watered: kingdom enough for any man. A river runs through the middle of its grain fields, seemingly as far from the sea as a sinner's heart is far from the gods. But this is the Scamander River, and twenty miles downstream it once ran red with the blood of Achilles' victims. Ida's native son cannot stay in Dardania; Aeneas has to lead the survivors back home. All his life he has complained about his treatment by Priam and his sons, and now that they are gone, Aeneas is heir to the throne. On his broad shoulders lies the fate of Troy. Or so we may imagine him thinking one day, not long after the Greeks had left and the fires had died down in the ruins of the city.

Legend has it that Troy was completely destroyed, but in fact the city was soon rebuilt. The new Troy was once again a great center. It was not as rich or as grand as Priam's city and it was not inhabited by the same people. But there were sources of continuity, and none greater than Aeneas himself.

Epic tradition offers several versions of Aeneas' fate, from captivity under Neoptolemus in Greece, to triumph in Italy near the future site of Rome—after an amorous detour in Carthage. But the *Iliad* is clear. Achilles scoffs at Aeneas for wanting to replace Priam as king, when everyone knows that one of Priam's many sons will inherit the throne. But Poseidon knows better. As the god predicts of Troy after the war,

> *For Priam now, and Priam's faithless kind,*
> *At length are odious to the all-seeing mind;*
> *On great Aeneas shall devolve the reign,*
> *And sons succeeding sons the lasting line sustain.*

The way to the throne of Troy began on Mount Ida, where tradition says that Aeneas gathered together the refugees from the defeated city.

The refugees might have meditated on the irony of Troy's fate. For all their fury, the Greeks never surrounded the city or sealed it off from the outside world. They tried to storm Troy's walls but failed. Nor did pitched battle between armies led by heroes succeed in the conquest of Troy. Only the steady pressure of Greek raids on Troy's hinterland, which lay open to Greek sea power, bled the city white. And in its vulnerable state, Troy fell prey to a fatal act of espionage. It was cunning and not courage that killed Troy.

We in turn may reflect on the ironies of epic. Like a chronicle of the pharaohs or the annals of a Hittite king, the *Iliad* idealizes war. The focus is on divinely inspired heroes who carry out superhuman deeds and suffer only clean wounds. The Greeks crowd the stage and Troy is doomed, although the struggle is so grand that it takes ten years. Yet Homer is honest enough to hint at the real war of far shorter duration; a war of filth and disease, of attacks on civilians, and of ordinary men who died lonely deaths. Helen is not only a beautiful but also a light-fingered cause of war, since she made off with her husband's treasure as well as his honor, and the Greeks wanted the gold back. Besides, they were far more interested in capturing enemy women than in regaining Menelaus's runaway bride.

Both in his exaggerations and his honesty Homer is truer to the Bronze Age than is usually recognized. Bronze Age poets regularly inflate battlefield deeds, but other Bronze Age texts preserve the truth: a way of war that was sometimes low-intensity, often devious, and always squalid. Thanks both to oral tradition and also perhaps to non-Greek written sources, Homer preserves these truths even though Troy fell centuries before his lifetime.

As they returned to their ships from the ruins of Troy, the Greeks would have carried their wounded and the bodies of their dead, and driven a crowd of captive Trojans forward, with cartloads of booty following. The art of the Bronze Age shows many such lines of prisoners, naked as often as not, hands tied behind their backs or locked in wooden beams. Then the plunder and women had to be divided among the army. The chiefs, naturally, got first pick. Neoptolemus, for example, is said to have chosen Andromache, Hector's widow; the other heroes accepted his choice, no doubt glad to have satisfied his considerable ego. The sons of the late, great Athenian hero Theseus, Acamas and Demophon, were content to rescue their mother, Aethra; according to Athenian tradition, she had gone to Troy as Helen's lady-in-waiting. At least they were content according to one story; another version says that Agamemnon gave them "many gifts" as well.

Like many a conquering army, the Greeks fell out with each other as soon as the war was over. The immediate cause of the quarrel was the question of Locrian Ajax and his sacrilege against Athena or her Trojan equivalent, by having inadvertently taken a statue of her when he grabbed Cassandra from the goddess's temple. By violating the goddess's image, Locrian Ajax subjected the whole army to her vengeance. Agamemnon and Menelaus, brothers and now rivals, argued in front of the troops. Agamemnon wanted to put off their departure until he could make amends by carrying out a big sacrifice to Athena; Menelaus wanted to go home. The Greeks had already stoned Ajax, and Menelaus no doubt reminded the men of this punishment. Agamemnon said that wasn't enough.

No ancient army, in any period, would think of making a long journey having incurred the wrath of a god. But Menelaus, Diomedes, and Nestor sailed away with their men the next day anyhow. As Nestor later explained it, Athena's punishment had already started with the royal quarrel; the safest course seemed to be to get far away from Troy. Nestor reached Pylos without incident. Likewise, Diomedes made it home safely to Argos, and Neoptolemus went to his father's ancestral land, Phthia, which he had never seen before, having grown up on the island of Scyros. But he played it safe by avoiding the treacherous sea and traveling overland.

Locrian Ajax escaped Athena, only to run afoul of Poseidon, who let him survive a shipwreck only to drown the man for his blasphemy. Menelaus lost most of his ships in a storm and was blown off course to Egypt with the rest. By the time he finally reached Sparta, the news was waiting of his brother's fatal homecoming. When Agamemnon returned to Mycenae, he was murdered by his wife, Clytemnestra, and the lover whom she had taken in his absence, Aegisthus, who was engaged in a blood feud with Agamemnon.

The sons of Atreus were never lucky in love. Menelaus brought back his prize, Helen. The *Odyssey* depicts the couple reunited and ruling in Lacedaemon, surrounded by war-won trophies in the royal palace. They lived to celebrate the marriage of their daughter to Neoptolemus. So the king was certainly better off than his butchered brother. Yet Helen's practice of slipping drugs into Menelaus's wine suggests that not all was happy in the royal halls.

Odysseus took ten years before reaching home—no doubt another case of the Bronze Age expression for "a long time until finally." In the Bronze Age, being blown off course, being shipwrecked or marooned were not uncommon occurrences, so there is some plausibility in the outline of the *Odyssey*. When Odysseus at last reached Ithaca he found his enemies in charge of his household and battled them to restore his authority.

The tales of trouble in Mycenae and Ithaca perhaps offer a hint of the violence that in fact struck the Mycenaean palaces. Sometime around 1190/1180 B.C. a wave of destruction hit the major centers on the Greek mainland, including Pylos, Tiryns, Athens, and Mycenae itself. Archaeology shows that life continued in the lower towns but the palaces on the citadels were destroyed, and with them went a way of life that included luxury goods, manorial estates, and scribes keeping written records. Greek civilization continued but at a lower level of complexity and wealth.

A similar fate was in store for many of the citadels of Anatolia, Cyprus, Canaan, and Mesopotamia. Egypt weathered the storm but it felt its force nonetheless. Clearly, it was a disastrous time throughout the Bronze Age world of the Eastern Mediterranean and Near East.

The causes of this decline are unclear. Earthquakes appear to have played a role, but they were probably not the only source of trouble. Dynastic disputes, imperial overstretch in adventures like the Trojan War, bad harvests, peasant unrest, may all have contributed. In Anatolia, grain was scarce shortly before 1200 B.C., perhaps suggesting climate change that affected Greece as well.

There is only weak evidence for foreign invasion, whether by the Sea Peoples or the Dorians. The Dorians were Greek-speakers from northwestern Greece. Contrary to popular misconception, they did not come south until much later, so they could not have destroyed the Mycenaean palaces. But the Sea Peoples do fit chronologically. They attacked and destroyed the city of Ugarit around 1190 B.C. They seem to have played a role in the fall of the city of Hattusha around the same time, and they attacked Egypt but were driven back. They were more successful in Canaan, where they settled down as the people known later as the Philistines.

Who were the Sea Peoples? The answer is not yet clear, but we do know that they were a coalition, and there is good reason to think that some of them were Greeks. So, if the Sea Peoples sacked the Mycenaean palaces, they might better be thought of as a faction in a Greek civil war rather than as foreign invaders.

The Hittites, at any rate, had other problems besides the Sea Peoples. Well before the city of Hattusha was sacked, it suffered decline and depopulation. Parts of the Hittite Empire in southern and southeastern Anatolia had become separate kingdoms. Various branches of the Hittite ruling dynasties were enmeshed in intermittent feuds that sometimes turned very nasty. Although Hattusha fell, marking the end of the Hittites' great central Anatolian empire, the Hittite kingdoms in the south managed to survive for centuries more.

We are only beginning to understand why most of the palaces of the eastern Mediterranean were in ruins by not long after 1200 B.C. Future research should shed much new light on the matter. But whatever the truth was, it was probably as complex as the process that left most of the cities of Europe and Japan in ruins by 1945. Just as no single cause can explain World War II, so the Sea Peoples alone cannot explain the end of the palace civilization of the Bronze Age.

Archaeology shows that after the burning and probable sacking of Troy VIi, the city was reconstructed—and in no mean way. Wherever possible, old buildings were repaired and streets were repaved, but new structures went up as well. Troy VIj (formerly known as Troy VIIb1)—to use the archaeologists' ungainly name for this new Troy—was not poor. Gold and bronze jewels, an iron ax, and a carnelian seal have all been found there. And it is to this city, several generations later (ca. 1130 B.C.) that prehistoric Troy's only inscription may be dated, the married couple's seal referred to earlier.

Of course the new Troy was not as rich as the old one. Agriculture provides a clue here. While Priam's Troy produced wheat, Troy VIj subsisted on barley, a poorer grain, which ancient peoples usually fed to animals. And the new Troy was not inhabited by the same people—not after the deaths and deportations. So a new population emerged in Troy VIj: a mixture of old Trojans and newcomers from the Balkans.

Imagine Aeneas back again in Troy. He lives with the din of carpenters, stonemasons, and brick bakers. The dead have been buried, the rubble cleared, the stones replaced. Sheep and cattle have been herded to their pens within the walls. Libations have been poured to the gods.

From his half-built home on the citadel, one evening Aeneas might have looked out on the plain, a tawny sea of grain lying still in the pale blue light. Turning, he would see Poseidon's realm, a silvery ribbon stretching as far as the islands' walls. And as a brisk breeze of Boreas ruffled his hair, he might have looked down on the new town rising. With all the inevitable problems, Aeneas might have been proud of his role in lifting up Troy like a stone out of deep water, to use a Hittite expression. The lofty works of the gods, the peaks of Mount Ida and of Samothrace, would soon be replicated once again by the proud man-made towers of Troy.

GLOSSARY OF KEY NAMES

Achaeans Along with Argives and Danaans, one of the three main names used by Homer for the people we call Greeks.

Achilles Mythical king of Phthia and heroic warrior whose rage is at the heart of the *Iliad*.

Aeneas Mythical figure, son of Anchises and goddess Aphrodite, kinsman of Priam, fights in Trojan War; rules in rebuilt, postwar Troy.

Agamemnon Mythical king of Mycenae, and leader of Greek expedition against Troy.

Ahhiyawa Powerful kingdom referred to by Hittite texts, probably to be identified with the land of Homer's Achaeans.

Ajax son of Oïleus of Locris Mythical figure, an especially rough and impious Greek warrior at Troy, also known as "Lesser Ajax" and "Locrian Ajax."

Ajax son of Telamon of Salamis Mythical character, immensely strong if slow Greek warrior at Troy, also known as "Greater Ajax."

Akkadian Dominant language and culture of Mesopotamia, 2350–1900 B.C., and widespread in its influence throughout Bronze Age Near East.

Alaksandu King of Wilusa, ca. 1280 B.C., made alliance with Hittites; his name recalls Homer's Alexander (Paris).

Amazons Women warriors, referred to by Homer and in Greek myth, vaguely recalled by Iron Age women warriors of southern Russia.

Amenhotep II King of Egypt, 1427–1392 B.C., victorious general in Canaan, Syria, and Mesopotamia.

Amenhotep III King of Egypt, 1382–1344 B.C., reigned at height of New Kingdom's power.

Amyclae Town in Laconia, site of Menelaion (shrine of Helen and Menelaus), possible site of Bronze Age palace.

Andromache Mythical character, wife of Hector, afterward widowed and taken as war-prize by Greeks.

Antenor Mythical figure, pro-Greek Trojan.

Antimachus Mythical character, anti-Greek Trojan.

Apasa Probably the later Ephesus, capital of kingdom of Arzawa.

Argives See ACHAEANS.

Arzawa Kingdom in western Anatolia.

Attarissiya Raider from Ahhiyawa, cited in Hittite texts, who attacked Anatolia and Cyprus, ca. 1400 B.C.; possibly to be identified with Atreus of Greek myth.

Aulis Bronze Age (and later) harbor town in east-central Greece; according to Homer the embarkation point of the Greek expedition against Troy.

Beşik Bay Modern name of Trojan Harbor, about five miles southwest of site of city of Troy.

Boreas North wind.

Briseis Mythical princess of Lyrnessus, taken as war-prize by Achilles and appropriated by Agamemnon as compensation for Chryseis.

Bronze Age Era, ca. 3000–1100 B.C., in which bronze was the primary metal for tools and weapons; iron was rare and expensive but it was known.

Cadmus Mythical king of Thebes.

Calchas Mythical Greek seer at Aulis and Troy.

Canaan Region of city-states dominated by Egypt and contested by Hittites, stretching from modern Turkish-Syrian border to Gaza.

Cassandra Mythical figure, daughter of Priam, minor character in Homer, but in Vergil the important but ignored prophetess of Troy's ruin.

Catalog of Ships Lines in which Homer (*Iliad* 2.484–787) lists all the captains, kings, and countries taking part in the Trojan War.

Chryseis Mythical figure, daughter of priest Chryses of city of Chryse in southwestern Troad, taken as war-prize by Agamemnon.

cuneiform Early writing system, widely used in ancient Near East.

Cycnus Mythical character, king of town of Colonae on west coast of Troad, whose name recalls the historical figure Kukkunni, King of Wilusa.

Danaans See ACHAEANS.

Dardanian Valley Fertile region of middle Scamander River in Troad, mythical home of Aeneas.

Dardanians Mentioned in Egyptian text as Hittite allies who sent chariots to fight at Battle of Qadesh.

Deïphobus Mythical figure, Trojan prince who marries Helen after death of his brother, Paris.

Diomedes Mythical king of Argos, the youngest and one of the doughtiest Greek warriors at Troy.

Dolon Mythical figure, vain and incompetent Trojan spy, killed by Diomedes.

Eëtion Mythical king of Thebes-under-Plakos and father of Andromache, killed by Achilles.

Epic Cycle Ancient Greek epics *(Cypria, Aethiopis, Little Iliad, Sack of Ilium, The Returns)* describing Trojan War and aftermath: survives only in a few quotations.

Euphorbus Mythical figure, son of Panthous, young Trojan warrior specially trained in chariot fighting, wounds Patroclus severely.

Eurypylus Mythical figure, son of Telephus of Mysia, brings contingent to fight for Troy.

Gallipoli Fertile peninsula opposite the Troad, on northern shore of the Dardanelles.

Gilgamesh Popular ancient Near Eastern epic poem, ca. 2000 B.C. or earlier, originally in Akkadian but often translated.

Glaucus Mythical warrior, son of Hippolochus of Lycia, leading lieutenant of Trojan ally Sarpedon.

Hammurabi Babylonian king (1792–1750 B.C.), great warrior and codifier of law, conquered Mari.

Hattusha City in central Anatolia, Hittite capital.

Hattushilish I Great Hittite king, 1650–1620 B.C.

Hattushilish III Hittite king (reigned 1267–1237 B.C.), negotiated with Egypt and Ahhiyawa and fought western Anatolian rebel Piyamaradu.

Hector Mythical figure, son of Priam and Hecuba; Troy's crown prince and greatest warrior.

Hecuba Mythical character, wife of Priam and queen of Troy.

Helen Mythical figure, wife of King Menelaus of Lacedaemon; ran off with Trojan prince Paris, sparking the Trojan War.

Helenus Mythical character, brother of Hector and wise seer.

Hellenes In Homer, refers only to inhabitants of part of Thessaly in central Greece, but in Iron Age name for all Greeks.

Hisarlık "Fortified place" in Turkish, the modern-day name for the site of ancient Troy.

Hittites Also known as Hatti, between 1600s and ca. 1180 B.C. ruled an empire in Anatolia and Syria.

Ida Mountain in southern Troad, sacred to inhabitants.

Idomeneus Mythical character, king of Crete and great spearman, fought at Troy.

Ilion Another name for Troy; in early Greek, it was Wilion, but the "W" later dropped out. Source of name of the epic poem the *Iliad*.

Indo-European Language group and culture of its speakers, spread in ancient times from India to Britain; includes Greeks, Trojans, and Hittites.

Iphigenia Mythical character, daughter of Agamemnon and Clytemnestra, victim of human sacrifice at Aulis.

Iron Age First millennium B.C., when iron replaced bronze as main medium for tools and weapons.

Ishtar Near Eastern goddess of love, war, and fertility.

Ithaca Island off western Greece, legendary home of Odysseus.

Iyarri Anatolian god of war and plagues, known as an archer ("Lord of the Bow"), similar to Greek god Apollo.

Kukkunni King of Wilusa at some date before ca. 1280 B.C.

Kurunta Anatolian god, represented by stag; often a city's protector.

Lacedaemon Southern Greek region later also known as Laconia, kingdom of Menelaus and Helen.

Laocöon Mythical figure, anti-Greek priest of Troy, killed along with sons by sea monster.

Levant Region of southwestern Asia roughly equivalent to today's Israel, Jordan, Lebanon, Palestine, and Syria.

Levirate marriage Common ancient Near Eastern custom of a man marrying his deceased brother's widow.

Linear B Bronze Age Greek writing system used by Mycenaean scribes.

Luwian Indo-European language and culture of southern and western Anatolia, closely related to Hittite; possibly the language of Troy.

Lycia Region of southwestern Anatolia, probably the same area as the "Lukka Lands" of Hittite texts.

Lyrnessus In Homer, town in Troad conquered by the Greeks.

Machaon Along with brother Podalirius, mythical physician in Greek army at Troy.

Madduwatta Untrustworthy Hittite vassal in western Anatolia ca. 1400 B.C.

Mari City-state in northwestern Mesopotamia (modern Syria), well documented in decades before being sacked by Hammurabi in 1757 B.C.

Megiddo City in Canaan, site of major battle in 1479 B.C.

Melanippus Mythical character, son of Hicetaeon, fled hometown of Percote on the Dardanelles when the Greeks came; fought for Troy.

Memnon Mythical figure, prince of Aethiopia (possibly Nubia) and kinsman of Priam who brings contingent to fight for Troy.

Menelaus Mythical figure, husband of Helen and king of Lacedaemon as well as brother of Agamemnon.

Miletus City on Anatolia's Aegean coast, colonized by Minoans and Mycenaeans in turn.

Minoan The people and culture of Bronze Age Crete, at its height ca. 1800–1490 B.C.

Mira Western Anatolian state in Late Bronze Age; a successor state of Arzawa.

Murshilish II Hittite king, 1321–1295 B.C., conquered kingdom of Arzawa.

Mycenae Powerful city of mythical King Agamemnon; the adjective "Mycenaean" refers in general to Greeks and Greek civilization of the Late Bronze Age.

Mysia Region in northwestern Anatolia bordering the Troad.

Neoptolemus Mythical figure, son of Achilles and conqueror of Troy.

Nestor Mythical character, elderly king of Pylos and the Greeks' best counselor at Troy.

New Kingdom In both Egypt (1550–1075 B.C.) and Hatti (1400–1180) the Late Bronze Age era of expansion and empire.

Nubia Southern Nile region conquered by Egyptians, inhabited by black Africans, some of whom rose to high positions in New Kingdom Egypt.

Odysseus Mythical figure, king of Ithaca and most cunning and resourceful Greek warrior at Troy.

Old Babylonian literature Body of poetry and prose, ca. 2000–1600 B.C., whose influence may have reached as far as Homer.

Palaic Indo-European language of northern Anatolia, possibly language of Troy.

Palladium Mythical wooden statuette in Troy of goddess Athena.

Pandarus Mythical figure, son of Lycaon and great archer; Trojan ally.

Paris Mythical character, prince of Troy, seduced Helen and thereby caused the Trojan War; also known as Alexander, recalling Alaksandu, historical king of Wilusa.

Patroclus Mythical figure, son of Menoetius; Achilles' chief general and closest comrade.

Pellana Village in northern Laconia, site of Mycenaean buildings and tombs, possibly including palace of Helen and Menelaus.

Penthesilea Mythical figure, Thracian Amazon who brings contingent to fight for Troy.

Pergamos In Homer, citadel of Troy.

Philoctetes Mythical personage, Greek from Thessaly and mighty archer.

Piyamaradu Luwian raider who successfully defied Hittites in western Anatolia ca. 1250 B.C.; allied with Ahhiyawa.

Polites Mythical character, brother of Hector; fast runner and lookout.

Polydamas Mythical personage, son of Panthous of Troy; seer and shrewd tactician.

Priam Mythical figure, king of Troy.

Protesilaus Mythical figure, king of Phylace in Thessaly, first Greek killed at Troy.

Puduhepa Wife of Hattushilish III and one of the Hittites' most powerful queens.

Pylos In Homer, great kingdom in southwestern Greece, well-attested archaeologically by great palace, Linear B texts, and other remains.

Qadesh Canaanite city and site of great battle between Egyptians and Hittites, 1274 B.C.

Rameses II Long-reigning Egyptian King, 1279–1213 B.C., fought Hittites at Qadesh and later made peace with them.

Rameses III Egyptian king, 1184–1153 B.C., defeated Sea Peoples.

Sarpedon Mythical Lycian king and son of Zeus as well as commander of important allied contingent fighting for Troy; killed by Patroclus.

Scaean Gate In Homer, main gate of Troy.

Scamander River Main river of the Troad, flows from Mount Ida past Troy and into Dardanelles.

Sea Peoples Loose and shifting coalition, possibly including Greeks, that attacked eastern Mediterranean lands 1200–1100 B.C. and did great damage.

Shardana Mercenaries in and sometimes pirates against Egypt in 1200s–1100s B.C.

Shuppiluliuma I One of the strongest Hittite kings, 1344–1322 B.C., crushed Mitanni and rebuilt Hattusha.

Shuppiluliuma II Last Hittite king (1207–? B.C.), fought sea battles off Cyprus.

Simoeis River A river of the Troad that flows into the Scamander north of Troy.

Sinon Mythical figure, duplicitous Greek who tricks Trojans into accepting the Trojan Horse.

Storm God Sky god such as Zeus or Teshub, chief deity of Greeks and Anatolian peoples alike.

Taruisa A kingdom referred to in Hittite documents, possibly to be identified as Troy.

Tawagalawa Brother of king of Ahhiyawa, he aided Piyamaradu's rebellion in western Anatolia against the Hittites; possibly equivalent to Eteocles.

Telephus Mythical king of Mysia.

Teucer Mythical figure, brother of Ajax son of Telamon of Salamis, a great archer among the Greeks at Troy.

Thebes A major Mycenaean city in central Greece, destroyed violently ca. 1250 B.C.

Thebes-under-Plakos Trojan-allied city on Gulf of Adramyttium (Edremit); its site has not been identified.

Thersites Mythical character, malcontent and rabble-rouser in Greek army at Troy.

Tiryns Heavily fortified Bronze Age Greek city near Mycenae.

Tlepolemus Mythical figure, son of Heracles and king of Rhodes, fought with Greeks at Troy.

Troad Region of Troy, about 650 square miles in size.

Trojan Harbor See BEŞIK BAY.

Trojan Plain Broad area west of city of Troy, whose northern part was largely underwater in Bronze Age; in Homer, site of pitched battles of Trojan War.

Tukulti-Ninurta Assyrian king, 1244–1208 B.C.

Tyndareus Mythical personage, king of Lacedaemon, father of Helen.

Ugarit Wealthy and literate Canaanite city, commercial and naval power, Hittite ally, destroyed by Sea Peoples ca. 1187 B.C.

Ur Wealthy city in southern Mesopotamia.

Vergil Also known as Virgil, Roman poet (70–19 B.C.), author of the *Aeneid*, epic of Aeneas's struggles after the Trojan War.

Walmu Exiled king of Wilusa, ca. 1225 B.C.; vassal of Hittites.

wanax Linear B term for "king," perhaps recalled in Homer's use of term *anax* for Greece's leading king, Agamemnon.

Wilusa A kingdom referred to in Hittite documents, thought to be the Greek (W)ilion, that is, Troy.

NOTES

In citing ancient Greek and Roman authors, I follow the abbreviations of the standard reference work, the *Oxford Classical Dictionary*, 3rd edition (Oxford: Oxford University Press, 1999). I cite the titles of Greek and Latin works, however, in English translation. For Near Eastern texts I refer, wherever possible, to common English designations and to easily accessible English translations. EA ("El Amarna") designates a tablet of the Amarna Letters.

INTRODUCTION

1 makes it likely that the Trojan War indeed took place: I follow the arguments set forth by Joachim Latacz in his *Troy and Homer: Towards a Solution of an Old Mystery*, translated by Kevin Windle and Rosh Ireland (Oxford: Oxford University Press, 2004).

2 in its heyday: Manfred Korfmann, "Die Arbeiten in Troia/Wilusa 2003," *Studia Troica* 14 (2004): 17.

3 ninth year of the long conflict: For an argument that the *Iliad* is set in the ninth and not the tenth year of the Trojan War (as is usually thought), see Ernst Aumueller, "Das neunte Jahr. Ilias B 134-295-328," in Joachim Latacz and Heinrich Hettrich with Guenter Neumann, eds., *Wuerzburger Jahrbuecher fuer Die Altertumswissenschaft*, Neue Folge 21 (1996/97): 39–48.

7 "nine times and then a tenth": William L. Moran, ed. and trans., *The Amarna Letters* (Baltimore: Johns Hopkins University Press, 1992), EA 81, l. 24, p. 50, and p. 151 n. 6; cf. EA 82, l. 39, p. 52.

CHAPTER ONE: WAR FOR HELEN

13 Helen is dressed: My description is based on Homer, *Iliad* 3.121–71, 380–447; *Odyssey* 4 *passim*, 15.58, 104–8, 124–30, 171, and Ione My-

Ionas Shear, *Tales of Heroes: The Origins of the Homeric Texts* (New York: Aristide D. Caratzas, 2000), 61–72; Elizabeth Barber, *Prehistoric Textiles* (Princeton: Princeton University Press, 1991), 170–73. See the descriptions in Bettany Hughes, *Helen of Troy: Goddess, Princess, Whore* (London: Jonathan Cape, 2005), 42, 65–66, 109–11.

13 Hittite proverb: Billie Jean Collins, "Animals in Hittite Literature," in Collins, ed., *A History of the Animal World in the Ancient Near East* (Leiden: Brill, 2002), 243; Harry A. Hoffner Jr., "The Song of Hedammu," in *Hittite Myths*, 2nd edition (Atlanta: Scholars Press, 1998), 54.

14 Menelaus's palace: That palace has not yet been discovered, so I use features from other Bronze Age Greek palaces such as Pylos and Mycenae.

14 rich hills of Lacedaemon: A region better known today as Sparta, although technically Sparta is only a small part of Lacedaemon. Sparta was not a city yet in the Bronze Age, but the name is much better known than Lacedaemon, so it is used here.

14 the company sits: C. W. Shelmerdine, "Review of Aegean Prehistory VI: The Palatial Bronze Age of the Southern and Central Greek Mainland," *American Journal of Archaeology* 101:3 (1997): 578–80; reprinted with an addendum on the period 1997–99 in Tracey Cullen, ed., *Aegean Prehistory: A Review*, Supplement 1 to *American Journal of Archaeology* (Boston: Archaeological Institute of America, 2001), 370–72.

15 *Pari-zitis:* Calvert Watkins, "Troy and the Trojans," in Machteld J. Mellink, ed., *Troy and the Trojan War*, from a symposium held at Bryn Mawr College, October 1984 (Bryn Mawr, Pa.: Bryn Mawr College, 1986), 57.

15 "Trojan": Michael Ventris and John Chadwick, *Documents in Mycenaean Greek*, 2nd edition (Cambridge, England: Cambridge University Press, 1973), PY 57, p. 190; cf. pp. 103–5.

15 "Trojan Woman": Ventris and Chadwick, *Documents in Mycenaean Greek*, PY 143, pp. 258–59; cf. pp. 103–5.

15 "Lacedaemonius": His father was Cimon son of Miltiades, a leading politician of classical Athens. See J. K. Davies, *Athenian Propertied Families 600–300 B.C.* (Oxford: Clarendon Press, 1971), 306.

16 not that he was fooled: *Odyssey* 4.264.

17 he was no-nonsense: *Iliad* 3.213–15.

17 his rival Paris: *Iliad* 3.54, 393–95.

17 "feeble" or "despicable": For example, James K. Hoffmeier, "The Gebel

Barka Stele of Thutmose III," and K. A. Kitchen, "The Battle of Qadesh—
The Poem, or Literary Record," in W. W. Hallo, ed., *The Context of Scripture: Canonical Compositions from the Biblical World*, vol. 2 (Leiden: Brill, 2000), 16, 33.

17 "soft spearman": *Iliad* 17.588.

17 the Greek historian Herodotus: Hdt 1.4.1.

17 Near Eastern kings proclaim in their inscriptions: For the items in this paragraph, see James K. Hoffmeier, "The Memphis and Karnak Steleae of Amenhotep II," in Hallo, ed. *Context of Scripture*, vol. 2, p. 20; K. A. Kitchen, "First Beth Shean Stela, Year 1," in ibid., 25; K. A. Kitchen, "Karnak, Campaign Against the Hittites," undated, in ibid., 28; Richard H. Beal "The Ten Year Annals of Great King Muršili II of Hatti," in ibid., 84; Itamar Singer, "Treaty Between Šupiluliuma and Aziru," in ibid., 93–94; Douglas Frayne, "Rim-Sin," in ibid., 253; Douglas Frayne, "Iahdun-Lim," in ibid., 260.

18 A Hittite king says: Murshilish II (r. ca. 1321–1295 B.C.); see Beal, "Ten Year Annals," in Hallo, ed., *Context of Scripture*, vol. 2, pp. 82–83.

18 example from Canaan in the 1300s B.C.: Moran, *Amarna Letters*, EA 250, ll. 15–27, p. 303.

18 king of Troy, Alaksandu: Gary Beckman, "Treaty Between Muwattalli II of Hatti and Alaksandu of Wilusa," in *Hittite Diplomatic Texts*, 2nd edition (Atlanta: Scholars Press, 1996), 87–93.

18 "soldier servant": On the expression, see J. D. Hawkins, "Tarkasnawa King of Mira," *Anatolian Studies* 48 (1998): 14. For the alliance between the Hittites and Wilusa (Troy), see Beckman, "Treaty," in *Hittite Diplomatic Texts*, 87–93.

19 Cadmus: The reinterpretation of this letter was announced by Frank Starke in summer 2003, but a full scholarly version has not yet been published. See Frank Starke, "Ein Keilschrift-Brief des Königs von Theben/Ahhijawa (Griechenland) an den König des Hethitischen Reiches aus dem 13. Jh. v. Chr." handout, August 2003, and Michael Siebler, "In Theben Ging's Los," *Frankfurter Allgemeine Zeitung*, August 12, 2003, p. 31, http://www.faz.net/s/RubF7538E273FAA4006925CC 36BB8AFE338/Doc~EC6CFECB6D44B4344B70010A6675AF6A3~ ATpl~Ecommon~Scontent.html. For an argument against the thesis that the Hittite document reveals an ancestor of a king of Ahhiyawa named Kadmos, see Joshua T. Katz, "Review of Joachim Latacz's *Troy and Homer: Towards a Solution of an Old Mystery*, Version 1.0, December

2005, Princeton/Stanford Working Papers in Classics, http://www
.princeton.edu/~pswpc/pdfs/katz/120503.pdf.

19 Tawagalawa: He appears in a document known as the Tawagalawa Letter or Piyamaradu Letter. See the discussion with translated excerpts in
Trevor Bryce, *Letters of the Great Kings of the Ancient Near East: The
Royal Correspondence of the Late Bronze Age* (New York: Routledge, 2003),
199–212. An English translation of the letter is available online (as "The
Piyama-radu Letter") at http://www.hittites.info/translations.aspx?
text=translations/historical%2fPiyama-radu+Letter.html.

19 Walmu: Gary Beckman, "Letter from a King of Hatti to an Anatolian
Ruler," in *Hittite Diplomatic Texts*, 145.

20 "For beauteous Helen": *Iliad* 3.70.

21 Aeschylus: Aeschylus, *Agamemnon* 687–89.

21 In Hittite society it was possible for a man to marry: Trevor Bryce,
Life and Society in the Hittite World (Oxford: Oxford University Press,
2002), 124.

21 the same may have been true for Greece: Shear, *Tales of Heroes*, 139–40.

23 "How would the sons of Troy": *Iliad* 6.441–43.

24 Queen Puduhepa: See Ekrem Akurgal, *The Hattian and Hittite Civilizations* (Ankara: Republic of Turkey Ministry of Culture, 2001), 101–2;
Trevor Bryce, *The Kingdom of the Hittites* (Oxford: Clarendon Press,
1998), 315–20; Bryce, *Life and Society*, 13–14, 136–37, 174–75.

24 "prizes": For example, *Iliad* 1.185.

25 a woman without a husband: Moran, *Amarna Letters*, e.g., EA 90, ll.
36–47, p. 163.

25 Madduwatta married off his daughter to King Kupanta-Kurunta: Gary
Beckman, "Indictment of Madduwatta," in *Hittite Diplomatic Texts*,
§§16–17, p. 157.

26 "You have become a wolf": Gary Beckman, "Hittite Proverbs," in
Hallo, ed., *Context of Scripture*, vol. 1, p. 215; Harry A. Hoffner Jr., *The
Laws of the Hittites: A Critical Edition* (Leiden: Brill, 1997) §37, p. 44,
plus commentary, 186–87; Bryce, *Life and Society*, 126.

26 Adultery: Hoffner, *Laws of the Hittites*, §197, p. 156; Bryce, *Life and Society*, 128.

26 Zannanza: Bryce, *Kingdom of the Hittites*, 193–99. The Pharaoh Ay
maintained his innocence but he was the chief suspect.

27 Thucydides dismisses this story: Thuc. 1.9.3.

27 war as a lawsuit before the gods: Th. P. J. Van den Hout, "Bellum Ius-

tum, Ius Divinum: Some Thoughts About War and Peace in Hittite Anatolia," in *Grotiana*, New Series 12–13 (1991–92 [1994]): 26.

27 Hattushilish I (1650–1620 B.C.), whose armies plundered: P. H. J. Houwink ten Cate, "The History of Warfare According to Hittite Sources: The Annals of Hattusilis I (Part II)," *Anatolica* 11 (1984): 49.

28 "manly deeds": For example, the ancient title of what is now commonly referred to as the "Comprehensive Annals" of King Murshilish II was "The Manly Deeds of Murshilish"; see Beal, "Ten Year Annals," in Hallo, ed., *Context of Scripture*, vol. 2, p. 82.

28 seven thousand Hittite subjects were transplanted: Tawagalawa Letter §9.

28 King Zimri-Lin of Mari: Barber, *Prehistoric Textiles*, 27–28; cf. W. Heimpel, *Letters to the King of Mari: A New Translation, with Historical Introduction, Notes, and Commentary* (Winona Lake, Ind.: Eisenbrauns, 2003), 27 85, p. 440.

28 "extremely beautiful" female cupbearers: Moran, *Amarna Letters*, EA 369, ll. 15–23, p. 366.

28 "captives": Ventris and Chadwick, *Documents in Mycenaean Greek*, PY 16, p. 161; cf. pp. 156, 579.

28 Herodotus commented: Hdt. 1.3–5.

28 when an ant is struck: Moran, *Amarna Letters*, EA 252, ll., 16–22.

CHAPTER TWO: THE BLACK SHIPS SAIL

31 a big man, healthy and muscular: This hypothetical description of Agamemnon's body, clothing, and arms is based on Homer and the royal skeletons of Mycenae. See Yiannis Tzedakis and Holley Martlew, eds., *Minoans and Mycenaeans: Flavours of Their Time* (Athens: Production Kapon Editions, 1999), 220–27.

32 "opener of canals": Frayne, "Iahdun-Lim," in Hallo, ed., *Context of Scripture*, vol. 2, p. 260.

33 "scepter-bearing king": *Iliad* 1.279.

33 symbol of power in Sumer: J. S. Cooper, "Enmetana," in *Reconstructing History from Ancient Inscriptions: The Lagash-Umma Border Conflict*, vol. 2, fasc. 1 in *Sources from the Ancient Near East* (Malibu, Calif.: Undena Publications, 1983), §v, p. 50.

33 cooling their heels on rocky Ithaca: *Odyssey* 24.118–19.

34 "of the great war cry": *Iliad* 5.855.

34 ghee-and-honey paste: A. K. Grayson, "Erishum I," in *Assyrian Royal*

Inscriptions, vol. 1, *From the Beginning to Ashur-resha-ishi* (Wiesbaden: Otto Harrassowitz, 1972), 7.62 and n. 36, p. 10.

34 prison or mutilation: Heimpel, *Letters to the King of Mari*, 27 161, p. 467; A.486+, p. 508; 26 282, p. 283; 26 257, p. 276.

34 to follow on foot while they rode in their chariots: As Ahmose son of Abana followed three pharaohs in the 1500s B.C.; see Miriam Lichtheim, "The Autobiography of Ahmose Son of Abana," in *Ancient Egyptian Literature: A Book of Readings*, vol. 2, *The New Kingdom* (Berkeley: University of California Press, 1976), 11–15, esp. 12.

35 "sacker of cities": For example, *Odyssey* 8.3.

35 Attarissiya: See Beckman, "Indictment of Madduwatta," in *Hittite Diplomatic Texts*, 153–60.

35 Piyamaradu: See note above on Tawagalawa.

35 Linear B tablets refer: For the points in this paragraph, see Thomas G. Palaima, "Mycenaean Militarism from a Textual Perspective: Onomastics in Context: *Lāwos, Dāmos, Klewos*," in Robert Laffineur, ed., *Polemos: Le Contexte Guerrier en Égée à l'âge du Bronze*, vol. 2, *in Aegaeum* 19 (1999): 367–80.

36 "the infantry and the chariotry": See, e.g., Gary Beckman, "Letter of Hattusili III of Hatti to Kadashman-Enlil II of Babylon," in *Hittite Diplomatic Texts*, 23 §7, p. 141; Itamar Singer, "Mursili's 'Fourth' Plague Prayer to the Assembly of Gods (Arranged by Localities)," in *Hittite Prayers* (Leiden: Brill, 2002), 13 §11, p. 67.

37 chain of beacon fire messages: Aeschylus, *Agamemnon* 293.

37 the tale of Iphigenia is preserved in other sources: It is in the Epic Cycle, in the *Cypria*.

37 "priestess of the winds": Ventris and Chadwick, *Documents in Mycenaean Greek*, 127, 304.

39 the galley: Ugarit also had a navy (as did Egypt and the Minoans) and it is possible that it too had galleys, perhaps even before the Greeks. See Elisha Linder, "Naval Warfare in the El-Amarna Age," in D. J. Blackman, ed., *Marine Archaeology*, Proceedings of the Twenty-third [sic] Symposium of the Colston Research Society Held in the University of Bristol April 4th to 8th, 1971 (London: Archon Books, 1973), 317–25; Paul Johnstone, *The Sea-Craft of Prehistory*, prepared for publication by Seán McGrail (Cambridge, Mass.: Harvard University Press, 1980), 79–82.

39 lion, griffin, or snake: The Minoans decorated their ships thus in the

Acrotiri frescoes (pre–ca. 1625 B.C.); see L. Kontorli-Papadopoulou, "Fresco-Fighting: Scenes as Evidence for Warlike Activities in the LBA Aegean," *Polemos*, vol. 2, p. 333.

40 "get there firstest with the mostest": Confederate cavalry General Nathan Bedford Forrest.

40 the whip and the stick: Steve Vinson, *The Nile Boatman at Work* (Mainz: von Zabern, 1998), 132.

40 sail weavers: F. Tiboni, "Weaving and Ancient Sails: Structural Changes to Ships as a Consequence of New Weaving Technology in the Mediterranean Late Bronze Age," *Nautical Archaeology* 34:1 (2005): 127–30.

40 It took six months: J. R. Steffy, as cited in T. G. Palaima, "Maritime Matters in the Linear B Tablets," *Thalassa: L'Égée Prehistorique et la Mer*, in *Aegaeum* 7 (1991): 288.

40 "Famous Ship" and "Fine Sailing": "Nausikles" and "Euplous" in Ventris and Chadwick, *Documents in Mycenaean Greek*, 95, 97; Palaima, "Maritime Matters," 284.

41 Ugarit was said in 1187 B.C.: J. Hoftijzer and W. H. Van Soldt, "Appendix: Texts from Ugarit Pertaining to Seafaring," in S. Wachsmann, *Seagoing Ships and Seamanship in the Bronze Age Levant* (College Station: Texas A&M University Press, 1998), 336 = M. Dietrich, O. Loretz, and J. Sanmartín, *The Cuneiform Alphabetic Texts from Ugarit, Ras Ibn Hani and Other Places: (KTU: second, enlarged edition)* 2 (Münster: Ugarit-Verlag, 1995), 47.

41 "who knock me far off my path": *Iliad* 2.132–33.

42 Pharaonic Egypt used merchant ships: Donald B. Redford, *The Wars in Syria and Palestine of Thutmose III* (Leiden: Brill, 2003), 204–5; James K. Hoffmeier, "Military: Materiel," in Donald B. Redford, ed., *Oxford Encyclopedia of Ancient Egypt*, vol. 2 (New York: Oxford University Press, 2001), 410.

42 found fruits on the trees: John A. Wilson, "The Asiatic Campaigns of Thut-Mose III, Subsequent Campaigns: Fifth Campaign," in J. B. Pritchard, *Ancient Near Eastern Texts Relating to the Old Testament*, revised edition (Princeton: Princeton University Press, 1969), 239.

43 "Then launch": *Iliad* 1.478–82.

44 "cast a glance": Th. P. J. Van den Hout, "Apology of Hattušili III," in Hallo, ed., *Context of Scripture*, vol. 1, p. 200.

44 "although they inhabited the lowlands they were not sea-goers": Thuc. 1.7.

45 "knew how to make, with his hands": *Iliad* 5.60–61.

45 "Thy father's skill, O Phereclus! was thine": *Iliad* 5.60–64.

45 "well-balanced ships": *Iliad* 5.62.

46 "the border of the sea": Th. P. J. Van den Hout, "The Proclamation of Telepinu," in Hallo, ed., *Context of Scripture*, vol. 1, p. 194.

46 "filled the streets with widows": *Iliad* 5.642.

46 Ammurapi: Hoftijzer and Van Soldt, "Appendix: Texts from Ugarit," RS 1.1, RS 20.238, pp. 343–44.

48 "horse-nourishing": See, e.g., *Iliad* 2.287.

CHAPTER THREE: OPERATION BEACHHEAD

49 "Behold, the troops and chariots": Itamar Singer, "Treaty Between Muršili and Duppi-Tešub," in Hallo, ed., *Context of Scripture*, vol. 2, p. 97.

50 Shuppiluliuma II: Harry A. Hoffner Jr., "The Hittite Conquest of Cyprus: Two Inscriptions of Suppiluliuma II," in Hallo, ed., *Context of Scripture*, vol. 1, p. 193.

50 "Nations on nations fill": *Iliad* 2.808–10.

50 the historian Thucydides: Thuc. 1.11.1.

51 Hittite king told his young Babylonian counterpart: A. L. Oppenheim, "A Letter from the Hittite King," in *Letters from Mesopotamia* (Chicago: University of Chicago Press, 1967), 145–46.

52 the crushing embrace of an enemy siege: Houwink ten Cate, "Annals of Hattusilis I," 66.

52 held Priam and his people closer: *Iliad* 4.45.

52 "iron heart": *Iliad* 24.521.

52 No one in the region was more blessed: *Iliad* 24.546.

52 "border guards" and "watchmen": See, e.g., Beckman, "Indictment of Madduwatta," in *Hittite Diplomatic Texts*, 29, 157.

52 "Little Gnat": J. M. Sasson, *The Military Establishments at Mari*, no. 3 of *Studia Pohl* (Rome: Pontifical Biblical Institute, 1969), 38.

52 "coastal watchers": Ventris and Chadwick, *Documents in Mycenaean Greek*, PY 56, p. 189; cf. p. 544.

53 no, two hundred!: *Iliad* 8.228–34.

54 Halizones from Halube: Watkins, "Troy and the Trojans," in Mellink, ed., *Troy and the Trojan War*, 52–55.

54 Alaksandu Treaty: Beckman, "Treaty Between Muwattalli II of Hatti and Alaksandu of Wilusa," in *Hittite Diplomatic Texts*, 87–93.

54 repay each gift with another gift: *Odyssey* 24.284–85.

55 stripped his kingdom of silver: Miriam Lichtheim, "The Kadesh Battle Inscriptions of Rameses II: The Poem," in *Ancient Egyptian Literature*, vol. 2, p. 64.

55 "Such clamors rose": *Iliad* 4.437–38.

55 fought by national unit, as the Greeks did: *Iliad* 2.362.

56 "happy with words": Heimpel, *Letters to the King of Mari*, 26 366, p. 321.

56 Hana warriors: Heimpel, *Letters to the King of Mari*, A.486+, p. 507.

56 "Death is the worst": *Iliad* 15.494–99.

56 Hittite soldiers: Billie Jean Collins, "The First Soldiers' Oath" and "The Second Soldiers' Oath," in Hallo, ed., *Context of Scripture*, vol. 1, pp. 165–68.

57 "Ah! would the gods": *Iliad* 4.288–89.

57 "Inglorious Argives!": *Iliad* 4.242–43.

57 Storm God of the Army: Beckman, "Treaty Between Muwattalli II of Hatti and Alaksandu of Wilusa," in *Hittite Diplomatic Texts*, §20, p. 92; H. Craig Melchert, ed., *The Luwians*, vol. 68 of *Handbuch der Orientalistik* (Leiden: Brill, 2003), 221.

57 pen them up like pigs in a sty: A Hittite expression; see Van den Hout, "Apology of Hattušili III," 203.

57 "Bitter cries": J. S. Cooper, *The Curse of Agade* (Baltimore: Johns Hopkins University Press, 1983), ll. 166–69, p. 59.

59 "horses of the sea": *Odyssey* 4.708.

59 as an ancient Athenian general would note: Thuc. 4.10.5.

60 a style mentioned in Homer: *Iliad* 10.261.

60 "swift-footed": See, e.g., *Iliad* 1.58; cf. the discussion in Robert Drews, *The End of the Bronze Age: Changes in Warfare and the Catastrophe c. 1200 BC* (Princeton: Princeton University Press, 1993), 141–47, 211.

61 "send me stallions!": Adapted from Beckman, "Letter from Hattušili III of Hatti to Kadasman-Enlil II of Babylon," in *Hittite Diplomatic Texts*, §17, p. 143.

61 he reared some of his horses: *Iliad* 24.279–80.

61 Amenhotep II: Miriam Lichtheim, "The Great Sphinx Stela of Amenhotep II at Giza: The Narration," in *Ancient Egyptian Literature*, vol. 2, p. 42.

61 "a dispersed battle": *Iliad* 15.329, 510.

61 "how impossible it is": Thuc. 4.10.5.

62 Phrontis son of Onetor: *Odyssey* 3.279–83.

62 half its length up onto the beach: *Odyssey* 13.113–15.

62 Euphorbus son of Panthous: *Iliad* 16.811; cf. 3.146.

63 lion, bulls, or falcons: Thera-fresco warships are painted with hunting lions as emblems. See Nanno Marinatos, *Art and Religion in Thera: Reconstructing a Bronze Age Society* (Athens: D. I. Mathioulakis, 1994), 54. "Wild Bull" and "Falcon" are among the recorded names of Egyptian warships; see Lichtheim, "The Autobiography of Ahmose Son of Abana," in *Ancient Egyptian Literature*, vol. 2, pp. 12, 14.

63 Shalmaneser I: A. K. Grayson, "Shalmaneser I," *Assyrian Royal Inscriptions*, vol. 1, *From the Beginning to Ashur-resha-ishi* (Wiesbaden: Otto Harrassowitz, 1972), l. 536, p. 80.

63 "With shouts incessant": *Iliad* 13.833–37.

63 Protesilaus: Possibly just a symbolic name, since in Greek it means "First to Land."

64 Pharaoh Rameses II killed so many: Lichtheim, "The Kadesh Battle Inscriptions of Rameses II: The Poem," in *Ancient Egyptian Literature*, vol. 2, p. 69.

64 Egyptian sculpted relief: At Medinet Habu, 20th Dynasty, Rameses III (1184–1153 B.C.); see Yigael Yadin, *The Art of Warfare in Biblical Lands in the Light of Archaeological Discovery*, vol. 2 (London: Weidenfeld & Nicolson, 1963), 340–41.

64 even lacked sandals: Miriam Lichtheim, "Papyrus Lansing: A Schoolbook," in *Ancient Egyptian Literature*, vol. 2, p. 171.

64 as crocodiles fall: Lichtheim, "The Kadesh Battle Inscriptions of Rameses II: The Bulletin," in *Ancient Egyptian Literature*, vol. 2, p. 62.

65 as one Greek common soldier boasts: Thersites, *Iliad* 2.231. For an image of how Egyptians bound their prisoners, see the Medinet Habu relief, in Yadin, *Art of Warfare in Biblical Lands*, vol. 2, pp. 342–43.

65 Great Sea God: In Near Eastern myth, see, e.g., Itamar Singer, "Mursili's Hymn and Prayer to the Sun-Goddess of Arinna (CTH 376.A)," in *Hittite Prayers*, 51–57.

65 Bronze Age gesture of respect: See, e.g., Rameses II as a god in Lichtheim, "The Kadesh Battle Inscriptions of Rameses II: The Poem," in *Ancient Egyptian Literature*, vol. 2, p. 67.

65 Kukkunni: Beckman, "Treaty Between Muwatttalli II of Hatti and Alaksandu of Wilusa," in *Hittite Diplomatic Texts*, no. 13, §3, p. 87.

66 the watchmen might anticipate: Cf. Miriam Lichtheim, "The Poetical Stela of Merneptah (Israel Stela)," in *Ancient Egyptian Literature*, vol. 2, p. 77.

66 verdict of Thucydides: Thuc. 1.11.1.

67 battle on the Sangarius River: *Iliad* 3.184–90.

CHAPTER FOUR: ASSAULT ON THE WALLS

69 double doors: Cf. Yadin, *Art of Warfare in Biblical Lands*, vol. 1, pp. 21–22.

69 the build of a boxer: *Odyssey* 18.66–74. For clothes, see *Odyssey* 19.225–43; cf. Nestor's clothes at *Iliad* 10.131–34.

70 bull that represented the army's god: The bull was a common Anatolian symbol of the Storm God, see Ann C. Gunter, "Animals in Anatolian Art," in Collins, ed., *History of Animal World in the Ancient Near East*, 90; the Storm God was the symbol of Troy's army, see Beckman, *Hittite Diplomatic Texts*, 92; a bull figure has been found recently in Troy VIi, see Wendy Rigter and Diane Thumm-Dograyan, "Ein Hohlgeformter Stier Aus Troia," *Studia Troica* 14 (2004): 87–100.

70 It was unmanly, said a Hittite king: Hattushilish III (1267–1230 B.C.), as cited in Van den Hout, "Bellum Iustum," 26.

71 a "tablet of war" and a "tablet of peace": Van den Hout, "Bellum Iustum," 17, 25.

71 as a Greek king once sent to the Hittite monarch: *Keilschrifturkunden aus Boghazköi* V (Berlin: Zu beziehen durch die Vorderasiatische Abteilung der Staatlichen Museen, 1921–25): 6, (E. Laroche, *Catalogue des Textes Hittites* ii (Paris: Klincksieck, 1971): 57–64; cf. Bryce, *Kingdom of the Hittites*, 238–40; Bryce, *Life and Society*, 168.

72 "This is what Zeus has given us": *Iliad* 14.86–87.

73 "disgraceful" and "an outrage": *Iliad* 11.142.

73 it was the gods and not she who were responsible: *Iliad* 3.164.

73 One Canaanite mayor confessed his fear of his own peasantry: Moran, *Amarna Letters*, EA 117, ll. 83–94, p. 194.

73 driven into exile by a younger brother who despised him: Moran, *Amarna Letters*, EA 137, ll. 14–35, p. 218.

73 could force a city into surrendering: Houwink ten Cate, "Annals of Hattusilis I," 67.

75 against the armed might of the Greeks: *Iliad* 13.101–6.

75 Hector once barely escaped Achilles' charge: *Iliad* 9.352–55.

75 this postern gate lacked protective bastions: *Iliad* 5.789.

76 three ways to conquer a fortified city: Adapted from Yadin, *Art of Warfare in Biblical Lands*, vol. 1, pp. 16–18.

76 Mesopotamian proverb: John A. Wilson, "Akkadian Proverbs and Counsels," in Pritchard, *Ancient Near Eastern Texts*, 425.

76 when men mount swift-footed horses: *Odyssey* 18.263–64.

76 when he said goodbye to his wife Penelope: *Odyssey* 18.258.

76 Thucydides is the source: Thuc. 1.11.1.

77 "a hateful path": *Odyssey* 14.235–36.

77 "as many as the leaves": *Odyssey* 9.51.

77 Pithana and his son Anitta: Harry A. Hoffner Jr., "Proclamation of Anitta of Kuššar," in Hallo, ed., *Context of Scripture*, vol. 1, pp. 182–83.

77 One ancient Greek literary critic: Aristarchus; see discussion by G. S. Kirk, *The Iliad: A Commentary*, vol. 2, on Books 5–8 (Cambridge, England: Cambridge University Press, 1990), 217–18; cf. ibid., vol. 1, on Books 1–4, pp. 38–43.

78 "That quarter most": *Iliad* 6.433–39.

79 a painted pottery fragment: Shear, *Tales of Heroes*, 29 and fig. 42, p. 31.

79 Ajax could defeat Achilles: *Iliad* 13.324–25.

79 "the bulwark of the Greeks": *Iliad* 7.211.

80 favorite of the goddess Ishtar: Van den Hout, "Apology of Hattušili III," in Hallo, ed., *Context of Scripture*, vol. 1, p. 201.

80 "mistress of strife and battle": A. Kirk Grayson, "Tukulti-Ninurta I," in *Assyrian Rulers of the Third and Second Millennia BC (to 1115 BC)*, Royal Inscriptions of Mesopotamia, Assyrian Periods/vol. 1, (Toronto: University of Toronto Press, 1987), 1.v, 2–22, p. 238.

81 The outer wall: The existence of a wall around the lower city is likely but not certain. For arguments in favor of its existence, see D. F. Easton, J. D. Hawkins, A. G. Sherratt, and E. S. Sherratt, "Troy in Recent Perspective," *Anatolian Studies* 52 (2002): 91–93; for arguments against, see D. Hertel and Frank Kolb, "Troy in Clearer Perspective," *Anatolian Studies* 53 (2003): 77–81.

84 heaps of blood: Lichtheim, "The Kadesh Battle Inscriptions of Rameses II: The Poem," in *Ancient Egyptian Literature*, vol. 2, p. 70.

CHAPTER FIVE: THE DIRTY WAR

86 "Sole Companion": John A. Wilson, "Texts from the Tomb of General Hor-em-Heb," in Pritchard, *Ancient Near Eastern Texts*, 251.

87 no one could match Achilles for his looks or physique: *Odyssey* 11.469–70.

87 big and beautiful: *Iliad* 21.108.

87 "None of the bronze-wearing Greeks is my equal": *Iliad* 18.105–6.

87 Achilles claimed to have destroyed: *Iliad* 9.328–29.

87 Anum-Hirbi: Kemal Balkan, *Letter of King Anum-Hirbi of Mama to King Warshama of Kanish* (Ankara: Türk Tarih Kurumu Basımevi, 1957), 16; Houwink ten Cate, "Annals of Hattusilis I," 69–70.

88 sea raiders: Bryce, *Kingdom of the Hittites*, 368, 369.

88 Egyptian, Mesopotamian, and Hittite texts: Wilson, "The Asiatic Campaigns of Thut-Mose III: The Battle of Megiddo" and "Subsequent Campaigns," in Pritchard, *Ancient Near Eastern Texts*, 234–41 passim; Heimpel, *Letters to the King of Mari*, 27 112, p. 449; Harry A. Hoffner Jr., "Deeds of Šupululiuma," in Hallo, ed., *Context of Scripture*, vol. 1, pp. 185–92 passim; cf. Bryce, *Life and Society*, 104–7.

88 Attarissiya: Beckman, "Indictment of Madduwatta," in *Hittite Diplomatic Texts*, 27 §19, p. 158.

88 Melanippus son of Hicetaeon: *Iliad* 15.546–51.

89 engineers from Lycia: Pausanias 2.16.5, 25.8.

89 "making war on other men over their women": *Iliad* 9.327.

89 Egyptian and Hittite booty lists: Wilson, "The Asiatic Campaigns of Thut-Mose III: The Battle of Megiddo" and "Subsequent Campaigns," in Pritchard, *Ancient Near Eastern Texts*, 234–41 passim; Hoffner, "Deeds of Šupululiuma," in Hallo, ed., *Context of Scripture*, vol. 1, pp. 185–92 passim; cf. Bryce, *Life and Society*, 104–7.

89 Linear B tablets: Ventris and Chadwick, *Documents in Mycenaean Greek*, PY 16, p. 161; cf. pp. 156, 579.

89 eleven were in the vicinity of Troy: *Iliad* 9.326.

89 But there were surely some refugees: Dozens of large storage jars were sunk to their full height (up to six and a half feet) beneath the floor of the houses of Troy VIi. This suggests crowding, which was once attributed to a surge of refugees during the Trojan War. Yet the houses date not to Troy VIi's end but to its early years, so they must refer to something other than the Trojan War—they may be a sign of squatters during the rebuilding of the city after the earthquake of ca. 1300 B.C. See P. A. Mountjoy, "Troy VII Reconsidered," *Studia Troica* 9 (1999): 296–97.

90 "Where Trojan dames": *Iliad* 22.155–56.

90 "like locusts": D. Pardee, "The Kirta Epic," in Hallo, ed., *Context of Scripture*, vol. 1, pp. 334–35.

90 Roman-era collection of myths: Pseudo-Apollodorus, *Epitome*, 3.33.

90 Thermi: Excavations in the 1930s dated the destruction to ca. 1250, but the recent redating of Trojan pottery might suggest a later date for the destruction—and hence, a date that fits the Trojan War.

91 naval battle took place between Hittite and Cypriot ships: Hoffner, "The Hittite Conquest of Cyprus," in Hallo, ed., *Context of Scripture*, vol. 1, pp. 192–93.

91 sculpted Egyptian relief: See the illustrations of Rameses III's relief at Medinet Habu in Yadin, *Art of Warfare*, vol. 2, pp. 250–52, 340–41.

92 the "holy city of Eëtion": *Iliad* 1.366.

92 described as "high-gated": *Iliad* 6.416.

92 "we destroyed it and brought everything here": *Iliad* 1.367.

93 "The distant Trojans never injured me": *Iliad* 1.153.

93 "The well wrought harp from conquered Thebae came": *Iliad* 9.186–88.

94 died in their house "of Artemis's arrows": *Iliad* 6.428.

94 According to an ancient commentary: *Iliad* 1.366–69, Scholion on 1.366; see Kirk, *The Iliad*, vol. 1, p. 91.

95 "Zeus / Preserved me": *Iliad* 20.92–93.

95 The arms of the Greeks: For the image, see Cooper, *Curse of Agade*, l. 159, p. 59.

95 fell on the town: Bronze Age Anatolians used the expression "fall on" to mean "invade," e.g., Balkan, *Letter of King Anum-Hirbi*, 1.0, p. 8, comm. p. 14.

95 more steadfast than a row of bricks: Compare Moran, *Amarna Letters*, EA 296, ll. 17–22, p. 338.

96 a silver drinking cup from Mycenae: Commonly known as the Silver Siege Rhyton, the vessel was found in Shaft Grave 4.

96 the Pharaoh Kamose: John A. Wilson, "The War Against the Hyksos (continued)," in Pritchard, *Ancient Near Eastern Texts*, 554.

96 Better-documented, later periods of ancient Greek history: See, e.g., Diodorus Siculus 13.14.5; cf. Aeneas Tacticus, *Siegecraft*, 40.4–5.

96 "Thy friendly hand": *Iliad* 19.295–97.

97 "I trampled the country of Hassuwa": Amelie Kuhrt, *The Ancient Near East: c. 3000–330 BC*, vol. 1 (London: Routledge, 1995), 242.

97 Seti I: John A. Wilson, "Campaigns of Seti I in Asia," in Pritchard, *Ancient Near Eastern Texts*, 254–55.

97 common practice in Late Bronze Age Egypt: Andrea Gnirs, "Military: An Overview," in Redford, ed., *Oxford Encyclopedia of Ancient Egypt*, vol. 2, p. 401.

97 Shalmaneser I: Grayson, "Shalmaneser I," in *Assyrian Rulers*, vol. 1, ll. 56–87, p. 184.

98 "I used to like to spare Trojans": *Iliad* 21.101–2.

98 Lycaon: *Iliad* 21.34–53, 23.740–47.

98 the people of Apasa: On this episode, see Bryce, *Kingdom of the Hittites*, 209–11; Akurgal, *Hattian and Hittite Civilizations*, 82–83; Hawkins, "Tarkasnawa," 24.

99 "Now shameful flight": *Iliad* 2.119–22.

CHAPTER SIX: AN ARMY IN TROUBLE

101 well-known gripers: See the letter to the King of Mari from Bahdi-Addu in ARM 2 118 in Oppenheim, *Letters from Mesopotamia*, 106.

101 softwood: The likeliest woods available around Troy are pine, laurel, juniper, heather-stems, and dried willow. Animal dung too might have been used as kindling.

102 "evil smelling smoke": Balkan, *Letter of King Anum-Hirbi*, 8, p. 16.

102 "bring much fever": *Iliad* 22.31.

103 Hittite and other ancient rituals: See, e.g., Richard H. Beal, "Assuring the Safety of the King During the Winter (KUB 5.4 + KUB 18.53 and KUB 5.3 + KUB 18.52)," in Hallo, ed., *Context of Scripture*, vol. 1, 1.79, §ii. 1–4, p. 210.

103 "Lord of the Bow": Maciej Popko, *Religions of Asia Minor*, trans. Iwona Zych (Warsaw: Academic Publications Dialog, 1995), 93.

103 "of the glorious bow": *Iliad* 15.55.

103 that the Storm God washed them away!: *CTH* 7, obv. 10–18, in Gary Beckman, "The Siege of Uršu Text (CTH 7) and Old Hittite Historiography" *Journal of Cuneiform Studies* 47 (1995): 25.

103 "What girl?": Literally, "prize," *Iliad* 1.123.

104 "best of the Greeks": Literally, "best of the Achaeans," e.g., *Iliad* 1.244.

104 "youths of the Achaeans": *Iliad* 1.473.

105 Archaeology confirms: Shelmerdine, "Review of Aegean Prehistory VI," 577–80 = 369–372.

105 at Thebes a sacrifice: Robin Hägg, "State and Religion in Mycenaean Greece," in R. Laffineur and W. D. Niemeier, eds., *Politeia: Society and State in the Aegean Bronze Age*, in *Aegaeum* 12 (1995). 388.

106 Hittite music: Monika Schuol, *Hethitische Kultmusik: Eine Untersuchung der Instrumental-und Vokalmusik anhand hetitischer Ritualtexxte und von archaeologlogischen Zeugnissen*, Deutsches Archaeologisches Institut

Orient-Abteilung, Orient-Archaeologie, Band 14 (Rahden/Westfalen, Germany: Verlag Marie Leidorf, 2004), 60.

107 Gilgamesh: E. A. Speiser, "The Epic of Gilgamesh," in Pritchard, *Ancient Near Eastern Texts*, 87; cf. M. L. West, *The East Face of Helicon* (Oxford: Clarendon Press, 1997), 231–32.

107 Teshub: "The Song of Hedammu" and "The Song of Ulikummi," in Hoffner, *Hittite Myths*, 51–52, 60.

107 the Canaanite epic hero Kirta: Pardee, "Kirta Epic," in Hallo, ed., *Context of Scripture*, vol. 1, p. 333.

107 Egyptian tale of Wenamun: Miriam Lichtheim, "The Report of Wenamun," in *Ancient Egyptian Literature*, vol. 2, p. 229.

107 Hattushilish I: Kuhrt, *Ancient Near East*, vol. 1, p. 238.

107 Tukulti-Ninurta: Grayson, "Tukulti-Ninurta I," in *Assyrian Rulers*, vol. 1:1.1, 1–20, p. 233.

107 Abi-Milki: Moran, *Amarna Letters*, EA 147, p. 233.

107 governor of the Mesopotamian city of Nippur: Oppenheim, "The Court of the Kassite Kings [BE 17 24]," in *Letters from Mesopotamia*, 116–17.

107 "fast runner": See, e.g., *Iliad* 21.265.

108 companies of soldiers or rowers at Pylos: Ventris and Chadwick, *Documents in Mycenaean Greek*, 183–94.

108 "Ranks wedged in ranks": *Iliad* 16.211–18.

109 Naramsin: Cooper, *Curse of Agade*, l. 86, p. 55.

109 Hattushilish III: Harry A. Hoffner Jr., "Apology of Hattušili III," in Hallo, ed., *Context of Scripture*, vol. 1, p. 200.

109 Merneptah: A. J. Spalinger, *War in Ancient Egypt: The New Kingdom* (Oxford: Blackwell Publishing, 2005), 239.

109 Xerxes: Hdt. 7.12–19.

109 "Our cordage torn": *Iliad* 2.135.

109 "Now, for five months": Shlomo Izre'el and Itamar Singer, *The General's Letter from Ugarit, A Linguistic and Historical Reevaluation of RS 20.33 (Ugaritica V, no. 20)* (Tel Aviv: Tel Aviv University, 1990), 25.

109 "Fly, Grecians, fly": *Iliad* 2.141–42.

110 Tukulti-Ninurta: Grayson, "Tukulti-Ninurta I," in *Assyrian Rulers*, vol. 1: l.i 21–36, p. 234.

110 "To one sole monarch": *Iliad* 2.205–6.

110 serious business to Bronze Age commanders: See, e.g., Sasson, *Military Establishments at Mari*, 41.

110 "Whate'er our master craves": *Iliad* 2.232–38.

110 or even a traitor: For example, see Heimpel, *Letters to the King of Mari*, 62–63.

111 fine Thracian vintages brought by ship to Agamemnon daily: *Iliad* 9.71–72.

111 round-shouldered: *Odyssey* 19.246.

111 the soldiers had leather shields: *Iliad* 10.152.

111 the laces that made sandals fit comfortably to the foot: *Iliad* 10.132.

112 axes made of dull bronze rather than sharp iron: *Iliad* 23.118–19.

112 cleaned the camp of animal dung: Cf. *Odyssey* 17.296–99.

112 swarms of flies: *Iliad* 19.25.

112 fasted until dusk because they worked so hard: Cf. *Odyssey* 18.369–70.

112 gainsaid Hector in the Trojan assembly, much to his annoyance: *Iliad* 12.211–14.

112 kiss his hand: *Odyssey* 24.398.

112 honor him like a god: *Iliad* 10.32–33.

112 picking up the royal cloak when Odysseus dropped it: *Iliad* 2.183–84.

112 "visitation of foreign dogs": *Iliad* 8.526–27.

113 "Have we not known thee, slave!": *Iliad* 2.248–51.

113 The Hittites knew the value of slapstick humor: Harry A. Hoffner Jr., "Daily Life Among the Hittites," in Richard E. Averback, Mark W. Chavalas, David B. Weisberg, *Life and Culture in the Ancient Near East* (Bethesda, Md.: CDL Press, 2003), 112.

113 "Encouraged hence": *Iliad* 2.354–56.

114 "by peoples and groups": *Iliad* 2.362.

114 Shuppiluliuma I: Hoffner, "Deeds of Šupiluliuma," in Hallo, ed., *Context of Scripture*, vol. 1, p. 190; cf. Bryce, *Kingdom of the Hittites*, 192.

115 "Like some proud bull": *Iliad* 2.480–81.

CHAPTER SEVEN: THE KILLING FIELDS

117 hymns to the war-god: Schuol, *Hethitische Kultmusik*, 207–8.

117 buried at home with their mothers: Calvert Watkins, "A Latin-Hittite Etymology," *Language* 45 (1969): 240–41.

117 "messengers of death": Yadin, *Art of Warfare in Biblical Lands*, vol. 1, p. 8.

117 hit a target at 300–400 yards: Yadin, *Art of Warfare in Biblical Lands*, vol. 1, pp. 7–8.

117 a top slinger: Hoffmeier, "Military: Materiel," in Redford, ed., *Oxford Encyclopedia of Ancient Egypt*, vol. 2, 406–12, 410.

118 "girl crazy": *Iliad* 3.39.

118 Yashmah-Addu and his older brother: André Parrot and Georges Dossin, eds., *Archives royales de Mari*, vol. 1 (Paris: Impr. Nationale, 1955), 69.

119 Two kings could fight it out: On Hattushilish III (1267–1237 B.C.), see Van den Hout, "Apology of Hattušili III," in Hallo, ed., *Context of Scripture*, vol. 1, p. 201; Harry A. Hoffner Jr., "A Hittite Analogue to the David and Goliath Contest of Champions?" *Catholic Biblical Quarterly* 30 (1968): 220–25; W. K. Pritchett. *The Greek State at War*, part 4 (Berkeley: University of California Press, 1985): 15–21. Another king who may have fought a champion battle is the Mesopotamian Ishme-Dagan, although perhaps he merely led the army into a battle where the enemy leader was killed; Parrot and Dossin, eds., *Archives royales de Mari*, 69.

119 or two corporals: Richard H. Beal, *The Organisation of the Hittite Military* (Heidelberg: Carl Winter Universitaetsverlag, 1992), 509–13.

119 Attarissiya: Beckman, "Indictment of Madduwatta," in *Hittite Diplomatic Texts*, 27§12, p. 156.

119 every king claimed to have a patron god: See various examples in Grayson, *Assyrian Rulers*, vol. 1, 206; Van den Hout, "Apology of Hattušili III," in Hallo, ed., *Context of Scripture*, vol. 1, pp. 200–1; Lichtheim, "The Kadesh Battle Inscriptions of Rameses II: The Poem," in *Ancient Egyptian Literature*, vol. 2, p. 66; cf. West, *East Face of Helicon*, 209.

120 Iron weapons existed in Bronze Age Anatolia: To be sure, Bronze weapons predominated, but the Hittites produced some iron daggers, knives, axes, spears, and lanceheads, so iron arrowheads are also likely. See J. O. Muhly, R. Maddin, T. Stech, and E. Özgen, "Iron in Anatolia and the Nature of the Hittite Iron Industry," *Anatolian Studies* 35 (1985): 67–84.

120 an ancient commentator suggested: Scholion on *Iliad* 4.218–19.

120 honey: Ventris and Chadwick, *Documents in Mycenaean Greek*, e.g., KN 206, p. 310; cf. Tzedakis and Martlew, eds., *Minoans and Mycenaeans*, 266.

120 "No rest, no respite": *Iliad* 2.385–90.

121 forty kings: Grayson, "Tukulti-Ninurta I," in *Assyrian Rulers*, vol. 1: 5.23–47, p. 244; 18.1–28, p. 266; 20.1–10, p. 268; 23.27–55, p. 272.

122 "fore-fighters" *(promachoi)*: See, e.g., *Iliad* 3.31, 4.354.

122 "the first men": See, e.g., *Iliad* 5.536.

126 Tudhaliya IV: Itamar Singer, "Tudhaliya's Prayer to the Sun-Goddess of Arinna for Military Success (CTH 385.9)," in *Hittite Prayers*, 108.

126 how thirsty warriors were: *Iliad* 22.2.

126 mind over matter: See, e.g., the Old Babylonian poem, Joan Goodnick Westenholz, "Sargon, the Conquering Hero," in *Legends of the Kings of Akkade: The Texts* (Winona Lake, Ind.: Eisenbrauns, 1997), 63, 65, 69.

126 "The great, the fierce Achilles": *Iliad* 4.512–13.

127 "How dear, O kings!": *Iliad* 7.327–30.

128 "Oh, take not, friends!": *Iliad* 7.400–3.

CHAPTER EIGHT: NIGHT MOVES

131 an imposing monument: Among many examples from Bronze Age Mesopotamia, Anatolia, and Egypt, see Kitchen, "First Beth Shean Stela, Year 1," "Second Beth-Shan Stela, [Year Lost]"; Frayne, "Iah-dun-Lim," in Hallo, ed., *Context of Scripture*, vol. 2, pp. 25, 28, 260; Hawkins, "Tarkasnawa," 4–10 (the Karabel Relief).

132 Murshilish II: Beal, "Ten Year Annals," Year 3, in Hallo, ed., *Context of Scripture*, vol. 2, p. 85.

132 Babylonian prayer: Benjamin R. Foster, "IV. Adad (a) Against Thunder," in *Before the Muses: An Anthology of Akkadian Literature*, vol. 2, *Mature, Late*, 2nd edition (Bethesda, Md.: CDL Press, 1996), 540–41.

132 dog: Moran, *Amarna Letters*, EA 76, p. 146.

132 "son of a nobody": A. K. Grayson, "Ashur-Uballit I," in *Assyrian Royal Inscriptions*, vol. 1: 15*.325, p. 50.

132 should turn into a woman: Collins, "The First Soldiers' Oath," in Hallo, ed., *Context of Scripture*, 166.

132 "Go, less than woman": *Iliad* 8.163.

132 "Trojans and Lycians": *Iliad* 8.173–74.

133 "his manhood dwindle away": Grayson, "Tukulti-Ninurta I," in *Assyrian Rulers*, vol. 1: 1.vi 2–22, p. 238.

133 Purple was the royal color: Gary Beckman, "Edict of Suppiluliuma I of Hatti Concerning the Tribute of Ugarit," in *Hittite Diplomatic Texts*, 166–68.

133 Mesopotamian saying: Sasson, *Military Establishments at Mari*, 42.

133 dogs were the favorite animal for insults: Among many examples, consider the Hittite King Shuppiluliuma I's characterization of the tribal chief Huqqana of Hayasa as "a lowly dog" (Beckman, "Treaty Between Suppiluliuma I of Hatti and Huqqana of Hayasa," in *Hittite Diplomatic Texts*, 27) and a Canaanite mayor's assertion that only a dog would disobey the orders of Pharaoh (Moran, *Amarna Letters*, EA 314, ll. 11–16, p. 347).

134 "the bridges of war": *Iliad* 4.371; 8.378, 555; 11.160; 20.427.

134 food served by Syrian towns: Moran, *Amarna Letters*, EA 55, ll. 10–15, p. 127; EA 324, ll. 10–15, p. 352.

134 sound the alarm: Heimpel, *Letters to the King of Mari*, 26 168, p. 239.

134 "This night will": *Iliad* 9.78.

135 sentinels: Beal, *Organization of the Hittite Military*, 251–60.

135 whose property was as wide as the sea: For the phrase, see Moran, *Amarna Letters*, EA 89, ll. 39–47, p. 162.

136 "a razor's edge": *Iliad* 10.173.

138 "man of tongue": Heimpel, *Letters to the King of Mari*, s.v. "informer," 585; S. Dalley, *Mari and Karana: Two Old Babylonian Cities* (New York: Longman, 1984), 150. Cf. Gabriel Lemkin, *My Just War: The Memoir of a Jewish Red Army Soldier in World War II* (Novato, Calif.: Presidio, 1998), 154.

138 white horses: Dalley, *Mari and Karana*, 161; Moran, *Amarna Letters*, EA 16, 9–12, pp. 39, 40 n. 3.

139 guerrilla war: Richard Holmes, ed., *Oxford Companion to Military History* (Oxford: Oxford University Press, 2001), 383–86.

139 "the war of the flea": The phrase comes from Robert Taber, *The War of the Flea: The Classic Study of Guerrilla Warfare* (Dulles, Va.: Brassey's, 2002).

139 staple techniques of Mesopotamian warfare: Sasson, *Military Establishments at Mari*, 39–42.

140 Hittite laws: Albrecht Goetze, "The Middle Assyrian Laws," in Pritchard, *Ancient Near Eastern Texts*, 188–97.

140 breaking and entering: S. N. Kramer, "Lipit-Ishtar Lawcode," in Pritchard, *Ancient Near Eastern Texts*, 160.

140 raids on merchant caravans: Dalley, *Mari and Karana*, 150.

140 Egyptians decry: Miriam Lichtheim, "The Autobiography of Weni," in *Ancient Egyptian Literature*, vol. 1, *The Old and Middle Kingdoms*, 20.

141 merchant counted himself lucky: Dalley, *Mari and Karana*, 150.

141 foiled an assassin: Moran, *Amarna Letters*, EA 81, ll 14–24, p. 150.

141 elder brother: Miraim Lichtheim, "The Two Brothers," in *Ancient Egyptian Literature*, vol. 2, *The New Kingdom*, 205.

141 macehead: Grayson, "Shalmaneser I," in *Assyrian Rulers*, vol. 1: 22, pp. 210–11.

141 farmers of Late Bronze Age Ugarit: Sylvie Lackenbacher, *Textes Akkadiens d'Ugarit: Textes provenants des vingt-cinq premières campagnes* (Paris: Les Éditions du Cerf, 2002), RS 17.341 = PRU IV, 161s. et pl. L, pp. 143–44.

141 "miserable Asiatic": Miriam Lichtheim, "The Instruction Addressed to King Merikare," in *Ancient Egyptian Literature*, vol. 1, *The Old and Middle Kingdoms*, 103–4.

141 Scouting patrols: Sasson, *Military Establishments at Mari*, 18; Heimpel, *Letters to the King of Mari*, 26 156, p. 236; Beal, *Organization of the Hittite Military*, 260–63.

141 two Bedouin: Beal, *Organization of the Hittite Military*, 266–68.

142 Sumerian poem: Dina Katz, "Gilgamesh and Akka," in Hallo, ed., *Context of Scripture*, vol. 1, p. 551.

142 "hunger contorts": Piotr Michalowski, *The Lamentation over the Destruction of Sumer and Ur* (Winona Lake, Ind.: Eisenbrauns, 1989), ll. 390–91, p. 61.

142 the chief magistrate of the Bronze Age city of Byblos: Moran, *Amarna Letters*, EA 125, ll. 14–24, 25–32, pp. 204–5.

142 mayor of Byblos: Moran, *Amarna Letters*, EA 85, ll. 6–15, p. 156.

142 "rivaling in height heaven and earth": The phrase comes from Moran, *Amarna Letters*, EA 29, ll. 16–27, p. 93.

143 "My early youth was bred": *Iliad* 6.444–46.

CHAPTER NINE: HECTOR'S CHARGE

146 "All males": *Iliad* 6.493–94.

146 an ancient talisman for bringing back a man: Barber, *Prehistoric Textiles*, 372–73.

147 as an Assyrian text put it: Grayson, "Shalmaneser I," in *Assyrian Rulers*, vol. 1: 1.88–106, p. 184.

147 Hammurabi: Heimpel, *Letters to the King of Mari*, 26 379, p. 329.

147 details of an operation: See, e.g., Heimpel, *Letters to the King of Mari*, 26 170, p. 240.

147 Repair the gate: Heimpel, *Letters to the King of Mari*, 26 221–bis, p. 263.

147 "A chosen phalanx": *Iliad* 13.126–31, 133–35.

148 "a man insatiable for war": *Iliad* 13.746–47.

149 like frightened cattle or sheep: *Iliad* 15.321–26.

149 "Bring fire!": *Iliad* 15.718.

149 "Zeus has granted us today": *Iliad* 15.719–21.

150 showers that deposit red dust: *Iliad* 16.458; Richard Janko, *The Iliad: A Commentary*, vol. 4, on books 13–16 (Cambridge, England: Cambridge University Press, 1992), 377. The sirocco (ancient Greek Notos or Lips) sometimes brings red rain in the form of dust-laden air from the Sahara. See J. B. Thornes and John Wainwright, *Environmental Issues in the Mediterranean* (New York: Routledge, 2002), 80; cf. Jamie Morton, *The Role of the Physical Environment in Ancient Greek Seafaring* (Leiden: Brill, 2001), 50–51.

151 "that war was sweeter": *Iliad* 11.14–15.

152 As a Babylonian hymn says: Foster, "To Nergal (a) Nergal the Warrior," in *Before the Muses*, vol. 2, p. 612.

152 "If thou but lead": *Iliad* 11.796–800.

153 "Think your Achilles sees": *Iliad* 16.269–74.

154 "smashing his belly": Izre'el and Singer, *General's Letter from Ugarit*, 27, with an argument on 49–50 for this rendition of a difficult original in Akkadian.

155 like pharaoh's war cry: Moran, *Amarna Letters*, EA 147, ll. 9–15, p. 233; John A. Wilson, "The Egyptians and the Gods of Asia," in Pritchard, *Ancient Near Eastern Texts*, 249.

155 "So may his rage be tired": *Iliad* 18.282–83.

156 "useless weight on the ground": *Iliad* 18.104.

156 "Let me this instant": *Iliad* 18.120–21.

157 thirty-six miles or more: Luce, *Celebrating Homer's Landscapes*, 103.

CHAPTER TEN: ACHILLES' HEEL

159 Like Hittite and Egyptian generals: For examples, see Billie Jean Collins, "The 'Ritual Between the Pieces,'" in Hallo, ed., *Context of Scripture*, vol. 1, pp. 160–61. More than one example of this ritual is known: Billie Jean Collins, "The Puppy in Hittite Ritual," *Journal of Cuneiform Studies* 42 (1990): 211–26; Wilson, "The Egyptians and the Gods of Asia," in Pritchard, *Ancient Near Eastern Texts*, 248.

160 a classic gesture: See, e.g., Moran, *Amarna Letters*, EA 64, p. 135; EA 151, p. 238; EA 314, p. 377.

160 signal his surrender: Houwink ten Cate, "Annals of Hattusilis I," 66–67.

161 "women who are equivalent to men": *Iliad* 3.189, 6.186.

161 several hundred thousand women: http://www.womensmemorial.org/PDFs/StatsonWIM.pdf.

162 surely were not cheap: *CTH* 7, rev. 31–32; Beckman, "The Siege of Uršu Text (CTH 7) and Old Hittite Historiography," *Journal of Cuneiform Studies* 47 (1995): 27, comm. 31.

163 Arzawa: Kuhrt, *Ancient Near East*, vol. 1, pp. 250–52, citing EA 31–32.

163 king of Mira: Bryce, *Kingdom of the Hittites*, 308–9.

165 "Talk not of ruling in this dolorous gloom": *Odyssey* 11.488–81.

165 "children of the Trojans": *Odyssey* 11.547.

166 "the king": *Little Iliad*, frag. 3.

167 "like Artemis with her golden arrows": *Odyssey* 4.122.

168 Eurypylus's mother: Odyssey 11.519–21; *Little Iliad*, frags. 6–7.

169 figurines were a familiar way of representing a deity: See the illustrations in O. Tashin, *Die Hethiter und ihr Reich: Das Volk der 1000 Götter* (Stuttgart: Theiss, 2002), 227–31, 344–47.

169 wealthy Hittite capitals had monumental sculptures of the gods: Ekrem Akurgal, *The Art of the Hittites*, photographs by Max Hirmer, trans. Constance McNab (New York: H. N. Abrams, 1962), 108–10.

169 sacred medicine bundles: See under "medicine bundle," in Arlene Hirschfelder and Paulette Molin, *The Encyclopedia of Native American Religions: An Introduction* (New York: Facts on File, 1992), 176.

169 the Hittites: Houwink ten Cate, "Annals of Hattusilis I," 70.

169 the Romans: See under "evocatio," *Oxford Classical Dictionary*, 580.

169 leave an enemy town unscathed: Houwink ten Cate, "Annals of Hattusilis I," 73.

CHAPTER ELEVEN: THE NIGHT OF THE HORSE

172 "horses of the sea": *Odyssey* 4.708.

173 Hittite military doctrine: Richard H. Beal, "Le Strutture Militari Ittite di Attaco e di Difesa," in M. C. Guidotti and Franca Pecchioli Daddi, eds., *La Battaglia di Qadesh* (Livorno: Sillabe, 2000), 111, 114–15.

173 siege of one Mesopotamian city: Heimpel, *Letters to the King of Mari*, xxii–xxiii, 67–69; 14 104, pp. 496–97.

173 Marathon: Hdt. 6.115.

174 Tarentum: Appian, *Foreign Wars*, 6.32–33; Plutarch, *Fabius Maximus* 21–22.

174 rate of about five knots: See John Coates, "Power and Speed of Oared Ships," in Christopher Westerdahl, ed., *Crossroads in Ancient Shipbuilding: Proceedings of the Sixth International Symposium on Boat and Ship Archaeology Roskilde 1991*, ISBSA 6 (Oxford: Oxbow Books, 1994), 249–56.

175 Bronze Age armies knew how to march by night: The Mesopotamian city of Kahat was captured at night by the army of Attaya in the 1700s B.C.; see Heimpel, *Letters to the King of Mari*, 26 317, p. 299. On Hittite marches at night, see Beal, "Le Strutture Militari Ittite," 112; Houwink ten Cate, "Annals of Hattusilis I," 68.

175 covered the distance: On marching rates of infantrymen, ancient and modern, see http://carlisle.www.army.mil/usamhi/bibliographies/referencebibliographies/marching/rates.doc.

175 Thargelion: Dionysius of Halicarnassus, *Roman Antiquities* 1.63.1.

175 "dissatisfaction and treachery": Michalowski, *Lamentation over the Destruction of Sumer and Ur*, ll. 297–99, p. 55.

176 shipwrights and carpenters: Ventris and Chadwick, *Documents in Mycenaean Greek*, 123; KN 47, p. 179; PY 51, p. 182; PY 189, p. 298.

176 realistic figures of wild animals: Moran, *Amarna Letters*, ll. 29–42, EA 8, p. 19; n. 10, p. 20.

176 often sent horses as a gift: See, e.g., Dalley, *Mari and Karana*, 153; Moran, *Amarna Letters*, EA 16, p. 39.

176 found a clay model of a horse: Manfred Korfmann et al., *Traum und Wirklichkeit: Troia* (Stuttgart: Theiss Verlag, 2001), 402.

178 had never given Aeneas the honor: *Iliad* 13.460–61.

179 Shuppiluliuma I conquered the city of Carchemish: Cited in Van den Hout, "Bellum Iustum," 27.

179 Lagash and Umma: Cooper, *Lagash-Umma Border Conflict*, 40, 48, 52.

CONCLUSION

184 "For Priam now": *Iliad* 20.306–8.

185 many such lines of prisoners: See, e.g., Royal Standard of Ur War Panel; relief in the tomb of Anta, Deshashe, Upper Egypt, Late Vth Dynasty, each depicted in Yadin, *Art of Warfare*, vol. 1, pp. 132–33, 146;

and relief at Medinet Habu, XXth Dynasty, Rameses III (1192–1160 B.C.), depicted in Yadin, *Art of Warfare*, vol. 2, pp. 342–43.

186 "many gifts": *Sack of Troy*, frag. 4.

189 like a stone out of deep water: Itamar Singer, "Hattusili's Exculpation to the Sun-Goddess of Arinna," in *Hittite Prayers*, 99.

A NOTE ON SOURCES

No one has read everything about the Trojan War. The sheer amount of scholarship on Homer, the archaeology of Troy, Mycenaean civilization, and Bronze Age warfare, not to mention Anatolia and the ancient Near East, is as long as it is exciting. This section lists only the main works used in writing this book. The focus is on scholarship in English and on publications of the last twenty years.

THE TROJAN WAR

Among several recent and important introductions, pride of place belongs to Joachim Latacz, *Troy and Homer: Towards a Solution of an Old Mystery*, translated by Kevin Windle and Rosh Ireland (Oxford: Oxford University Press, 2004). This fundamental work rethinks the historicity of the Trojan War in the light of recent archaeology, Hittite studies, and work on Homer. But it is not always easy going for nonscholars. Some of the same ground is covered, although in much less detail, in Carol G. Thomas and Craig Conant's very good *The Trojan War*, Greenwood Guides to Historic Events of the Ancient World (Westport, Conn.: Greenwood Press, 2005). The volume includes a selection of primary documents. Trevor Bryce, *The Trojans and Their Neighbours* (London: Routledge, 2006), is an excellent introduction to the Late Bronze Age historical context, if debatable on certain points. Slightly out of date but still very good and very readable is Michael Wood's *In Search of the Trojan War*, updated edition (Berkeley: University of California Press, 1996), which scans the subject from Homer to modern archaeology to the Hittites. A shorter survey is available in N. Fields, *Troy c. 1700–1250 BC* (Osceola, Fla.: Osprey Direct, 2004). A number of valuable essays appear in Ian Morris and Barry Powell, eds., *A New Companion to Homer* (Leiden: Brill, 1997). There is much helpful introductory material in Bettany Hughes, *Helen of Troy, Goddess, Princess, Whore* (London:

Jonathan Cape, 2005). Archaeologist and historian Eric Cline has recorded a series of lectures, "Archaeology and the Iliad: Did the Trojan War Take Place?" for Recorded Books/Modern Scholar (2006).

The reader will quickly note that the Trojan War is a story not just of historical data but of the varying ways of interpreting those data. An introduction to the range of scholarly opinion can be found in these collections of essays: Machteld J. Mellink, ed., *Troy and the Trojan War*, from a symposium held at Bryn Mawr College, October 1984 (Bryn Mawr, Pa.: Bryn Mawr College, 1986), and a special issue of the journal *Classical World* 91:5 (1998). A good summary of the state of debate at the end of 2006 can be found in Malcolm H. Wiener, "Homer and History: Old Questions, New Evidence," in a forthcoming issue of *Aegaeum* containing papers from the 11th International *Aegaeum* Conference (April 2006), "EPOS: Reconsidering Greek Epic and Aegean Bronze Age Archaeology."

Ever since the modern study of history began in the 1800s, there have been two broad schools of thought about Troy. The *positivists* believe that the Trojan War really happened and that there is a kernel of historical truth—and then some—in Homer. The *skeptics* think there is no more truth in Homer than in a fairy tale. Heinrich Schliemann brought the positivists to prominence and they remained active through the mid-twentieth century. Important examples of the argument that there really was a Trojan War and that Homer's narrative reflects the Bronze Age are such books as T. B. L. Webster, *From Mycenae to Homer*, 2nd edition (New York: Norton, 1964), D. L. Page, *History and the Homeric Iliad* (Berkeley: University of California Press, 1959), and J. V. Luce, *Homer and the Heroic Age* (New York: Harper & Row, 1975).

In the decades after World War II, the skeptics gained the upper hand. The excavations of Troy in the 1930s pointed to a small and unimposing place—not the grand city of the *Iliad*. Linguists and students of inscriptions picked holes in the ancient texts that were supposed to provide written confirmation of the truth of Homer's tale. Finally, the bitter experience of the Second World War rendered unfashionable all heroic narratives, such as the Trojan War.

In the English-speaking world, the most prominent postwar skeptic is M. I. Finley, who argued that there is more in Homer of the early Iron Age than of the Bronze Age; see his *World of Odysseus*, revised edition (New York: Viking Press, 1978); his contribution to M. I. Finley, J. L. Caskey, G. S. Kirk, and D. L. Page, "The Trojan War," *Journal of Hellenic Studies* 84

(1964): 1–20; or "Lost: The Trojan War," in his *Aspects of Antiquity: Discoveries and Controversies* (London: Penguin, 1991). See also several of the essays and the editors' conclusions in J. K. Davies and L. Foxhall, eds., *The Trojan War: Its Historicity and the Context—Papers of the First Greenbank Colloquium* (Liverpool: Bristol Classical Press, 1981). More recent examples of skepticism about Homer's Bronze Age credentials can be found in several of the chapters of Morris and Powell, eds., *A New Companion to Homer*, as well as in Ian Morris, "The Use and Abuse of Homer," *Classical Antiquity* 6 (1986): 81–138. But for a reassessment in light of the new evidence, see Ian Morris, "Troy and Homer," Version 1.0, November 2005, Princeton/Stanford Working Papers in Classics, http://www.princeton.edu/~pswpc/pdfs/morris/120506.pdf. (For skepticism about the new excavations at Troy, see below.)

Now the pendulum is swinging again. Prominent positivists in the last decade include Latacz in his *Troy and Homer*; Bryce, in his *Trojans and Their Neighbours*, and the late Ione M. Shear, an Aegean–Bronze Age archaeologist, in her *Tales of Heroes: The Origins of the Homeric Texts* (New York: Aristide D. Caratzas, 2000). G. S. Kirk offers a concise and cogent case for positivism in "History and Fiction in the *Iliad*," in his *The Iliad: A Commentary*, vol. 2, Books 5–8 (Cambridge, England: Cambridge University Press, 1990), 36–50. Hughes offers a vivid and well-researched study of Helen as a real-life Bronze Age Greek woman in *Helen of Troy*. She anticipates my conclusions about Helen's lack of passivity and about the personal nature of Bronze Age notions of interstate relations.

Two revolutions have shaped the study of the Trojan War in the last two decades, one in archaeology and the other in epigraphy (the study of inscriptions). For the results of new excavations at Troy since 1988 and for the debate about them, see below, and the overview in W. D. Niemeier, "Greeks vs. Hittites: Why Troy Is Troy and the Trojan War Is Real," *Archaeology Odyssey* 5:4 (2002): 24–35. The latest Hittite epigraphical research increases the likelihood that Troy (Ilion) was the city that the Hittites called Wilusa; that the people whom Homer calls Achaeans and we call Mycenaeans or Bronze Age Greeks were the Ahhiyawa of Hittite texts; that the Achaeans considered themselves equal to the Hittites; that they expanded from the Greek mainland to the southern Aegean islands such as Crete and Rhodes and to the Anatolian mainland; and that they were piratical raiders whose ships struck as far afield as Cyprus and Lebanon. On recent discoveries in Hittite epigraphy, see J. D. Hawkins,

"The End of the Bronze Age in Anatolia: New Light from Recent Discoveries," in A. Çilingiroğlu and D. French, eds., *Anatolian Iron Ages 3* (London: British Institute of Archaeology at Ankara, 1994), 91–94; J. D. Hawkins, "Tarkasnawa King of Mira," *Anatolian Studies* 48 (1998): 1–31; Michael Siebler, "In Theben ging's los," *Frankfurter Allgemeine Zeitung*, August 12, 2003, 31, http://www.faz.net/s/RubF7538E273FAA4006925CC 36BB8AFE338/Doc~EC6CFECB6D44B4344B70010A6675AF6A3~ATpl~ Ecommon~Scontent.html; and F. Starke, "Ein Keilschrift-Brief des Königs von Theben/Ahhijawa (Griechenland) an den König des Hethitischen Reiches aus dem 13. Jh. V. Chr," handout, August 2003. Archaeology adds the information that Late Bronze Age Greeks colonized the city of Miletus on Anatolia's Aegean coast. See W. D. Niemeier, "Miletus in the Bronze Age: Bridge Between the Aegean and Anatolia," *Bulletin of the Institute of Classical Studies* 46 (2002–03): 225–27.

The positivists fall into several different categories. Some date the Trojan War to around 1300 B.C. (at the end of Troy VIh) and others to around 1210–1180 (at the end of Troy VIIa—also known as Troy VIi). This book adheres to the latter view, as does Shear in her *Tales of Heroes*. Advocates of a date around 1300 B.C. include Michael Wood and D. F. Easton, "Has the Trojan War Been Found?" *Antiquity* 59 (1985):188–95. Others agree that Homer reflects the genuine historical memory of the Greek people, but deny that there was ever one Trojan War. Instead, they say, Homer took several centuries of wars in Anatolia and turned them into a single conflict. His poems are a smorgasbord of events; most of them really happened but not in any one time or place. The current excavators of Troy tend to this view. Emily Vermeule and Sarah P. Morris date the core material of Homer's poems back to the early Mycenaean era; see E. D. T. Vermeule, "Priam's Castle Blazing: A Thousand Years of Trojan Memories," *Troy and the Trojan War* (Cambridge, Mass.: Harvard University Press, 1986): 77–92, and Sarah Morris "A Tale of Two Cities: The Miniature Frescoes from Thera and the Origins of Greek Poetry," *American Journal of Archaeology* 93:4 (October 1989): 511–35.

This book argues that the Trojan War was caused by a combination of fear, honor, and self-interest: Thucydides' trio of motives underlying international relations. There has been no shortage of other theories. To cite just one category, for clashing economic interests as a cause of war between Greeks and Anatolians (including Trojans), see E. H. Cline, *Sailing the Wine-Dark Sea: International Trade and the Late Bronze Age Aegean* (Ox-

ford: Tempus Reparatum, 1994); Christopher Mee, "Aegean Trade and Settlement in Anatolia in the Second Millennium B.C.," *Anatolian Studies* 28
(1978): 122–55; Christopher Mee, "Anatolia and the Aegean in the Late
Bronze Age," in Eric H. Cline and Diane Harris-Cline, eds., *The Aegean and
the Orient in the Second Millennium B.C.*, Proceedings of the Fiftieth An-
niversary Symposium, Cincinnati, April 18–20, 1997, *Aegaeum* 18 (1998):
137–48; Trevor R. Bryce, "The Nature of Mycenaean Involvement in
Western Anatolia," *Historia* 38 (1989): 1–21.

The Trojan War is not just a war but a cultural icon. Films, novels,
fashions, and current events shape perceptions of it; there are influences
from which not even scholars are immune. Barbara Tuchman saw Homer
through the lens of the Vietnam War in *The March of Folly from Troy to
Vietnam* (New York: Ballantine Books, 1984): 35–50. On Troy and contemporary culture, see Johannes Haubold, "Wars of *Wissenschaft:* The New
Quest for Troy," *International Journal of the Classical Tradition* 8:4 (Spring
2002): 564–79; my "Why Is Troy Still Burning?" *Historically Speaking: The
Bulletin of the History Society,* 8:1 (September–October 2006: 18–20; Martin
M. Winkler, ed. *Troy, From Homer's Iliad to Hollywood's Epic* (Oxford:
Blackwell Publishing, 2007).

TROY AND ARCHAEOLOGY

Troy was excavated from 1871 to 1891 by Heinrich Schliemann and Wilhelm Dörpfeld, and then again in 1932–1938 by Carl W. Blegen. In 1988,
excavations at Troy were resumed after a fifty-year hiatus, having been
preceded a few years earlier by a dig about five miles away at Beşik Bay (the
Trojan Harbor). These new excavations are directed by Ernst Pernicka,
successor to the late Manfred Korfmann, with the cooperation of Brian
Rose. In addition to archaeologists, the excavation team includes anthro-
pologists, art historians, chemists, computer scientists, epigraphers, geolo-
gists, Hittite specialists, Homerists, students of ancient plant life
(archaeobiologists), and others. Reports of "Project Troia," the ongoing
excavations at Troy, as well as articles on the archaeology of Troy and the
Troad, may be found in *Studia Troica*, a scholarly journal published annually since 1991. Articles appear in English or German, each with a brief
summary in both languages. Since 1998, the annual archaeological report
has been published in both languages; earlier reports are in German with
an English summary. News, bibliography, and other valuable information

are also available in English on the Internet at http://www.uni-tuebingen
.de/troia/eng/index.html. For a 2003 summary of the state of the excavations at Troy, see http://www.uni-tuebingen.de/troia/deu/trier_deu.pdf
and an update in 2006 at http://www.uni-tuebingen.de/troia/eng/work
shop_report.pdf. An excellent introduction to the excavations and their
meaning for historians is found in Latacz, *Troy and Homer*, 15–100.

The excavators have written a guide to the site, available in English.
See Manfred Korfmann and Dietrich Mannsperger, *Troia/Wilusa—
Overview and Official Tour* (Istanbul: Ege Yayınları, 2005); it is still hard to
find outside of Turkey. In German, there is a highly readable and reliable
introduction, with beautiful color photos and remarkable, if hypothetical,
reconstructions by Birgit Brandau, Hartmut Schickert, and Peter Jablonka,
Troia wie es wirklich Aussah (Munich: Piper, 2004). One of the more innovative (and controversial) aspects of Project Troia is the use of computer
models to create hypothetical reconstructions of the various ancient cities
of Troy. For an introduction on the Internet, see http://www.uni-
tuebingen.de/troia/vr/index_en.html. The lavishly illustrated catalog to a
2001 museum exhibit contains fine introductory essays (in German) by
leading scholars on a wide range of topics concerning Troy: Manfred
Korfmann et al., *Troia: Traum und Wirklichkeit* (Stuttgart: Theiss Verlag,
2001). Two important statements of the Anatolian character of Troy are
Manfred Korfmann, "Troia, An Ancient Anatolian Palatial and Trading
Center," *Classical World* 91.5 (1998): 369–85 and F. Starke, "Troia im Kon-
text des historisch-politischen und sprachlichen Umfeldes Kleinasiens im
2. Jahrtausend," *Studia Troica* 7 (1997): 447–87.

On the biconvex hieroglyphic seal found at Troy, see J. David Hawkins
and Donald F. Easton, "A Hieroglyphic Seal from Troy," *Studia Troica* 6
(1996): 111–18. On the bronze figurine, see Manfred Korfmann, "Aus-
grabungen 1995," *Studia Troica* 6 (1996): 34, 36; Machteld J. Mellink and
Donna Strahan, "The Bronze Figurine from Troia Level VIIa," *Studia
Troica* 8 (1998): 141–49. On the steles outside the gates of Troy, see Manfred Korfmann, "Stelen vor den Toren Troias, Apaliunas-Apollon in Tru-
isa/Wilusa?" in Güven Arsebük, Machteld J. Mellink, and Wulf Schirmer,
eds., *Light on Top of the Black Hill, Studies Presented to Halet Çambel* (Istanbul: Ege Yayınları, 1998), 471–78. An inscribed silver bowl may attest to a
victory over Troy by a Hittite king, probably an early one, but the subject
is still under debate: J. David Hawkins, "A Hieroglyphic Inscription on a
Silver Bowl," *Studia Troica* 15 (2005): 193–204.

For an introduction to the Troad, the region of Troy, in light of Homeric scholarship and recent archaeology, see J. V. Luce, *Celebrating Homer's Landscapes: Troy and Ithaca Revisited* (New Haven: Yale University Press, 1999), 21–164; see Cook's meticulous if now partly outdated *The Troad: An Archaeological and Topographical Survey* (Oxford: Clarendon Press, 1973). A detailed study of the excavations at Beşik Bay (the Trojan Harbor), including the cemeteries, may be found in Maureen A. Basedow, *Beşik Tepe: Das spätbronzezeitliche Gräberfeld* (Munich: Verlag Philipp von Zabern, 2000). On the Mycenaean-style seal stone with smiling face, found in the harbor excavations, see Ingo Pini, "Zu den Siegeln aus der Beşik-Necropole," *Studia Troica* 2 (1992): 157–64, esp. 157–58. Rüstem Aslan and Gerhard Bieg, with Peter Jablonka and Petra Krönneck, "Die Mittel-Bis Spätbronzezeitliche Besiedlung (Troia VI und Troia VIIa) der Troas unter der Gelibolu-Halbinsel, Ein Überblick," *Studia Troica* 13 (2003): 165–213, is a fundamental survey of archaeological research in the Middle and Late Bronze Age Troad outside the city of Troy. Fascinating details of the ecology and geology of the region appear in G. A. Wagner, Ernst Pernicka, and Hans-Peter Uerpmann, *Troia and the Troad: Scientific Approaches* (New York: Springer, 2003). For an argument on following Homer when it comes to locating the Greeks' ship station, see J. C. Kraft, "Harbor Areas at Ancient Troy: Sedimentology and Geomorphology Complement Homer's Iliad," *Geological Society of America* 31:2 (2003): 163–66. Botanist Martin Rix offers an appreciation of the plant life of Mount Ida in "Wild About Ida: The Glorious Flora of Kaz Dagi and the Vale of Troy," *Cornucopia* 5:26 (2002): 58–75.

There is a discussion of the fossils of the Troad in A. Mayor, *The First Fossil Hunters* (Princeton: Princeton University Press, 2000). On the winds in the Dardanelles and their impact on Troy's prosperity, see J. Neumann, "Number of Days That Black Sea Bound Sailing Ships Were Delayed by Winds at the Entrance to the Dardanelles Near Troy's Site," *Studia Troica* 1 (1991): 93–100.

A considerable minority of scholars reject a number of the Troia Project's conclusions; that is, they doubt that the lower city has really been found, that Troy was a major center of commerce, that Troy and Wilusa are one and the same—and some question even the identification of Hisarlık with Troy, an equation that goes back to Schliemann. The leading skeptics are the ancient historian Frank Kolb and the archaeologist Dieter Hertel, and they are joined by Hittitologists and experts in the ancient

Near East as well as ancient historians and archaeologists. In English, see Frank Kolb, "Troy VI: A Trading Center and Commercial City?" *American Journal of Archaeology* 108:4 (2004): 577–613, and D. Hertel and Frank Kolb, "Troy in Clearer Perspective," *Anatolian Studies* 53 (2003): 71–88. Christoph Ulf edited a collection of articles (in German) largely critical of the excavators' conclusions in *Der neue Streit um Troia, Eine Bilanz* (Munich: C. H. Beck Verlag, 2003).

But most of these criticisms have been convincingly answered: see D. F. Easton, J. D. Hawkins, A. G. Sherratt, and E. S. Sherratt, "Troy in Recent Perspective," *Anatolian Studies* 52 (2002): 1–35, and P. Jablonka and C. B. Rose, "Late Bronze Age Troy: A Response to Frank Kolb," *American Journal of Archaeology* 108:4 (2004): 615–30. In 2006 an important new section of the lower town's defensive trench was found, strengthening their theories: http://www.uni-tuebingen.de/uni/qvo/pm/pm2006/pm-06-128.html. It is not certain that Wilusa equals Troy or that the Ahhiyawa of Hittite texts are Homer's Achaeans, that is Greeks, but both conclusions are likely. The evidence of Late Bronze Age trade between the Aegean and the Black Seas is stronger than the skeptics allow, although it requires more investigation. See Olaf Höckmann, "Zu früher Seefahrt in den Meerengen," *Studia Troica* 13 (2003): 133–60.

The results of the University of Cincinnati's excavations at Troy between 1932 and 1938 are published in four volumes edited by Carl W. Blegen, John L. Caskey, and Marion Rawson, *Troy: Excavations Conducted by the University of Cincinnati, 1932–1938* (Princeton: Princeton University Press, 1950–53), as well as in three supplementary monographs (1951–63). Blegen summarized his conclusions in *Troy and the Trojans* (New York: Praeger, 1963). Wilhelm Dörpfeld's excavations at Troy are described in an English-language book by Herbert Cushing Tolman, *Mycenaean Troy* (1903). Heinrich Schliemann famously began the modern excavation of Troy in 1871, and he published the pioneering results in volumes called *Ilios* (1881) and *Troja* (1884).

HOMER

Most readers get to know Homer in translation. While they are no substitute for the Greek original, many excellent translations are available. This book uses Alexander Pope's dignified and lapidary *Iliad* of 1720 and *Odyssey* of 1725–26, which render Homer in heroic couplets. Among recent translations, the two outstanding formal renderings of the *Iliad* are Richmond Lattimore, *The Iliad of Homer* (Chicago: University of Chicago Press, 1951) and Robert Fagles, *The Iliad/Homer* (New York: Penguin Books, 1991). Fagles's *Odyssey* is particularly beautiful: *Odyssey/Homer* (New York: Penguin Books, 1996). But perhaps the outstanding translation is Stanley Lombardo's rendition of Homer in ordinary English: *Iliad/Homer* and *Odyssey/Homer* (Indianapolis: Hackett Publishing Company, 2000).

Indispensable for serious study of the *Iliad* is a six-volume scholarly commentary by G. S. Kirk, Mark W. Edwards, Richard Janko, J. B. Hainsworth, and N. J. Richardson, *The Iliad: A Commentary* (Cambridge, England: Cambridge University Press, 1985–93). A scholarly commentary in English on Books I–XVI of the *Odyssey* is available in A. W. Heubeck, Stephanie Hainsworth, and J. B. Hainsworth, *A Commentary on Homer's Odyssey*, 2 vols. (Oxford: Clarendon Press, 1990). For an introduction to what little survives of the other poems of the Greek Epic Cycle, see M. Davies, *The Epic Cycle* (Bristol: Bristol Classical Press, 1989). M. P. O. Morford and Robert J. Lenardon, *Classical Mythology* (New York: Longman, 1971) is useful.

Scholarly books and articles on Homer are almost innumerable. A good starting point is Barry Powell, *Homer* (Malden, Mass.: Blackwell, 2004), or Mark W. Edwards, *Homer, Poet of the Iliad* (Baltimore: Johns Hopkins University Press, 1987), while Morris and Powell, eds., *A New Companion to Homer*, offers expert essays on topics ranging from poetic meter to the experience of battle. A number of important essays on a variety of related subjects are found in Jane B. Carter and Sarah P. Morris, eds., *The Ages of Homer: A Tribute to Emily Townsend Vermeule* (Austin: University of Texas Press, 1995). On Homer as an oral poet, the basic book remains A. B. Lord, *The Singer of Tales* (Cambridge, Mass.: Harvard University Press, 1960). There is much of value in Gregory G. Nagy, *The Best of the Achaeans* (Baltimore: Johns Hopkins University Press, 1999).

On the impact of the ancient Near East on Homer, see M. L. West, *The East Face of Helicon* (Oxford: Clarendon Press, 1997), and Webster, *From Mycenae to Homer*, 27–64; Walter Burkert, *The Orientalizing Revolution: Near Eastern Influence on Greek Culture in the Early Archaic Age*, trans. Margaret E. Pinder and Walter Burkert (Cambridge, Mass: Harvard University Press, 1992), 1–6, 88–100. Calvert Watkins has done groundbreaking work on the possible Trojan roots of the Homeric poems. See "The Language of the Trojans," in Mellink, ed., *Troy and the Trojan War*, 45–62; "Homer and Hittite Revisited," in P. Knox and C. Foss, eds., *Festschrift Wen-*

dell Claussen (Stuttgart: Leipzig, 1998), 201–11; "Homer and Hittite Revisited II," in K. Alishan Yener and Harry A. Hoffner Jr., eds., *Recent Developments in Hittite Archaeology and History: Papers in Memoriam of Hans G. Güterbock* (Winona Lake, Ind.: Eisenbrauns, 2002), 167–76. On the possible Hittite roots of certain images, verb forms, and similes in the *Iliad,* see Jaan Puhvel, *Homer and Hittite,* Innsbrucker Beiträge zur Sprachwissenschaft, Vorträge und Kleinere Schriften 47 (Innsbruck: Inst. F. Sprachwiss. D. Univ., 1991). Sarah P. Morris's innovative work on the relationship of Greek and Near Eastern art and poetry includes her *Daidalos and the Origins of Greek Art* (Princeton: Princeton University Press, 1992) and her "The Sacrifice of Astyanax: Near Eastern Contributions to the Siege of Troy," in Carter and Morris, eds., *The Ages of Homer,* 221–45.

There are unusual and original insights into the mentality of early poets such as Homer in Elizabeth Wayland Barber and Paul T. Barber, *When They Severed Earth from Sky: How the Human Mind Shapes Myth* (Princeton: Princeton University Press, 2004).

WARFARE

For all his prominence in Western culture, Homer's description of warfare remains highly debated, and poetry is often ambiguous. A fundamental study of the Homeric battlefield is Joachim Latacz, *Kampfparänese, Kampfdarstellung und Kampfwirklichkeit in der Ilias, bei Kallinos und Tyrtaios* (Munich: Beck, 1977). Latacz argues convincingly that pitched battle in Homer is mainly a matter of mass combat rather than individual duels, yet he contends that rather than Homer describing the Bronze Age battlefield, the poet describes Greek warfare of his own day, shortly before 700 B.C. Hans Van Wees wrote a thorough and astute study of the varieties of Homeric warfare, including raiding, although there is more of the Bronze Age in Homer's battles than Van Wees allows. See, among other works, his *Status Warriors: War, Violence and Society in Homer and History* (Amsterdam: J. C. Gieben, 1992) and his "The Homeric Way of War: The 'Iliad' and the Hoplite Phalanx (I)," *Greece and Rome,* 2nd series, 41:1 (1994): 1–18 and "The Homeric Way of War: The 'Iliad' and the Hoplite Phalanx (II)," *Greece and Rome,* 2nd series, 41: 2 (1994): 131–55; also *Greek Warfare, Myths and Realities* (London: Duckworth, 2004), 151–65, 249–52, 290–94. Like Latacz, Van Wees largely removes Homeric battle from the Bronze Age. He differs from Latacz in dating Homer to the 600s B.C. and in taking heroic duels literally. He reconstructs Homeric battle as a matter of the constant ebb and flow of group and individual, which he compares to war in New Guinea. Latacz's reconstruction is more persuasive, but he underestimates the presence of Bronze Age arms and armor in Homer and the existence of mass combat in the Bronze Age. For a corrective, see Shear, *Tales of Heroes*. As Pritchett argues, the phalanx was hardly an invention of Archaic Greece but dates back to the Sumerians: Pritchett, *Greek State at War*, part 4: pp. 5–32. Still useful on raiding is Walter Leaf, *Troy: A Study in Homeric Geography* (London: Macmillan, 1912).

Van Wees and Ralph Gallucci are among those arguing, against the skeptics, that the chariot tactics in Homer are realistic and historical. See Gallucci, "Studies in Homeric Epic Tradition," in Karlene Jones-Bley et al., eds., *Proceedings of the Tenth Annual UCLA Indo-European Conference, Los Angeles 1998* (Washington, D.C.: Institute for the Study of Man, 1999), 165–82. In this same piece Gallucci shows that Bronze Age Assyrians named their siege engines after horses, and suggests that the Trojan Horse is a dim, mythic memory of that.

Skeptics will doubt the relevance of Bronze Age warfare to Homer, but nothing could be more pertinent to the premise of this book. Although four decades old, Yigael Yadin's two volumes are the best introduction to Bronze Age warfare: *The Art of Warfare in Biblical Lands in the Light of Archaeological Discovery* (London: Weidenfeld & Nicolson, 1963). There is much of value in Nigel Stillman and Nigel Tallis, *Armies of the Ancient Near East, 3000 B.C. to 539 B.C.* (Worthington, England: Wargames Research Group, 1984). There are good but brief discussions of Bronze Age warfare in General Sir John Hackett, ed., *Warfare in the Ancient World* (New York: Facts on File, 1989) and in Simon Anglim, Phyllis G. Jestice, Rob S. Rice, Scott Rusch, and John Serrati, *Fighting Techniques of the Ancient World 3000 BC–AD 500: Equipment, Combat Skills, and Tactics* (New York: Thomas Dunne Books, 2002). Robert Drews offers many important insights into conflict in the Late Bronze Age in his *The End of the Bronze Age: Changes in Warfare and the Catastrophe c. 1200 BC* (Princeton: Princeton University Press, 1993); his theories of chariot warfare, the limited role of infantry, and the disconnection between Homeric and Mycenaean society are, however, unconvincing. A. Harding's thoughtful essay considers war and the era's culture: "Warfare: A Defining Characteristic of Bronze Age Europe?" in John Carman and Anthony Harding, eds., *Ancient Warfare: Archaeological Perspectives* (Stroud, England: Sutton Publishing, 1999), 157–74.

Archaeological artifacts, military architecture, and the Linear B tablets are rich in detail about Late Bronze Age Greek warfare. For an overview of the subject, see Sarah Monks, "The Aegean," in R. Osgood, Sarah Monks, and Judith Toms, *Bronze Age Warfare* (Phoenix Mill, England: Sutton Publishing, 2000), 115–37. The first generation of Linear B evidence is discussed in Michael Ventris and John Chadwick, *Documents in Mycenaean Greek*, 2nd edition (Cambridge, England: Cambridge University Press, 1973); for the recent evidence, see Thomas G. Palaima, "Mycenaean Militarism from a Textual Perspective: Onomastics in Context: *Lāwos, Dāmos, Klewos,*" in Robert Laffineur, ed., *Polemos: Le Contexte Guerrier en Égée à l'âge du Bronze*, vol. 2, in *Aegaeum* 19 (1999): 367–80. On Mycenaean arms and armor, see Shear, *Tales of Heroes*, 29–60, and A. M. Snodgrass, *Arms and Armour of the Greeks* (Ithaca: Cornell University Press, 1967), 14–34.

For an introduction to Hittite warfare, see P. H. J. Houwink ten Cate, "The History of Warfare According to Hittite Sources: The Annals of Hattusilis I (Part II)," *Anatolica* 11 (1984): 47–83; Richard H. Beal, *The Organisation of the Hittite Military* (Heidelberg: Carl Winter Universitaetsverlag, 1992); Richard H. Beal, "Hittite Military Organization," in Sasson, ed., *Civilizations of the Ancient Near East*, vol. 1, pp. 545–54; Richard H. Beal, "Le Strutture Militari Ittite di Attaco e di Difesa" [in Italian], in M. C. Guidotti and Franca Pecchioli Daddi, eds., *La Battaglia di Qadesh* (Livorno: Sillabe, 2000), 109–21. There is much of importance in these specialized studies: Kemal Balkan, *Letter of King Anum-Hirbi of Mama to King Warshama of Kanish* (Ankara: Türk Tarih Kurumu Basımevi, 1957); H. A. Hoffner, "A Hittite Analogue to the David and Goliath Contest of Champions?" *Catholic Biblical Quarterly* 30 (1968): 220–25; Hans G. Güterbock and Theo P. J. Van den Hout, eds., *The Hittite Instruction for the Royal Bodyguard, The Oriental Institute of the University of Chicago, Assyriological Studies*, no. 24 (Chicago: University of Chicago Press, 1991); Gary Beckman, "The Siege of Uršu Text (CTH 7) and Old Hittite Historiography," *Journal of Cuneiform Studies* 47 (1995): 23–32; Schlommo Izre'el and Itamar Singer, *The General's Letter from Ugarit* (Tel Aviv: Tel Aviv University, 1990); T. P. J. Van den Hout, "Bellum Iustum, Ius Divinum: Some Thoughts About War and Peace in Hittite Anatolia," in *Grotiana, New Series* 12–13 (1991–92 [1994]): 13–35.

New Kingdom Egyptian warfare is very well documented, and it is at a minimum suggestive of Late Bronze Age fighting more generally. See Ian Shaw's succinct *Egyptian Warfare and Weapons* (Buckinghamshire, England: Shire Publications, 1991) and A. J. Spalinger's more detailed *War in Ancient Egypt* (Oxford: Blackwell Publishing, 1991), as well as Andrea Gnirs, "Ancient Egypt," in Kurt Raaflaub and Nathan Rosenstein, eds., *War and Society in the Ancient and Medieval Worlds, Asia, the Mediterranean, Europe, and Mesoamerica* (Washington, D.C.: Center for Hellenic Studies, 1999), 71–104. See also J. K. Hoffmeier, "Military: Materiel," in D. B. Redford, ed., *Oxford Encyclopedia of Ancient Egypt*, vol. 2 (New York: Oxford University Press, 2001), 406–12, and D. B. Redford, *The Wars in Syria and Palestine of Thutmose III* (Leiden: Brill, 2003).

On Early Bronze Age warfare in Mesopotamia, see J. S. Cooper, *Reconstructing History from Ancient Inscriptions: The Lagash-Umma Border Conflict*, vol. 2, fasc. 1 of *Sources from the Ancient Near East* (Malibu, Calif.: Undena Publications, 1983). The rich evidence for Middle Bronze Age warfare at Mari can be found in J. M. Sasson, *The Military Establishments at Mari, Studia Pohl* (Rome: Pontifical Biblical Institute, 1969) and W. Heimpel, *Letters to the King of Mari: A New Translation, with Historical Introduction, Notes, and Commentary* (Winona Lake, Ind.: Eisenbrauns, 2003). For an introduction to Mari, see S. Dalley, *Mari and Karana: Two Old Babylonian Cities* (New York: Longman, 1984).

On set battles in the ancient Near East, see, for Megiddo (1479 B.C.), E. H. Cline, *The Battles of Armageddon* (Ann Arbor: University of Michigan Press, 2003), 6–28; and for Qadesh (1274 B.C.), W. J. Murnane, *The Road to Kadesh: A Historical Interpretation of the Battle Reliefs of King Sety I at Karnak* (Chicago: Oriental Institute of Chicago, 1990); and M. Healy, *Qadesh 1300 BC: Clash of the Warrior Kings* (Oxford: Osprey Publishing, 1993).

On chariots, see S. Piggott, *Wagon, Chariot, and Carriage: Symbol and Status in the History of Transport* (New York: Thames & Hudson, 1992), Mary Aiken Littauer et al., eds., *Selected Writings on Chariots, Other Early Vehicles, Riding and Harness*, in *Culture & History of the Ancient Near East*, vol. 6 (Leiden: Brill, 2002) and Juliet Clutton-Brock, *Horse Power: A History of the Horse and the Donkey in Human Societies* (Cambridge, Mass.: Harvard University Press, 1992).

On Bronze Age and Homeric naval history, see S. Wachsmann, *Seagoing Ships and Seamanship in the Bronze Age Levant* (College Station: Texas A&M University Press, 1998); Lionel Casson, *Ships and Seamanship in the Ancient World* (Baltimore: Johns Hopkins University Press, 1971), 30–35, 38–53, 445–46; Lucien Basch, *Le Musée Imaginaire de la Marine Antique* (Athens: Institut Hellénique pour la Préservation de la Tradition Nautique, 1987), 76–202; Shelley Wachsmann, "The Pylos Rower Tablets Reconsidered," *Tropis V, 5th International Symposium on Ship Construction in Antiquity: Nauplia, 26, 27, 28 August 1993, Proceedings*, ed. Harry Tzalas (Nauplion, Greece: Hellenic Institute for the Preservation of Nautical Tradition, 1993), 491–504; T. G. Palaima, "Maritime Matters in the Linear B Tablets," *Thalassa: L'Égée Prehistorique et la Mer*, in *Aegaeum* 7 (1991): 273–310; J. Crouwel, "Fighting on Land and Sea in Late Mycenaean Times," *Polemos*, 455–64. For arguments that the Mycenaeans invented the galley in the Late Bronze Age, see Michael Wedde, "War at Sea: The Mycenaean and Early Iron Age Oared Galley," *Polemos*, 465–78, as well as Michael Wedde, *Towards a Hermeneutics of Aegean Bronze Age Ship Imagery* (Mannheim: Bibliopolis, 2000). On the Egyptian navy, see E. Linder, "Naval Warfare in the El-Amarna Age," in D. J. Blackman, ed., *Marine Archaeology*, Proceedings of the Twentythird [sic] Symposium of the Colston Research Society Held in the University of Bristol April 4th to 8th, 1971 (London: Archon Books, 1973), 317–25; Steve Vinson, *Egyptian Boats and Ships* (Princes Risborough, England: Shire Publications, 1994). On Bronze Age shipwrecks, see George Bass, "Cape Gelidonya: A Bronze Age Shipwreck," *Transactions of the American Philosophical Society* 57, part 8 (1967), cf. http://ina.tamu.edu/capegelidonya.htm; W. Phelps, Y. Lolos, and Y. Vichos, eds., *The Point Iria Wreck: Interconnections in the Mediterranean ca. 1200 BC* (Athens: Hellenic Institute of Marine Archaeology, 1999); on the Ulu Burun wreck, see http://ina.tamu.edu/ub_main.htm.

Health conditions were surely no inconsiderable factor in the Trojan War. On war wounds and battlefield medicine, see Christine Salazar, *The Treatment of War Wounds in Greco-Roman Antiquity* (Leiden: Brill, 2000), 126–58; Guido Majno, *The Healing Hand: Man and Wound in the Ancient World* (Cambridge, Mass.: Harvard University Press, 1975), 142–47; Wolf-Hartmut Friedrich, *Wounding and Death in the Iliad: Homeric Techniques of Description*, trans. Gabriele Wright and Peter Jones (London: Duckworth, 2003); R. Arnott, "War Wounds and Their Treatment in the Aegean Bronze Age," *Polemos*, 499–506. There is much important and comparative information on malaria in Robert Sallares, *Malaria and Rome: A History of Malaria in Ancient Italy* (Oxford: Oxford University Press, 2002). There is an insightful discussion of battle stress in the *Iliad* in J. Shay, *Achilles in Vietnam* (New York: Maxwell Macmillan International, 1994). Poison in Homer is examined in A. Mayor, *Greek Fire, Poison Arrows & Scorpion Bombs* (Woodstock, N.Y.: Overlook Press, 2003).

On Amazons, see J. H. Blok, *The Early Amazons: Modern and Ancient Perspectives on a Persistent Myth* (Leiden: Brill, 1995); Lyn Webster Wilde, *On the Trail of the Women Warriors: The Amazons in Myth and History* (New York: Thomas Dunne Books, 2000); Jeanine Kimball-Davis, *Warrior Women: An Archaeologist's Search for History's Hidden Heroines* (New York: Warner Books, 2002); Renate Rolle, *World of the Scythians*, trans. F. G. Walls (Berkeley: University of California Press, 1989); and browse the archaeology links of the Web site of the Center for the Study of Eurasian Nomads, http://www.csen.org. On the female soldiers of Dahomey, see Stanley B. Alpern, *Amazons of Black Sparta: The Women Warriors of Dahomey* (New York: New York University Press, 1998) and Robert B. Edgerton, *Warrior Women: The Amazons of Dahomey and the Nature of War* (Boulder, Colo.: Westview Press, 2000). For a suggestion that the Amazons were really the female archers (or possibly male archers dressed as women) who took part in Hittite ritual, see Watkins, "The Language of the Trojans," in Mellink, ed., *Troy and the Trojan War*, 53, 55.

War and religion often go together. There are good insights into the religious milieu of Bronze Age Anatolia and its survival in Homer in Christopher Faraone, *Talismans and Trojan Horses* (Oxford: Oxford University Press, 1992). For an introduction to ancient Anatolian religion, see M. Popko, *Religions of Asia Minor* (Warsaw: Academic Publications, 1995); on Luwian religion, see Manfred Hutter, "Aspects of Luwian Religion," in H. Craig Melchert, ed., *The Luwians*, Handbuch der Orientalistik, vol. 68 (Leiden: Brill, 2003), 211–80. There is much on Mycenaean religion in the books below.

THE MYCENAEANS

Among several good and readable introductions to the subject are John Chadwick, *The Mycenaean World* (Cambridge, England: Cambridge University Press, 1976) and W. D. Taylour, *The Mycenaeans*, 2nd edition (London: Thames & Hudson, 1983). A more detailed and scholarly introduction is available in O. Dickinson, *The Aegean Bronze Age* (Cambridge, England: Cambridge University Press, 1994).

For a scholarly survey of fairly recent work, see C. W. Shelmerdine, "Review of Aegean Prehistory VI: The Palatial Bronze Age of the Southern and Central Greek Mainland," *American Journal of Archaeology* 101:3 (1997): 537–85, reprinted with an addendum on the period 1997–99 in

Tracey Cullen, ed., *Aegean Prehistory: A Review*, Supplement 1 to *American Journal of Archaeology* (Boston: Archaeological Institute of America, 2001), 329–82. Elizabeth French, *Mycenae, Agamemnon's Capital: The Site in Its Setting* (Charleston, S.C.: Tempus, 2004) is a succinct introduction to the most important Mycenaean site. An article on the excavations at Pellana and the purported palace of Menelaus and Helen is (in Greek) Theodore G. Spyropoulos, "The Palace of Menelaus and Helen in Mycenaean Lacedaemon," *Aeropos* 54 (March–April 2004): 4–15. An earlier candidate for the site of the palace is Therapne; see Hughes, *Helen of Troy*, 29–33.

On Linear B texts, see Ventris and Chadwick, *Documents in Mycenaean Greek*, and J. T. Hooker, *Linear B: An Introduction* (London: Bristol Classical Press, 1980). For an exciting tale of scholarship in action, see John Chadwick, *The Decipherment of Linear B*, 2nd edition (London: Cambridge University Press, 1967).

Earlier scholarship on the Mycenaeans, especially in light of Linear B texts, tended to regard Late Bronze Age Greek kingdoms as centralized, bureaucratic machines, and therefore utterly different from the ramshackle chiefdoms of the *Iliad*. For a corrective, see D. B. Small, "Surviving the Collapse: The Oikos and Structural Continuity Between Late Bronze Age and Later Greece," in Michael Galaty and William A. Parkinson, eds., *Rethinking Mycenaean Palaces* (Los Angeles: Cotsen Institute of Archaeology, 1999), 283–91; Ione Mylonas Shear, *Kingship in the Mycenaean World and Its Reflections in the Oral Tradition* (Philadelphia: INSTAP Academic Press, 2004). For Linear B texts and the Mycenaean military, see Palaima, "Mycenaean Militarism."

There are tantalizing suggestions of the impact of Anatolia on Mycenaean culture and society in such works as S. Morris, "Potnia Aswiya: Anatolian Contributions to Greek Religion," *Potnia: Deities and Religion in the Aegean Bronze Age*, in *Aegaeum* 22 (2001): 423–34; and Trevor R. Bryce, "Anatolian Scribes in Mycenaean Greece," *Historia* 48:3 (1999): 257–64.

For the possibility of Mycenaean mercenaries in the Egypt of King Tut, see R. Parkinson and Louise Schofield, "Images of Mycenaeans: A Recently Acquired Painted Papyrus from El-Amarna," in W. Vivian Davies and Louise Schofeld, eds., *Egypt, the Aegean and the Levant: Interconnections in the Second Millennium BC* (London: British Museum Press, 1995), 125–26.

On Mycenaean jewelry, see Eleni M. Konstantinidi, *Jewellery Revealed in the Burial Contexts of the Greek Bronze Age* (Oxford: J. & E. Hedges, distributed by Hadrian Books, 2001) and http://www.fhw.gr/chronos/02/mainland/en/mg/technology/index.html.

On Mycenaean food, drink, and perfume, see Y. Tzedakis and H. Martlew, *Minoans and Mycenaeans: Flavours of Their Time* (Athens: Production Kapon Editions, 1999) and Cynthia W. Shelmerdine, *The Perfume Industry of Mycenaean Pylos* (Göteborg, Sweden: P. Åström, 1985). The possibility of human sacrifice in Minoan Crete is explored in J. A. Sakellarakis and S. E. Sapouna, *Archanes* (Athens: Ekdotike Athenon S.A., 1991).

HITTITES AND OTHER ANATOLIANS

The interaction between man and nature in ancient Anatolia is explored in J. Yakar, *Ethnoarchaeology of Anatolia* (Jerusalem: Graphit Press, 2000). On the animal world, see Billie Jean Collins, ed., *A History of the Animal World in the Ancient Near East* (Leiden: Brill, 2002). For an introduction to archaeological sites in Turkey, see Ekrem Akurgal, *Ancient Civilizations and Ruins of Turkey* (Turkey: Guzel Sanatlar Matbaasi A.S., 2001). There is much of value in Bernard McDonagh, *Blue Guide: Turkey*, 3rd edition (New York: W. W. Norton, 2001). Bilge Umar has written many books on the historical geography of Turkey. It is not necessary to know Turkish to appreciate the photos in his *Türkiye'deki Tarıhsel Anıtlar* (Istanbul: Inkılâp Kitabevi, 1995).

Trevor Bryce, in his *The Kingdom of the Hittites*, new edition (Oxford: Clarendon Press, 2006) and his *Life and Society in the Hittite World*, new edition (Oxford: Oxford University Press, 2004), provides an excellent introduction to the Hittites, as does J. G. MacQueen, *The Hittites and Their Contemporaries in Asia Minor*, revised edition (London: Thames & Hudson, 1986); see also several good articles in Sasson, ed., *Civilizations of the Ancient Near East*, as well as the lavishly illustrated O. Tashin, *Die Hethiter und ihr Reich: Das Volk der 1000 Götter* (Stuttgart: Theiss Verlag, 2002 [in German]) and the guide to Hattusha by its current excavator, J. Seeher, *Hattusha Guide: A Day in the Hittite Capital*, revised edition (Istanbul: Ege Yayınları, 2002). On new theories about the destruction of Hattusha, see J. Seeher, "Die Zerstörung der Stadt Hattuša," *Akten der IV: Internationalen Kongresse für Hethitologie* (Wiesbaden, 2001), 623–34. H. A. Hoffner, "Daily Life among the Hittites," in R. E. Averbeck et al., eds. *Life and Culture in the Ancient Near East* (Bethesda, Md.: CDL Press, 2003), 95–120, is an excellent overview. There are important recent papers in K. Alishan Yener and Harry A. Hoffner Jr., eds., *Recent Developments in Hittite Archaeology and History: Papers in Memoriam of Hans G. Güterbock* (Winona Lake, Ind.: Eisenbrauns, 2002), and Gary Beckman, Richard Beal, and Gregory McMahon, eds., *Hittite Studies in Honor of Harry A. Hoffner, Jr: On the Occasion of his 65th Birthday* (Winona Lake, Ind.: Eisenbrauns, 2003). There is a great deal of value in the monographs by Gary Beckman, *Hittite Diplomatic Texts*, 2nd edition (Atlanta: Scholars Press, 1999); I. Singer, *Hittite Prayers* (Leiden: Brill, 2002); Harry A. Hoffner Jr., *The Laws of the Hittites: A Critical Edition* (Leiden: Brill, 1997); and Harry A. Hoffner, ed., *Hittite Myths* (Atlanta: Scholars Press, 1998). On Hittite music, see Stefano de Martino, "Music, Dance, and Processions in Hittite Anatolia," in Sasson, ed., *Civilizations of the Ancient Near East*, vol. 4, 2668–69.

For the Hittites' neighbors and the political geography of Anatolia, see H. Craig Melchert, ed., *The Luwians*, with important contributions by Trevor Bryce, J. D. Hawkins, Manfred Hutter, and others; J. D. Hawkins, "Tarkasnawa King of Mira"; Hawkins, "Anatolia: The End of the Hittite Empire and After," in Eva Andrea Braun-Holzinger and Hartmut Matthäus, eds., *Die nahöstlichen Kulturen und Griechenland an der Wende vom 2. zum 1. Jahrtausend v. Chr.: Kontinuität und Wandel von Strukturen und Mechanismen kultureller Interaktion*, Kolloquium des Sonderforschungsbereiches 295 "Kulturelle und sprachliche Kontakte" der Johannes Gutenberg-Universität Mainz, December 11–12, 1998 (Möhnesee: Bibliopolis, 2002), 143–51; M. Benzi, "Anatolia and the Eastern Aegean at the Time of the Trojan War," in Franco Montanari and Paola Ascheri, eds., *Omero Tremila Anni Dopo* (Rome: Edizioni di Storia e Letteratura, 2002), 343–409.

What language or languages did the Trojans speak? There is much of interest on this still-unanswered question in the works by Watkins and Melchert cited above; see also G. Neumann, "Wie haben die Troer in 13. Jahrhundert gesprochen?" *Würzburger Jahrbücher für die Altertumswissenschaften* 23 (1999): 15–23; Ruggero Stefanini, "Toward a Diachronic Reconstruction of the Linguistic Map of Ancient Anatolia," in S. De Martino and F. Pecchioli Daddi, eds., *Anatolia antica: Studi in Memoria di Fiorella Imparati, Eothen* 11 (Florence: Logisma editore, 2002), 783–806; Itamar Singer, "Western Anatolia in the Thirteenth-Century B.C. According to the Hittite Sources," *Anatolian Studies* 33 (1983): 206–17.

For relations between the Greeks and Anatolia, see H. G. Güterbock, "The Hittites and the Aegean World: Part 1, The Ahhiyawa Problem Reconsidered," *American Journal of Archaeology* 87:2 (1983): 133–38; M. J. Mellink, "The Hittites and the Aegean World: Part 2, Archaeological Comments on Ahhiyawa-Achaians in Western Anatolia," *American Journal of Archaeology* 87:2 (1983): 138–41; E. T. Vermeule, "Response to Hans Güterbock," *American Journal of Archaeology* 87:2 (1983): 141–43. See also Trevor Bryce, "Ahhiyawans and Mycenaeans: An Anatolian Viewpoint," *Oxford Journal of Archaeology* 8 (1989): 297–310; Trevor Bryce, "Relations Between Hatti and Ahhiyawa in the Last Decades of the Bronze Age," in Beckman et al., eds., *Hittite Studies* (2003): 59–72; E. Cline, "A Possible Hittite Embargo Against the Mycenaeans," *Historia* 40 (1991): 1–9; W. D. Niemeier, "Mycenaeans and Hittites in War in Western Asia Minor," *Polemos*, vols. 1–2, in *Aegaeum* 19, pp. 141–56; P. H. J. Houwink ten Cate, "Contact Between the Aegean Region and Anatolia in the Second Millennium B.C." (1973), in R. A. Crossland and Ann Birchall, eds., *Bronze Age Migrations in the Aegean: Archaeological and Linguistic Problems in Greek Prehistory* (Park Ridge, N.J.: Noyes Press, 1974), 141–61.

THE ANCIENT NEAR EAST BEYOND ANATOLIA

A succinct introduction to the ancient Near East is found in B. A. Knapp, *The History and Culture of Ancient Western Asia and Egypt* (Chicago: Dorsey Press, 1988). Two valuable reference books are Sasson, ed., *Civilizations of the Ancient Near East*, and Daniel C. Snell, ed., *A Companion to the Ancient Near East* (Oxford: Blackwell, 2005). Important collections of documents from the region include W. W. Hallo, ed., *The Context of Scripture: Canonical Compositions from the Biblical World*, 2 vols. (Leiden: Brill, 1997–2000); J. B. Pritchard, *Ancient Near Eastern Texts Relating to the Old Testament*, revised edition (Princeton: Princeton University Press, 1969); Amelie Kuhrt, *The Ancient Near East: c. 3000–330 BC*, 2 vols. (London: Routledge, 1995).

A selection of literature from New Kingdom Egypt is available in Miriam Lichtheim, *Ancient Egyptian Literature: A Book of Readings*, vol. 2, *The New Kingdom* (Berkeley: University of California Press, 1976). A good historical introduction can be found in Donald B. Redford, *Egypt, Canaan, and Israel in Ancient Times* (Princeton: Princeton University Press, 1992) while Redford, ed., *Oxford Encyclopedia of Ancient Egypt* (New York: Oxford University Press, 2001) is a valuable reference source. P. H. Newby, *Warrior Pharaohs: The Rise and Fall of the Egyptian Empire* (London: Faber & Faber, 1980) is very readable.

For the royal inscriptions of Assyria, see A. K. Grayson, *Assyrian Royal Inscriptions*, vol. 1, *From the Beginning to Ashur-resha-ishi* (Wiesbaden: Otto Harrassowitz, 1972) and Grayson, *Assyrian Rulers of the Third and Second Millennia BC (to 1115 BC)* (Toronto: University of Toronto Press, 1987). For an introduction to the history of Assyria see H. W. F. Saggs, *The Might That Was Assyria* (London: Sidgwick & Jackson, 1984).

Anthologies concentrating on texts from ancient Mesopotamia include B. R. Foster, *Before the Muses: An Anthology of Akkadian Literature* (Bethesda, Md.: CDL Press, 2005) and A. Leo Oppenheim, *Letters from Mesopotamia* (Chicago: University of Chicago Press, 1967). Two volumes of Mesopotamian poems about war and destruction are Piotr Michalowski, *The Lamentation over the Destruction of Sumer and Ur* (Winona Lake, Ind.: Eisenbrauns, 1989) and J. S. Cooper, *The Curse of Agade* (Baltimore: Johns Hopkins University Press, 1983). Among a number of good introductions to ancient Mesopotamia, one of the best is A. Leo Oppenheim, *Ancient Mesopotamia: Portrait of a Dead Civilization*, revised edition completed by Erica Reiner (Chicago: University of Chicago Press, 1977); for an update on more recent discoveries, see Stephen Bertman, *Handbook to Life in Ancient Mesopotamia* (New York: Facts on File, 2003). Stephanie Dalley and A. T. Reyes write about the impact of Mesopotamia on Bronze Age Greece in Stephanie Dalley et al., *The Legacy of Mesopotamia* (Oxford: Oxford University Press, 1998), 85–94.

For the Amarna Letters, see William L. Moran, ed. and trans., *The Amarna Letters* (Baltimore: Johns Hopkins University Press, 1992). For an analysis of the international relations system illustrated in these letters, see Raymond Cohen and Raymond Westbrook, eds., *Amarna Diplomacy: The Beginnings of International Relations* (Baltimore: Johns Hopkins University Press, 2000). See also Trevor Bryce, *Letters of the Great Kings of the Ancient Near East* (London: Routledge Taylor and Francis Group, 2003) and Mario Liverani, *International Relations in the Ancient Near East, 1600–1100 B.C.* (New York: Palgrave, 2001).

A selection of texts from Ugarit can be found in Michael David Coogan, *Stories from Ancient Canaan* (Louisville: Westminster John Knox Press, 1978); S. Lackenbacher, *Textes Akkadiens d'Ugarit: Textes Provenants des vingt-cinq Premières Campagnes* (Paris: Les Éditions du Cerf, 2002 [in French]). For a brief introduction to Ugarit and Bronze Age Canaan, see Cyrus H. Gordon and Gary Rendsburg, *The Bible and the Ancient Near East*, 4th edition (New York: W. W. Norton, 1998), 82–95.

The identification of the Hittite "Alashiya" as Cyprus is a virtual detective story. See Y. Goren et al., "The Location of Alashiya," *American Journal of Archaeology* 107 (2003): 233–55.

Much new research has been done in recent years on the Sea Peoples, and a good deal of it is available in Eliezer D. Oren, ed., *The Sea Peoples and Their World: A Reassessment* (Philadelphia: University of Pennsylvania Press, 2000). See also the essays in Seymour Gitlin et al., *Mediterranean Peoples in Transition: Thirteenth to Early Tenth Centuries BCE: In Honor of Professor Trude Dothan* (Jerusalem: Israel Exploration Society, 1998). An older but still valuable work is N. K. Sandars, *The Sea Peoples: Warriors of the Ancient Mediterranean, 1250–1150 BC* (London: Thames & Hudson, 1978).

ACKNOWLEDGMENTS

Many people on three continents helped me to write this book. Chapters were generously read in draft and improved by Judith Dupré, Mark Levine, Kim McKnight, Marcia Mogelonsky, Jan Parker, and Meredith Small. My mentor, Donald Kagan, offered valuable advice at the outset of this project. Getzel Cohen opened doors at Troy. I am greatly indebted to him and to the staff of the Troia Project, and in particular to its late director Manfred Korfmann; and to Peter Jablonka, Rüstem Aslan, Gerhard Bieg, and Hans Jansen. Mustafa Aşkin led me through the Troad; Selma and Iskender Azatoglu were hosts and guides to Mount Ida; and Serhan Güngör is Turkey's *guide extraordinaire.* Allen Ward introduced me to Elias and Maria Tomazos, who brought me to a conference on the recent excavations at Pellana, Greece, generously hosted by the local community; there I met Ralph Gallucci, Matthew Dillon, and the excavation director, Theodore Spyropoulos, who offered valuable scholarly advice. My Cornell colleagues John Coleman, Peter Kuniholm, Sturt Manning, Jon Parmenter, Hayden Pelliccia, Pietro Pucci, Hunter Rawlings, Eric Rebillard, Jeffrey Rusten, and James Weinstein shared their knowledge of matters ranging from Thucydides to Anatolian trees to Native American religion. Among scholars at other universities who helped me are Günhan Böreckci, Paul Cartledge, Eric Cline, Peter Dorman, Elizabeth S. Greene, Victor Davis Hanson, Simon Hillier, John Lee, Joseph Manning, Michelle Maskiel, Adrienne Mayor, Josiah Ober, Geoffrey Parker, Stephen Radentz, and Katerina Zacharias. Suzanne Lang provided invaluable secretarial and logistical assistance. Elizabeth Shedd did photo research and Susan Dixon designed and produced my Web site.

I would also like to thank Diane Barcelo, Nina Barclay, Stephan Blum, Susanne Bocher, Matthias Cieslak, Çiler Çilingiroğlu, Robert A. Graham, Pavol Hnila, Martin Loicano, Alison Minton, Bill Patterson, Kevin Rooney, Rabbi Eli Silberstein, Sevim Karabiyik Tokta, Sinan Unur, Steffen White, Janis Whitlock, Malcolm Wiener, and Chaya Rivka Zwolinksi.

The Department of History of Cornell University granted me leave to write this book. I am grateful to them, to Cornell's Department of Classics, and to the staff of Cornell's John M. Olin Library. I owe a debt to my students past and present, at Cornell and elsewhere, for their stimulation and support.

The people of Greece and Turkey proved as generous as ever.

I am greatly indebted to the wisdom and patience of my editor at Simon & Schuster, Bob Bender. His counsel is present on every page. I would also like to thank his assistant, Johanna Li, as well as Phil Metcalf and Tom Pitoniak. I am greatly indebted as well to my editor at Hutchinson, Paul Sidey, for his thorough, perceptive, and productive reading of the manuscript. I would also like to thank his assistant, Tiffany Stansfield. Without Howard Morhaim, best of literary agents, advisor, and friend, this book would not have come about.

My greatest debts are to my family. My mother continues to encourage me, as does the memory of my late father. The support and affection of my wife, Marcia, and my children, Sylvie and Michael, have made this project an odyssey and not a marathon. My brothers and sisters, both by birth and by marriage, are the greatest of friends, and I dedicate this book to them.

INDEX